WHO AM I?

THE SUPREME UNDERSTANDING
(THE ANATOMY OF EGO)

Bhagwan Ra Afrika

Compiled and Edited by Dharma Máji Ra Afrika

Published by Research Associates School Times Publications/
Frontline Distribution Int'l, Inc.
751 East 75th Street
Chicago, IL 60619
Tel: (773) 651-9888
Fax: (773) 651-9850
E-mail: Frontlinebooks@prodigy.net

Distributed in the Caribbean by
Frontline Books
Island Plaza Mall
Ocho Rios, St. Anns, Jamaica, Caribbean
Tel: (876) 974-5158

and

Headstart Books Distributors
54-56 Church Street
Kingston, Jamaica, Caribbean
Tel: (876) 922-3915

ISBN 0-94839-057-3

ABOUT THE AUTHOR

Bhagwan Ra Afrika (Leonard Ingram) is considered by many to be one of the greatest living Afrikan Mystics and Masters, known for his fierce and direct Zen-like style. Bhagwan is a scholar of world religions, the author of several books and is widely acclaimed for his innovative and critical synthesis of mystical traditions—Eastern, Western and Afrikan. He has been hailed by many as one of the brightest lights of the modern spiritual world.

Initiated in 1970 by Huzur Maharaji Charan Singh into the Radha Soami tradition, Bhagwan began his formal teaching of the "Path" in 1989. Deeply concerned about the complete absence of a "true" spiritual tradition (*parampara*) in the Afrikan-American community, Bhagwan founded the *House of Ra*. Since that time, the fire of his passion has sparked a spiritual revolution in the hearts and minds of many people in the Afrikan-American community, as well as the community of spiritual seekers in general, regardless of race or ethnicity.

Bhagwan is outspoken and more critical than most teachers of the superstitious belief systems that are invariably wrongly associated with genuine spiritual traditions, especially within the Afrikan-American community. This, coupled with his unwillingness to compromise in matters of the heart and intellect, has resulted in an original expression of a complete teaching that embraces both the practical and spiritual life in a way that calls any who would "hear" his teachings to seriously consider the true meaning of their life and the true purpose of their existence.

Those who have "heard" and been touched by Bhagwan Ra Afrika's teachings have found themselves immersed in a profound recognition of their own true nature and propelled into a thrilling discovery of what it really means to attain Self- and God-realization. Bhagwan shouts from his heart and implores each of us to take up the challenge to "Know thyself," and be spiritually transformed in the process.

The author can be reached at:

House of Ra
7115 North Avenue, PMB#288
Oak Park, IL 60302
(312) 490-4301
Website: http://www.angermgmt.com

ACKNOWLEDGMENTS

The enemy on the Path is the ego, and unless the ego is transcended, life simply remains a hell. This ego creates darkness, as well as spiritual and intellectual blindness. It is this ego that creates in human consciousness the "experience" of being separate from God. And this "feeling" of being separate from God breeds all kinds of additional miseries in our lives. It is like uprooting a tree from the earth, it starts dying. This is the same effect that ego has on mankind: It creates in us the experience of death and dying. It "separates" us from the source of our life . . . God.

I am happy that by the tremendous effort of my student and friend Dharma Máji Ra Afrika (Dorothy Johnson), this translation of a series of talks on the nature of ego is now available. It has been her long hours of transliteration of countless hours of audio and video cassette tapes that gave birth to this book, which contains the words and insights of "my Perfect Teacher," Huzur Maharaji Charan Singh. May this effort of my sister, Dharma Máji Ra Afrika, benefit ALL sentient beings. May her *seva* always bring her happiness and its causes forever.

October 1997   Bhagwan Ra Afrika
                                           Chicago, Illinois

PREFACE

During *satsang* at the *House of Ra*, the spiritual Adept, Bhagwan Ra Afrika, frequently gives discourses using a variety of words that are unfamiliar to most Western people. This created the necessity for a glossary or guidebook to enable those who are unfamiliar with some of the terms to gain a deeper understanding of the profound subjects that are discussed.

We have endeavored to make this glossary as inclusive as possible, but acknowledge that it is impossible to include every description from every tradition. We have, nonetheless, tried to include the most frequently used terms, especially those used at the *House of Ra*.

We have also tried to include the different spellings from the various traditions of words which have the same meaning. For example, the Sanskrit word for lust is "kam" and in Buddhism, it is "kama." Other examples are "ananda" (anand); "avidja" (avijja).

Also, some words are spelled the same, but have different meanings, e.g., "Brahma" has a different meaning in Hinduism than it does in Buddhism. Another example is "Yama." Still another is "nadi." Thus, in cases like these, where the difference is particularly important, we have noted the same.

Words from the same tradition may sometimes have slightly different spellings or meanings, depending upon the sect and other variables: e.g., "karma" is spelled with an "r" in some schools of Buddhism, but in Pali, one of the languages in which the Hinayana School was first written, it is spelled "kamma." Other examples are "dharma" (dhamma); "dukkha" (dukha). In those cases, the most widely used spelling is listed first and the less frequently used is placed in parentheses directly after it.

According to the lineage or tradition, and depending on the author, some proper names may also be spelled differently. For instance, there is "Mahavira" or "Mahavir"; "Mira Bai" or "Mirabai"; "Sahjo Bai" or "Sehjo Bai." Both spellings are included in those instances.

Following is a key to pronunciation as well as a list of abbreviations to further aid in the use of this glossary.

We hope you find this glossary useful in your spiritual search.

The Editors

Key to Pronunciation and Abbreviations

a is sounded as in sof*a* (or as in b*o*x—Bengali usage)
e is sounded as in pr*e*y
i is sounded as in s*i*t
o is sounded as in s*o*
u is sounded as in p*u*ll
ai is sounded as in *ai*sle
au is sounded as in n*ow*
y is sounded as in *y*ou
g is sounded as in *g*od
ng is sounded as in so*ng*
ch is sounded as in *ch*urch
h after the following consonants is pronounced hard:
  bh as in a*bh*or; dh as in a*dh*ere; gh as in le*gh*orn;
  kh as in in*kh*orn

ca.— circa (approximately)
e.g. — for example
i.e. — that is
l.c. — lower case
lit. — literally
specif. — specifically

CONTENTS

INTRODUCTION

Most of us have had Psychology 101 in college or have come across the word "ego." We have heard of the "id" and the "superego." *Webster's New World Dictionary* defines ego as "the self; the individual as aware of himself." In actuality, ego is much more complex. *Webster's* makes reference to the "psyche" and its relationship to the physical body; but the "self" referred to is self with a lowercase s. "Self" with a capital S is a much deeper dimension of our being and that, along with its varying degrees of consciousness, is what will be analyzed in this series of discourses given by Bhagwan Ra Afrika.

Ego is the feeling of being *separate* from God, from that which *is*. Since we feel we are separate or distinct from the Creator, as well as creation itself, there is no sense of connection with our inner essence, with the thing that has been in existence since beginningless time. Some of us call it the "soul," some of us call it the "spirit." In reality, it is nameless; it simply *is* (total *bliss*, total *oneness*). Most often, when people speak of the "soul," they are actually referring to the ego. The vast majority of us have no "conscious" perception of our souls, because in our ordinary, egoic condition we do not have access to that level of consciousness.

Our egos have completely obscured our intrinsic nature, and it usually takes tremendous effort to uncover our true Selves. Our "sense of self" has no "connection" with the inner Self, only with the body, emotions and mind. As the great Ma Yoga Shakti states in *Daughters of the Goddess*[*]: "Body, mind and spirit should be in harmony with each other. The spirit should speak through your intelligence and intelligence should direct your actions." Our egos dictate our actions.

The feeling of being separate arises because of the dual nature of our mind (subject and object), and that sense of separateness keeps us from experiencing the *oneness* of creation. This sense of separateness is perhaps the greatest *fallacy of being human (an ego)*: the nonrecognition of the fact that we are all interdependent and, at our deepest level, are all connected. *Connectedness* has nothing to do with race, culture, ethnicity or gender. It is about *oneness*: our oneness with creation, which includes *each other*, as well as the earth, animals and plants. Until one is able to *transcend* the ego (or sense of disconnectedness), one can never experience the true meaning of existence. Thus, *transcending the ego* is really the dropping of this feeling of separateness and realizing the essence of our oneness, or *elixir of being.*

Ego, at the stage of vanity, can also be described as the false basis of pride. It is based on the image we have formed of ourselves in order to maintain a certain persona, a certain "reputation." Bhagwan Ra Afrika often refers to it as our "ego mythology." More often than not, that image is based upon others' perceptions of who we are, and that perception is usually flawed because they also do not know who *they* are. Until we "mature" as egos and are able to peel away the layers of ignorance and see who we *really* are, underneath our *physical manifestation*, we will continue to suffer the effects thereof.

Our entire life is spent trying, in vain, to maintain a body that is slowly dying and an ego which will die along with that body. Therefore, as long as we do not realize the *impermanence* of all things, and through that understanding, transcend this egoic condition (and thereby reduce our "grasping" and "clinging" to phenomenal existence), we will continue to needlessly suffer. The effects of not striving to facilitate the maturation of our egos are the cause of all suffering, because suffering is ego's child. Our attempts to alleviate our suffering, in turn, give birth to (negative) *karma*, which produces more suffering. All spiritual traditions teach that we must "kill," or transcend, the self (ego) in order to realize our higher Self (God-nature), which will result in the cessation of the wheel of transmigration (rebirth).

My wish is that everyone who is exposed to the insights and wisdom of Bhagwan Ra Afrika be inspired to begin the journey toward Self-discovery that is the crux of *all* development, spiritual, mental and otherwise. With the publication of this book, may all sentient beings move a little closer to the experience of genuine happiness and freedom from *samsara* and suffering.

A special acknowledgment is due Shakti Devi Ra Afrika for her excellent work on Chapter One. May her *seva* benefit all sentient beings.

October 17, 1997   Dharma Máji Ra Afrika

---

*Daughters of the Goddess, The Women Saints of India, Linda Johnsen. Yes International Publishers: St. Paul Minnesota.

CHAPTER ONE
KNOW THYSELF!

No doubt, those of you who have studied spiritual traditions (particularly those of Afrika and India) know already that the *primary* criterion for initiation into the mystery systems of ancient Afrika was to "Know thyself." It is not by accident that this prerequisite of knowing thyself has been insisted upon in all authentic systems of spiritual cultivation, because it is the actual *context* in which the spiritual practice must occur. The early Ionic pre-Socratic philosophers, the forerunners of Plato and Aristotle—Thales, Anaximenes, Heraclitus, Pythagoras, and so on—all were, of course, initiated into the ancient Kemetic mystery systems and were, therefore, themselves made very aware of this criterion and condition for self-understanding. And like their great Afrikan teachers, when the Greek philosophers and mystics started their respective academies and *ashrams*, they very often would write across those academies, "Worship the gods if you must, but first know thyself."

Remember, to "know thyself" does not mean "knowing" in the very superficial way that you know *yourself.* You know your name; you know when you were born and who your parents and brothers and sisters are; you know your address and your social security number. Some of you (with excellent memories) have even managed to memorize your driver's licenses, but these are very mundane, peripheral things! This is *not* much knowledge of yourself! These mystics were not talking about *that* kind of superficial knowledge. They meant to *really* know thyself.

Therefore, when these Greek philosophers and sages transported the teachings, the *Dharma*, or "the Path" back into their respective cultures, towns or cities, they would always insist: "Worship the gods if you must, but *first* know thyself." Because in Athens, where Socrates set up his school, the principal strategy was the worship of a plenitude of gods, the Greek Pantheon, and all of that. And Socrates, like the mystics before him in that tradition said, "Okay, go ahead and worship your gods, if you must." It is understood that you must worship them because you are in search of *consolation.* You are in search of some kind of god that you can call upon to bring your misery to an end. Thus, the Greek mystics said, if you are not able to find any other way out of your misery, then of course, worship the gods if you must. We understand that this has been your custom. But your first order of business, if you are truly in search of the antidote to all of your suffering, should be to *know thyself.*

SELF-UNDERSTANDING: THE FOUNDATION OF THE PATH

To truly know (and understand) yourself is the *foundation* of the Path. And your *sadhana* cannot be more effective than your degree of self-understanding. Please make a note of that. If you have not understood much about yourself, then you will *not* be able to do much sadhana. Your sadhana will be very difficult. It will not be something that you will enjoy doing. We must look, then, into this whole notion of what it means to truly know thyself and to *see* the role that self-understanding plays on the Spiritual Path.

This is the argument that I offer to you today for your serious consideration: Do you *really* know yourself? Do you really, truly *understand* yourself beyond mundane and superficial knowledge? You know what kind of food and clothes you like and dislike, your favorite TV programs, etc. This is very shallow knowledge. This is ignorance. I call you to pause for a moment and really, truly go on the search for some *real* understanding of yourself. So today I feel we should take advantage of this time and explore this whole notion, because it is so fundamental. It is so essential that you truly, truly achieve at least some degree of self-understanding—that you truly understand yourself and really see the *true* nature of your living and your life until that understanding becomes *radical.*

I really want you to understand that without the solid foundation of self-understanding, you *cannot* follow the Path, by definition! To follow the Path, you *must* have some self-understanding, and no one can give that to you. I cannot give you that; I can only point to the methodology by which it can be obtained, which is simply looking at your life. But you must actually *do* that! *No one* can tell you who you are. *You* must discover that, and stop hiding from the reality of your true condition. Do not "glamorize" this hiding that you are calling searching or sit it on a pedestal. You are simply hiding from your own ignorance of who you really are. You have no idea of how you are really living, and there is *no* substitution for that knowledge! You must actually *see* this.

I have asked you, repeatedly, in the past *satsangs* to start taking a look at your life, at how you live. Some have said, "Well, Bhagwan,

I already know that. Let's go on to the next thing." No, we cannot go to the next thing! You must *do* this because all of the problems you are having are rooted in the fact that you truly do *not* understand yourself, simply because you have not *looked* at yourself. I understand because, by avoiding examining your life (and yourself) and preoccupying yourself with looking at a thousand and one other things, you can continually *hide* from the reality of your vast and deep ignorance of *who* you are.

You are interested in all kinds of things: "Bhagwan, what about karma? Bhagwan, what about destiny? How does that work? How many levels of creation are there?" You are simply preoccupied, to the point of fascination, with all of these tangent inquiries. You *refuse* to *look* at yourself, to truly try to understand yourself because of the *fear* that you will encounter the ignorance that is the case: *You really do not know who you are.* You do not have a clue because you have no *self-understanding.* You are afraid to confront your true spiritual condition; hence, your fascination with peripheral things related to the Path. But at some point, you see, you *must* truly enter into the ordeal that is self-understanding and accumulate *real* knowledge about yourself.

You would rather, of course, talk about philosophy and metaphysics and all of these things because, again, you can remain preoccupied. "Let's go into a deep discussion of religion. Now, let's talk about Jesus. Let's talk about Buddha. Let's talk about Kabir. Let's talk about Mahavira. Let's talk about these great men, these great paths." However, I want to talk about *you*, and this does not interest you! I want you to go on a journey and find out something about *yourself*! Why are you so concerned with Moses? How would you understand Moses, or Jesus, or Buddha if you *do not* even understand yourself? What is the point? You become fascinated with these people. Now, I am not condemning them, so please do not misunderstand me. I am simply putting things in their proper perspective.

You must take as much interest in yourself as you take in these historical, dead masters and begin to truly look and see yourself. Therefore, I have been asking you, over and over, to look into the nature of your *own* life (and activities), to look into all of your presumptions about happiness and so forth. You all are *not* doing that yet, because you do not *see* how it pertains to the Path! However, I want you to really try to *understand* that this *is* the very foundation of the Path. You must truly achieve self-understanding. You must, therefore, gather the courage and truly look at yourself to the point of "radical" understanding.

When you begin to make this self-observation, a few things will become immediately obvious. What you will find is that you are *always* in search of (or seeking union with) some kind of condition, or event, or thing, or person in the pursuit of happiness, and that *this* is your *constant* activity. Please note that you never search for something unless you first feel fundamentally *separate* from it! *All* seeking or searching is rooted in the *assumption* of separation. Why else would I seek anything? My "seeking" occurs from the assumption of my own separateness. *That* is what triggers the seeking! And this seeking and searching is always "stressful" and "agonizing"—*always!*

I have repeatedly told you that the problem is your feeling of separateness: *ego.* Ego *is* this feeling of being separate from that which you are in search of (and are trying to union with). You actually have to see this and lose all sympathy with your seeking. Become "unsympathetic" to your ego. This is the *minimal* criteria for the true application of the *self-discipline* that is sadhana; otherwise, you will not enter truly into spiritual practice. How can you? You have come to the Path searching for something that, fundamentally, you feel separate from. You are searching for "enlightenment." The fundamental feeling is that enlightenment is something *separate* from you and you are in *search* of it. You even use the seeking as part of your effort to console yourself. I want you to actually see the seeking, see the separateness that it is arising from, and be moved to transcend this whole affair. But you must first *look* deeply into your egoic activity and truly *see* it. There is no sense in playing games with it.

You see, by remaining preoccupied with all of these sundry and peripheral spiritual activities, we are able to fulfill our egos. To become lost in philosophy, religion, discussion, etc. is very consoling to the ego. It keeps that separateness alive and well. It relieves you, it consoles you—for a moment—through its preoccupation. Thus, we are in a sense really hiding from our own truth although, deep down inside, it is there.

Deep down (at the deepest parts of your living and your being), you *know* that you are not living a life anywhere near what you *feel* it should be! You *know* that! Deep down inside you know you are "pretending." You push this realization away the moment it surfaces, and replace it with some distraction, but there is always something deep down inside of you that knows you are just "faking" it! You are just an actor, a great pretender. You are not being "real" in anything that you are doing in any relationship. It is *all* hypocrisy. You are just pretending. We are *all* pretending. Something deep down inside of us reminds us that we are not real. And we know that this is directly related to the hiding that we are doing. This pretending is our hiding from the reality that we really do not know. We are afraid to encounter the ignorance.

You really do not know *what* you want! You really do not have a clue. You do not know what you want to do. But this is too much to admit! "Damn, I do not know what I want!" Now this sounds too threatening; this hurts the ego! You have all of these degrees, you have been on the planet for fifty years! Right? You have had all kinds of relationships, and so on, and to admit that you do not know *what* you want or *what* you are doing is just too much! But the truth is that in your ignorance, you *really* do not know what you want. You are just doing shit and *hoping* that it will result in happiness! However, deep down inside, you really do not *know* what you are doing.

You really do not know what you are doing, which means that you have not *looked* at *what* you are doing! It is almost like you do not even know what you have on. Do you see? You have on some clothes, but you do not know *what* you have on! It's like that. You have no idea of the way you *act*, or the way you *live*. You have no knowledge of your own activity, because you do not *see* your own activity. Do you see my point? I am saying that to know yourself is to know the *activity* that is making up your life, to know *what* it is that you are doing in terms of your activities—to actually *see* your life, the bottom line: *this* is what I am doing. Now the question is, what are you doing? What are you really doing that you are calling "living"? "I'm living, Bhagwan." That's too vague. Some may say, "Bhagwan, I'm living large!" Okay. What is it you are doing that you are calling living? What does that activity really consist of? What does it really look like? What is it really involved with?

I am telling you that when you begin to look at the activity that is your living, what you will find is that it is simply an activity of *continuous* searching or seeking for "union" with some event, condition, thing or person that you fundamentally feel separate from. And that activity, in addition to being comprised of the search, is also comprised of other activities to *console* you in the failure to obtain union with those very objects and conditions sought. Now, you've been seeking financial stability—a condition. Right? You've been seeking the condition that you have called "financial stability," but not only have you *not* achieved it, the *failure* to achieve it has created stress and strain in you! Then, you added some *more* activities—what I call egoity—to *console* yourself, to console this painful, stressful feeling of being separate from your goal. It's quite a thing. And you have to *see* this in your own life and living.

You must "know thyself." This was not something these mystics were saying just to be saying stuff. This is not a cliche! This is *fundamental*. You may pursue your Christianity, your Buddhism, your Hinduism, your philosophy or your this or that, if you *must*. Because it is understood that you must at least be able to function. And your misery is such that if you did not have these things you would *not* even be able to function! You would be "hysterically miserable," and we would have to lock you up somewhere! So, if you must have these things just to maintain a certain degree of functionality, okay: "Worship the gods if you must." But you must still get down to business, and the *first* thing on the Spiritual Path is you must *know yourself*—at some point in the journey. You are not able to truly take advantage of initiation unless you know yourself. There is really no way around it: You must truly understand yourself. Self-understanding is a condition, a prerequisite for the Spiritual Path. It is so!

QUESTIONS AND ANSWERS

Sat Rani: *So we have to get ourselves to the point where we are able to see what our greatest consolation is that we are seeking in our goals and relationships.*

What you will begin to discover is that you are not separate from any of the conditions you are seeking, that this feeling of being separate is an activity that *you* are doing, that *you* are creating moment to moment—"pinching yourself," as I call it. You, yourself, are creating this feeling of being separate from the very conditions that you are in search of. The reality is that there is *no* separateness, that you are intrinsically related to everything that exists. It is *already* the case. The act of separateness is an optical illusion occurring in your own consciousness. There is no reality to your feeling of being separate. It is profound.

I am not saying that this is readily and easily understood; it is not. It will, therefore, require very serious consideration. But you truly will have to do it; otherwise, there is no way to live the spiritual life. There just is no other way. You *cannot* live a so-called "spiritual life" without having some understanding of yourself. How is that possible? How can you say you are living a spiritual life if you have absolutely *no* self-understanding? What is that? *That* is a contradiction, by definition. The spiritual life is simply a life *lived* out of this self-understanding.

Self-understanding is fundamental. You *must* have it and you must, therefore, stop all of your avoidance and *look*. You must drop your preoccupation (and fascination) with all of your egoic activities that are consoling you, that are enabling you to continually hide from the reality of your ignorance. Now, you are ignorant of your own self and do not have a clue of what you are doing—at all! It hurts the ego to be told that, because it is not flattering. It does not feed into your vanity. It hurts! But the truth is you do not even *know* what is going on in your *own* life.

Rick: *So am I to understand—and I have a   limited understanding—that we are in denial of our true selves? When it comes to looking at your true nature, you are avoiding it by speaking in philosophical ways and creating distractions such as religion— anything except yourself and your shortcomings. You'll never get honest enough to look at yourself. You'll want to say, "I am an unselfish person," but then you deny someone one of your cookies. There are "stipulations" to your unselfishness. "Well, I only had two cookies so I couldn't give you one, but that doesn't make me a selfish person."*

It is even more radical and profound than that, brother. Of course, it is a kind of psychological thing. But I am saying that it is even *more* fundamental than that. It is to actually *look* at the activity because, first of all, *why* are you trying to hold on to the cookies? You are trying to keep possession of those cookies because you feel that by "possessing" them, you will have "happiness"! Do you see my point? The activity that is called "selfishness" is rooted (itself) in the seeking and searching for conditions that you feel will produce happiness or fulfillment. And I am saying that when you look at *that* activity, you will find that in *every* instance you have met with only minimum satisfaction, and can only sustain the condition for a little while. It is temporary, transient. Then you are on to some other seeking, and this kind of *endless* seeking characterizes every waking moment of your life! There is no ending.

Prem Bani: *Much of what has already been said gives me a better sense of what I was going to ask. The ego is so powerful. I heard you say that you will either have to kill it or it will kill you, and in the struggle to try to kill it you go through lots and lots of changes. My question is, how do you save yourself?*

That is the whole point: You are *not* trying to save yourself! Jesus said, "He who findeth (tries to save) his life shall lose it. . . ." (St. Matthews 10:39) You are not trying to "save" yourself, because *that* is ego. This is the whole point, Prem Bani: ego is an *activity*. It is an activity that is arising out of a feeling of being separate, and all that you must do is *transcend* it. It is like the thoughts that come into your mind. When one is a novice meditator, one is trying to "stop thinking," trying to stop the flow of thought. How can you do that? The thoughts are *not* even coming from you. That is the *illusion* you have. The thoughts that are "running" through your consciousness are independent of you. You are just *paying attention* to the thoughts. You think you are creating the thoughts, but you are not creating them at all! Do you see the fallacy?

It (ego) is an activity and it has to be transcended. Simply *seeing* the futility of the activity that is egoity will cause you to *transcend* it. When the understanding of it becomes "radical," full or mature, it will fall away. Because you will not (and cannot) be involved in an activity that you clearly see will *not* produce any happiness. You just cannot do it! There is no way to venture into it. *That* is the way the mind is constructed. It can *only* pursue pleasure and avoid pain, based on the presumptions it has formed. And when you actually see the activity that constitutes your life and living, actually see what you are doing (and its outcome), you stop! And that's why it is so important that you actually see your core or essential activity which is ego and its egoity. See it and see its failure. Really *see* it; do not take my word for it because that will not move you much. Do you see? Discount what I am saying or set it on the shelf. Do not make my words the principal motive behind your sadhana. *See* the futility of it with your *own* eyes for your *own* self, and seeing that futility, *automatically* the attention (and its energy) will come out of the activity that is ego. However, unless and until *you* see it, nothing the Guru says will break it. Now, this is absolutely and profoundly true.

You may come to satsang until the end of your life, but if you have not truly *understood* yourself, then the egoic activity will not be broken. In fact, you have not really benefitted from coming to satsang if you have not looked at the egoic activity. You have simply reduced satsang to another act of consolation. You have failed to truly take advantage of satsang. To truly take advantage of satsang means that you will enter into this great process of consideration: looking at the ego activity that is the sum total of your life. Thus, this ego, this feeling of being separate, has to be *really* understood.

The mystics' definition of ego is different from that of the psychologists. The mystics have *all* defined ego as this feeling of being separate. It is this feeling of being separate from your goal of union—be that with a person, event, condition or thing. It is this *feeling* that you are separate from your goal that "triggers" and fuels the search, because you will *never* search for that which you feel is *already* the case, will you? Seeking *always* comes out of the fundamental assumption of separateness from that which you are trying to achieve union with. It is this feeling of separateness that is your *own* activity which you are creating all the time, and *that* activity has to be transcended. This is what is meant by the phrase "dropping the ego." It really means the dropping of this *activity* that the ego is involved in, the dropping of this feeling of separateness. No, it is not easy. No one said it was easy. If it was easy, everybody would be enlightened. The reality is that just a handful of people will achieve it. Now, this is just the plain truth. Many are "called," but just a few attain it (are "chosen").

HEARING THE DHARMA

Gurudasa: *My question has to do with conditioning and where you've been and what is instrumental in all that, because you become a "composite" of all of these things and it's a matter of breaking this habitual conditioning and pattern. You said that we can't get into the sadhana unless we have some understanding of ourselves. But the sadhana is what helps us to have an understanding of ourselves! I see this cycle and I'm trying to figure out where you break into it to start one so it can help you with the other one.*

Actually, it starts with first hearing the Dharma, because there is
no possibility to practice something that you do not even know about.
Somebody has to first tell you about the sadhana. So it starts with
actually *hearing* the Dharma, then gaining the *understanding* that leads
to *practice*. *That* is the core of development. Someone has to tell you
that you are in a state of ignorance; otherwise *how* would you know?
Your ignorance is so deep that you have no way of knowing.
Therefore, if these great mystics are not moved out of their compassion
to point it out to us, we would *never* know.

In Buddhism they call it the "pointing out instructions." That is
what the Lama does—"point it out" to you. Many different methods
are used. In Zen, they may point it out by cracking you over the head
with a stick! We may go "Zen" at the House. What I have not
achieved with words, maybe a staff will work! Sometimes they will
use a *koan*, a device that is "nonsensical," that "shuts" the mind down,
just breaks the mind down, i.e. the sound of one hand clapping. For
years you will go on trying to solve that until you *exhaust* the mind,
simply run it down. There are many different devices used in many
different paths. In fact, the only things that distinguish these great
paths *are* their devices and technologies! Again, the essential thing,
Gurudasa, is *first* being fortunate enough to *hear* the Dharma or the
teachings.

As we discussed last time, your *receptivity* upon hearing the
teachings depends on your *own* qualities. The teachings say "know
thyself!" If you are a very intelligent person, you will hear the Dharma
and will understand it—instantly! You will then respond accordingly,
and truly enter into the discovery of Self. That is the person who is
highly intelligent; who has brought a lot of intelligence into this life;
who must have worked somewhere in a previous life. Upon *hearing*
the truth, they instantly *recognize* it and *understand* it.

Then you have the person who is "mediocre," average, not much
intelligence. They hear the Dharma, but they have to hear it about two
or three million times to get the point; hence, the repetition. The
mediocre person says, "Hmm, now *what* does that mean, 'know
thyself?' I know I'm a man (or a woman). I know my mama, my
daddy. I know where I live. What did they mean by that?" The
mediocre mind *cannot* understand: "What did Socrates mean, 'know
thyself'? That doesn't make sense." They then begin to try to make
sense out of it.

But if you are inferior, the lowest order or type of person, when you hear the Dharma, you will simply laugh! "What is this nonsense, 'know thyself'? What is Bhagwan talking about? Shit, I know myself! I *know* who *I* am!" You are mad! It will not make any sense to you. This is the low-rate person—not much intelligence at all. *That* is their natural response. Bukuju said that is how you know it was the Dharma: they (inferior people) laughed. You are able to tell it was the truth because an idiot will simply laugh and say, "This is just crap." That is the appropriate response. Actually, the idiot laughs because they are *frightened* and their laughter is nothing but a *cover-up* for their fear.

Samadhi, Dayal and I were having lunch and I said to Samadhi Ji that (at satsang) I have to say the same thing over and over. If you are mediocre, I have to say it about ten million times just for you to understand it *once!* Sooner or later, your mediocre mind *will* understand it. It is not that I am saying anything different. But it takes time when you are working with a mediocre intelligence. A great patience is required.

It is very interesting that the vast majority of us are mediocre! This may come as a heartbreak to some of you because I know how these egos are. However, even on ordinary intelligence tests, when psychologists compile the outcome, *one percent* of the population will score at the genius level, and *one percent* will score at the idiot level! The other *ninety-eight percent* is of *mediocre* intelligence. And they are the ones that Buddha had to talk to for forty years. In the case of a Mahakasyapa or a Sariputta, not even *words* were necessary: just *seeing* Buddha was enough! They *understood* the possibility of human life. They *saw* it—done! But the vast majority of us will have to hear the Dharma over and over. Therefore, we are fortunate that these great men and women have come into the world with the kind of patience to give us the Dharma over and over *until* we get it!

It is like that patient teacher, Gurudasa, who works with the student until they get it; they do not become frustrated. It is a very simple problem, and the child *should* be able to do it, but obviously they are missing the point. The teacher is very patient, and continually works with the student over and over until the student *gets* it. She does not become too frustrated with them. *That* is what makes a great teacher! As parents, we can't do that. We will "give him five more minutes," and if Junior doesn't get it, forget it! You might even whip Junior, right? "Why can't you get this problem right?" You might try to beat Junior into understanding his algebra! But you do not know anything about teaching. You have to be patient just as these great teachers are patient with us. But it all begins, Gurudasa, with hearing the Dharma.

THE PRINCIPAL "MISTAKEN" ACTIVITY

Malik: *Is there a lower self? And is there a difference between the lower self and higher self?*

Brother, when you go very *deep* into this process of self-discovery (and reach another level of understanding), you will discover that what you have been calling *yourself* is really a *caricature*! It is what we call the "lower self." You discover that, "My God, not only is this just egoic activity, it's *not* even really *me!*" It is amazing! You then come into a "higher" level of identity. So, yes, you begin to discover that there are "levels of identity." Yet, unless you really go into this, you will never see it, and you must truly *see* it as it pertains to *you*. Start with whatever concept you have of yourself now. That is fine; that is good enough. We do not have to get into trying to distinguish between higher self and lower self; we can save that work for a while. Just begin to *examine* yourself as you conceive of yourself *right now*, your life as it is flowing right now. Try to truly see and understand yourself, actually *observe* yourself. See what is the essential activity that constitutes your life and your living. What is the activity that is consuming all of your energy, all of your breaths, all of your time? What is the *principal* activity that you are *totally* and *always* focused on and *preoccupied* with?

Life is made up of activity, what we call *karma* or action. It's all karma, all action. You are always "active," you are always in motion, you are always *doing* something. Karma is *always* going on. What is the nature of *your* karma? You must *know* your karma. We talk about karma, but have you ever thought about it? You want to know about the different kinds of karma. "Bhagwan, what's the difference between *sinchit* karma, *pralabdha* karma, and *kriyaman* karma?" Fine. We will discuss that, but what is *your* karma? Do you know what your actual karma is? You really do not know, and *this* you must know. You must, therefore, begin to observe your own karma, your own *essential* activity, the activity that all other activities are connected to.

There is a major activity, just like on a rosary, you have that major bead. What is the core activity that you are involved in around which all other activities revolve? Knowing *that* is self-understanding. Knowing your address, your phone number, where you live is *no* understanding from the spiritual perspective. Knowing your social security number, how old you are, and all of this other stuff, is just peripheral nonsense. You must know the essential activity that you are engaged in. *That* is the beginning of real self-understanding. It is not complete, but it is the beginning. What is the essential activity that you are engaged in from morning, noon to night, from birth to death? Observe it, know it. *That* is knowing yourself—as you are. Is it clear? Because if it is not clear, we want to take more time to discuss it.

This is essential stuff. This is basic, this is fundamental. If you do not get this, you will not get anything else. So do not avoid your ignorance—at least not here! Satsang is a format where we can deal with our ignorance! It's all right. We are all here confessing our ignorance. It's okay. You can temporarily "drop your ego" and relax. No one is going to ridicule you. We understand. We are all in this situation. There is an atmosphere or milieu of truth here. You can tell the truth; you are not going to be condemned. But if you do not get these basics, you will miss. It is like when you are studying in school: If you do not know your ABCs, you will not learn how to read. How can you? You will not become literate. It begins with knowing the ABCs. The Pulitzer Prize begins by learning the alphabet! They are integrally connected. In the same way, this is the basic training. This is the beginning, the bedrock. If you do not have this, you will not get very much on the Path because you really will not have the basics down pat.

Theravadaji: *Bhagwan, it seems that the habit of avoiding the observation of our true nature, the accumulation of this momentum is (itself) causing our responsiveness to the habit, feeding into it. So it is going to take our concentrated consideration—being constantly focused—to penetrate it, to break this cycle.*

Spoken very well, Theravadaji, like a true elder! *That* is exactly the case: This egoic activity of avoidance is historical and has picked up a lot of momentum. We have become habituated, and therefore it will require a deliberate, conscious act to arrest it. However, even then we will find ourselves falling back into the habit of avoidance, and again we must catch ourselves and deal with it. We must wrestle with this, and struggle to come into this level of self-understanding. You are absolutely right: It will not be automatic. It will require a *sustained* effort. It must be a moment-to-moment effort, because moment-to-moment we are involved in this egoic activity of avoidance. It has to be met, therefore, with a moment-to-moment counter activity, and it will be arduous, no doubt about it. But the Path *is* arduous! However, you are absolutely right, Theravadaji. It will not be an easy thing, because you will be encountering all of the mental and emotional habits and strategies that you have devised to console yourself and hide from your ignorance, to avoid looking at the reality that you do not have a clue of *what* you are doing and you do not even know *who* you are!

Theravadaji: *But you can take consolation that you fight the good fight, and trying to keep the focus on the true search of who you are in the face of believing who you are—knowing actually who you are, but not knowing that you know—creates the energy that feeds the determination to keep the fight going.*

Sure! It keeps the stamina up. Perseverance keeps you strong. That is one of the functions of satsang: to keep you motivated, keep you up so that you do not get discouraged, because you could easily get discouraged. *That* is the whole purpose of the biographies of the Moseses and Buddhas and the Kabirs and St. Teresas, etc. These are our "spiritual" heroes. These are individuals whom we can look at, when we get a little discouraged and feel like giving up the battle, and be renewed and remotivated. From them we can take sustenance. Their function is somewhat like that of the ancestors: We can fall back on them and be renewed as a result. You are absolutely right. We will have to stand toe-to-toe with this thing, but when we *realize* what is at stake, *that* fuels us the more! Even if you have understood this much, that will motivate you because, look at what is at risk.

Do you want to continue to live like this? You have lived *millions* of lives like this! This is not the first one! For millions of lifetimes you have lived like this—in total ignorance. My God! It is time for this to end! You should have had enough of this. Enough is *enough!* For millions of lives, you have "hid out" in relationships with wives, husbands, jobs, philosophy, metaphysics, and this and that. You have done this *countless* times, and you have *still* never known yourself. Every lifetime you have died unfulfilled. Every single life you have lived, you have gone to your death *totally* unfulfilled, full of remorse and grief at having wasted it. And you are on your way to your death in this life in the same way. You will simply die and exit out of this life feeling, "Damn, I never even lived! I really didn't live." And you are right, you have not lived. You do *not* even *know* how to live. You do not know *who* you are; so *how* will you live? You never saw your principal error. You never discovered the error that is egoity. You never really got the point. You never really learned the greatest lesson of life: *Happiness cannot be achieved through these strategies that you have adopted.* All of your strategies are simply aimed at momentarily consoling yourself.

You have not truly *seen* that, even in those rare occasions when you were able to achieve union with the event, condition, thing or person in your pursuit of happiness, the union has produced *minimum* satisfaction and it has been *transient* or temporary at best. Under no instance has it been *permanent*; however, because you have not actually *looked* at your activity, you have not *realized* that. Thus, you continually make the *same* mistakes over and over! Every morning that you get up, you continue to make the same mistakes in your life that you have been making for *billions* of lives. And the result always remains the same: unsatisfactory. But you will never get it until you look and see! Yet you are still so preoccupied with coming up with more strategies. You are still so involved with the "tweaking" process of egoic strategies which themselves will always fail! You are hopelessly involved in attempting that which is impossible and you cannot even see the impossibility of it all. It's truly tragic!

It is because of our tragic situation that these mystics and sages are moved out of their great compassion to come and show us the way out. They come and tell us the way out of all this. They say, "You do not understand yourself! You are ignorant, and the only antidote is some knowledge." You must have some knowledge! It is obvious that the knowledge *you* have thus far been working from is insufficient; simply look at the results. You really do not have any knowledge, and you do *not* understand what the mystics mean by "knowledge." You think, "Oh! I have got to read the Vedanta, the Sutras, the Bible, the Gita and the Koran. I have got to memorize *all* of the scriptures and get some knowledge." *That* is not the kind of knowledge they are talking about! But this is the only kind of knowledge you are pursuing.

You are spending countless hours reading and accumulating data and information because you think *that* is the kind of knowledge the mystics are talking about! However, the knowledge that *liberates* is the knowledge of yourself! I want to be clear about this so that there is no misunderstanding! The *only* knowledge that liberates is knowledge of *yourself*, period! It is so, and if you do not believe it, then you all know the rest. Now, this is the case. The *only* function of satsang is to come together to be *inspired* and motivated to seek *true* knowledge. *All* other functions are truly peripheral.

Bharataji: *Bhagwan, if I understand you correctly, what you are saying is that there are many activities we are engaged in—going to work, relationships or whatever—and we may think that each of these activities has a different, underlying theme to it, but in reality it is not so much that these activities are different; there is <u>one</u> underlying theme for all of these activities, and that is what we need to see.*

Right, Bharataji, spoken beautifully. Absolutely! You have put into words what cannot be put into words. It is *one* underlying, recurring theme that is running through *all* of your activities. Do you really, truly know what it is? And *this* is the whole thing. That is why I say this (the Path) is a different thing. This is not your "hallelujah" religion. You have never encountered anything like this. I understand the difficulty, so I am sympathetic and bring great patience to the work. I understand that *this* is way beyond anything you have ever encountered in your life. You have truly never *heard* anything like this, and so it is *inconceivable* to you. You can hardly hold onto the insight; just a minute or two, and then it evaporates. You have not encountered anything like this because it does not exist in *our* 'hood. Buddha never came to the 'hood. You are not used to it, and it is going to take time. It is a miraculous insight: *One* principal activity is running through *all* of your activities. What is it?

Absolutely, there is only *one* thing that you are *always* doing. For instance, if any of you have ever taken higher math, you know that it requires a different species of intellect, a different kind of training. Solving the problem involves so many things, so many subtle executions. I can remember taking calculus, and calculus is one of those kinds of math where, because there are so *many* steps you need, you may work through five or six or seven pages and *still* come out with the wrong answers: "Where did I go wrong?" This is particularly the case in differential equations. You are just pouring over it and pouring over it, and then maybe if you are lucky, finally, you will see, "Oh, this is what it is." But that might be after two or three days of working on the problem. Some mathematicians work on solving a problem for years. Sometimes you will get a blind side and can't find the mistake, and you have to go to the professor. The professor will "point out" what you did wrong. And then you *see* it. Oh! And now you know *how* to do the thing.

In the same way, you have to discover *what* has been the subtle mistake you have been continuously making that has been producing the wrong answer. What is the subtle mistake? There is a principal activity that underlies all of your other activities, that *all* of your other activities are linked into, and this principal activity is the cause of all of your suffering, your unhappiness, your misery and your frustration. And unless you see what the principal mistaken activity is that you are engaged in, you will not be free. Are you following me? There is a principal mistaken activity that you are involved in, and it is because of *that* mistaken activity that you are *miserable*. Be motivated to find *what* is that mistaken activity. It's worth seven years. It's worth that struggle that Theravadaji talked about. It's worth going to war for. This is something worth fighting for! Because if I am ever to be happy, I *must* find out what is the principal mistaken activity that is the cause of my suffering and sorrow. Even if you only investigate the suffering itself—investigate it! Move into it!

Do not "anesthetize" yourself as most of us do. When suffering comes, we anesthetize ourselves to get it off of us: "Give me a drink. Let me shoot some dope. Let me watch some TV. Let me absorb myself in a book. Let me do something to dilute, to anesthetize, to relieve the suffering." You are *preoccupied* with the relieving of the suffering. However, I am saying, do *not* relieve it! *Go* into it! Move deep into the suffering. Trace your suffering down to this principal mistaken activity. Very radical! I am saying, stop *consoling* yourself, stop the egoity! Egoity is simply your strategies for consoling yourself during moments of misery and suffering. *That* is what egoity is about. Stop it! Interrupt it long enough to move deep into the nature of the suffering and investigate it, because it is a part of your biography. It holds the *truth*. Go deep into it until you are able to see the principal mistaken activity that is giving rise to your suffering. Seeing that, you will be released from your suffering. However, if you go on anesthetizing yourself, loading yourself up with aspirins, then you will go on deceiving yourself that there is no problem.

Bhakti Máji: *I've done some work on this and what I've come up with is that a lot of things in my life stem from a "mental conversation" I hold with myself, which began when I was younger. By really taking a look at this, I got some relief because it made me aware and when things that are really important to me, or even small things like being late occur, this conversation that I have about myself keeps coming up. But is there some work that I can do to not have that conversation come up, to have that activity not continue?*

You must go deep into the activity and *radically* see it in order to drop it. You simply have not entered into it at its *most* fundamental level. You may be still on the psychological surface, which is peripheral. I am talking about going much deeper into it, much deeper than psychoanalysis or psychotherapy. I am talking about all the way into the basement, the core. Yet, you will pass through psychology, psychoanalysis and psychotherapy because those are peripheral layers. You will see all of the things that make up those disciplines, but you must go *deeper* than that—down to the principal mistaken activity itself, which is your feeling of being separate. It is truly something.

Viveka: *Well, I was thinking the mistaken activity was actually consolation. So, what you are saying is that there is a mistaken activity that is different for each of us?*

Go deeper! It always becomes the *same*, but your insight is correct, Viveka Ra. As you move deeper, you will pass through layers, coming down to the essential activity, to the bedrock of it all. And you will pass through all kinds of things. The first discovery you will make is that this consolation (itself) is one of the mistaken activities! You are right, but you must trace that even *deeper*, until you get to the bedrock, the absolute core. And you will discover that it is the *feeling* of being separate. It is this very feeling of being *separate* (from that which I am in pursuit of) that sets up stress and strain in the mind/brain/body . . . the psycho-physical system. Hence, the need to be consoled arises.

Here is the object that I want to union with in order to become happy, and *until* that union is made, I am in a state of stress or strain!

There are things you have been trying to union with your *whole* life and you *still* have not achieved union with them! So this means that throughout your whole life there have been things that have caused you years of stress, which are still causing you stress, because you still have not achieved them. (From the sangat): *And you never will!* Right! *That* is a hell of an insight! You have been looking for that right man (or right woman) that you read about in some fantasy book when you were twelve years old, but you have *not* found him (or her)! Fifty years have gone by and for fifty *years* you have been in *stress* and strain because of your failure to achieve that goal. And this *consolation*, then, becomes an *activity* in which we involve ourselves in order to comfort us during the interim.

You are absolutely right, but we want to get down to the *root* of this thing. All of these other things are leading us there, so there is nothing wrong with them. We are moving in the right direction: We are trying to understand what it is that *we* are doing. You are trying to understand your *own* activity as a living human being. This consolation is the first thing that you come across, and you begin to really *see* it. *That* is a remarkable degree of progress because most of us will not even see our consolation! We will not see the egoity that is really generating all of this consolatory behavior in us. You will be surprised at all the things you are doing to console yourself, but what your *principal* activity of consolation is, you have *no* idea.

If you are serious about it, I call you to do some homework between this meeting and the next. Let that homework be looking into how you are living and locate your own principal activity of consolation. How are you principally consoling yourself? Really look at it. *This* is the part, Viveka Ra, you will find that is unique. It will *vary* from individual to individual because each of us has devised our *own* particular activities to console ourselves. And look for them at the level of the body, the emotions and the mind! I want those of you who choose to do the homework to do it *thoroughly*! In fact, send me your discoveries; I would like to see them! This is voluntary, but it will take courage. Now, some will not have the courage to do this because you *do not* even feel it is necessary: "I don't have to do it." You are simply an idiot! Do not be idiotic about this thing. Do not be so arrogant that you feel you do not have to subject yourself to this kind of stuff. You must *do* it to *see* it. There is simply no other way.

Look at those principal *physical* activities at the level of your body that you engage in to give yourself relief, to console yourself, to make yourself *feel better*, to help you *handle* the stress and the discomfort—the "existential stress"—that comes with being an ego. This kind of existential stress and strain that we feel (across the spectrum of our being) manifests at the bodily, emotional and mental levels and, therefore, must be identified at each of these levels. Now, there is stress because I have not *unioned* with some goal. That stress will be subjectively experienced bodily, emotionally and mentally: "I have not found the right man (or right woman)." The stress at the level of body may manifest as "I ate twelve gallons of ice cream." But it is *definitely* going to impact you at the level of your body and you will definitely *have* to develop a strategy to relieve yourself.

It will also impact you at an emotional level, and you will have to also develop a strategy to *relieve* the stress and strain you are experiencing at the emotional level (which means that you will fantasize): "I'm going to get this man. He's coming soon. God is going to send me a man!" Do you see what I am saying? You have *all* kinds of fantasies that you *create* to relieve yourself at the emotional level! And, finally, mentally or intellectually you begin to come up with concepts to relieve yourself—strategies and *more* strategies. But you need to really *do* the work to see it.

[Question from the Sangat:] *So do you want us to do this for each day?*

However you would like to do it. I will leave that up to you. I am just pleading with you to try to spend a week. It is too much to ask you to make this a way of life. I am simply asking you to please take just one week and *study* your life and search it for this principal mistaken activity and the principal activities of consolation. If you can just *do* that, it will make my work a lot easier because then we will be reading from the same "book." We will be on the same page. As I told you in the past, here at the House, there is only *one* book to read, and that is the book of your *life*. I know you all like fancy names, so we will call it your *Jnana Sutra*. So, whenever you come to satsang, bring *your* Jnana Sutras with you—the book of knowledge of your life—and we will *study* from it. See if you can just spend one week. Do not excuse yourself, because *this* pertains to everybody in the room! *Everybody* truly needs to *do* this.

Mahadasi: *You said it can start from your childhood?*

Yes. The *mind* actually constructs or formulates a new ego as it moves from lifetime to lifetime.[1]

Maha Seva: *My understanding when you were speaking of the mind and the body is that when we think and that thought comes down to the emotional level, it turns into something else; and when it comes down to the physical, it also turns into something else.*

That is another way of looking at it. You can almost see that stress is like an energy that manifests itself variously across the different categories of being. Thus, there are many metaphors or models by which you can understand it. The homework is to *really* identify those principal activities that *you* are engaged in, *your* strategies for relieving yourself of your sorrow and suffering—bodily, emotionally and mentally. At least you should be able to see *that.* You may not be able to go deep into the principal mistaken activity that underlies *all* of that; but certainly you should be able to see that.

If you do not see how you are hopelessly consoling yourself, it is really hard to help you spiritually. You will be walking around thinking, "Well, Bhagwan, I'm not involved in any acts of consolation, so none of what you say pertains to me. None of what Buddha said, none of what Jesus said, none of what Mahavira said and none of the things that Moses said—none of this *pertains* to me." Then you become a voyeur. You are simply here looking in, "eavesdropping" on the rest of us. You are a "peeping tom." You are *not* really involved; you are just looking through the keyhole. You are perverted, pathological, you are getting your "rocks off." But then maybe your principal strategy of consoling yourself is through looking at other people's suffering and then critiquing it. Looking at others (voyeurism, pathology, peeping-tomism) *is* your principal activity. *That* is how you get by. Everybody has one; see *yours.*

Bhakti Máji: *In everything we do there is a strategy going on?*

Everything that you are doing. Everything!

---

[1] A detailed discussion of the impermanent nature of ego follows in Chapter Two.

Bhakti Máji: *So, you can take even the smallest thing, like me asking you this question, as an example of seeing how there is a certain strategy operating in all of us?*

You are absolutely right, Bhakti Máji. Now, you are being honest. I told you from the beginning that *all* of this is egoity—from bottom to top! Simply see it and lose your fascination with it. We are *fascinated* with it. We are *sympathetic* toward it. See it and then break your sympathy to this egoity. Cease being fascinated with it. See it for what it *really* is and then be moved to transcend it. When you *see* the activity, this develops into self-understanding.

Remember, I am not just calling you to involve yourself in some kind of sophisticated psychotherapy. I am calling you to really *investigate* the nature of your own being; to really look at your life and living; to truly begin to *understand* yourself. You must see this as the starting point on the Path. Sadhana has to be done in the *context* of self-understanding! Spiritual practice has to actually dictate to what extent these gatherings will be beneficial. Because how long can I continue with spiritual "mythology"? There is a limit to this stuff. How have I served you if I do not call you to rise above this? You can go to see "Rev. C.T. Chicken Wing" if you are just looking to be consoled! Right? Truly! And if you want to find perfect, proven strategies for consoling yourself, you can go to a therapist! That is what a therapist does! A therapist gives you ways to console yourself, ways to go from being "hysterically" unhappy and miserable to being "ordinarily" unhappy and miserable.

Sat Rani: *The thought that came to me was, what role would forgiveness play?*

Well, that would be psychology. Right now, I am going *beyond* psychology. The function of psychology is to make you "normally" miserable. Forgiveness is a method that will lead to normal misery. Forgiving your mother or your father or somebody that has offended you or hurt you relieves you from the anger that had previously been destroying your mental "comfort." You still are miserable, unhappy, unenlightened and ignorant, but it is "comfortable." Those are "little" teachings. That is psychology, and its aim is to help you adapt, to adjust you, to make you "normal," like the rest of society. If you think society is messed up, then why are you trying to become adjusted to it in the first place? If "society" is the problem, why in the world are therapists trying to adjust you to society? It is more madness! They are helping you to be "normally" insane, and you are paying a lot of money for that. Is that right, Sat Ra? You make good money, brother! I am calling for something that *transcends* all of that, that is much *deeper* than that. I do not think that we are going to be better able to sum it up than what Bharataji has already said. *Find* that thing, that *thread* that is connecting *all* of your activity. Every last one of them—even the most insignificant activity that you are engaged in at the level of the body, emotions or mind—is connected to this principal mistaken activity that is the source or origin of all of your activity: *ego*. And, therefore, the pain and suffering continue.

I want to try to truly serve you, but you are going to have to help me. I can teach, but *you* must actually practice. *That* is the relationship. If we do not have that element in our relationship, then we do not *have* any relationship! Do you just want me to sit here and teach, and then you practice *if* you feel like it? What kind of relationship are you asking me to be in with you? To *entertain* you? Are you going to reduce me to playing a part in your strategy to be consoled? Should the House, should satsang, should I, simply become a place (or an occasion) for you to console yourself, to make you "feel better" about yourself? You remain ignorant, but you feel better about your ignorance.

You must find the principal activity. You must find it, and there is a way to find it. That is my *only* reason for even getting up and coming here: I am waiting. Even if there is just *one*, like Tilopa and Naropa, I am waiting. I am just waiting for one person to really be ready to enter upon this journey for knowledge. Brother, are you the one?

The spiritual process is a *whole* different experience! It is translogical, transrational, transpersonal and transpsychological. It is not just religious, not just about morals. We are going, as the Buddha called it, into "the deep course of wisdom." In the *Prajnaparamita*, the Buddha said, "From here where I am at looking down, there is no body, no mind." I am now talking about going into the deep, deep course of wisdom. This is a happy occasion because *this* is the whole purpose for which we have been meeting. It is time that we get down and let the chaff be separated from the grain, and let the weak be separated from the strong. I am ready to roll! There is *no* way to reduce the teachings to a lower form. I cannot go *any* lower than this.

RESPONSIBILITY TO SEEKERS

Gurudasa: *I'm trying to go back in my experience to before I was initiated. If you had said this then, I would have felt really, really lost because it was only after initiation that I even was aware of the stuff going on in my mind. So, what about those who have not yet been initiated? Saying to do these things and thinking that you can do them is one thing, but being actually able to consciously and deliberately look is difficult.*

That is the reason why each of you is as responsible as I am because, as new people come, *you* will have to render service to them and *help* them. That is the whole purpose of sponsoring them, but that also means you have to get busy. You have to get them to the "Wine Shop" and all of those kinds of things. That is why you are doing all of these things: You are setting up a "House" and Dharma Máji is writing books. She is doing that for the benefit of those who are yet to come. You *all* should be involved in that, and you also should be *practicing* so that you actually have some knowledge to give. If you do what you are supposed to do, they will be fine, Gurudasa. Right, Viveka Ra? Straighten the sister out!

Viveka: *What you are saying is that a new person, having not experienced meditation and the process therein, would not be able to come up with an understanding of a mistaken activity, because they do not know what it is?*

Unless they are very intelligent.

Dharma Máji: *Some initiates cannot even do it.*

Right, Dharma Máji! But we will give them the benefit of the doubt. I know that there are some initiates who *cannot* do it. But we won't have that kind of situation anymore. I did not give you as much time to really consider all of these things. In some instances, I was too quick; your pain was just *too* much. I was guilty of "idiot compassion." I will never be guilty of that again; I will be wise. But your suffering was so great. What could I do? I *had* to *do* something. And now I must suffer the consequences of that and work backwards.

Yet, all of this will fall into place. Maharaj Ji[2] obviously has a plan
here, and we must *trust* in that plan. The Masters are *never* wrong! It
has been my observation that how you get here is how you needed to
get here, period! It always works out. Nonetheless, as we continue, it
is really necessary that we all really begin to look into this thing very
much. Gurudasa, I think newcomers will be better benefitted because
I will not indulge their mythology. I will not spend so much time
consoling them just to undo it all. I will immediately service
them—and so will you. *That* is what part of your obligation as a Sat
Dasi is: You too *must* serve. So I am confident that together we can
do it. We are a *sangat*, and we *can* and *must* do this thing.

This is the challenge, this is the homework. Enter into it, search
out those activities that are your principal activities of consolation. If
you are truly ambitious, try to find that principal mistaken activity that
underlies and connects *all* of your activities. More than anything,
begin to start trying to truly understand yourself. My purpose today
was to simply emphasize that it is now time for you to really start
trying to understand yourself, to *know thyself.* And if I do not do that,
you understand, then I will not really serve you. It would just be more
philosophy, more bullshit! I am trying to point you in the right
direction as best that I know how. You *must* stop playing games.

You must truly become serious and disciplined. Get off the edge
of the bowl. Stop straddling the fence. Get on in here or step back,
because you will be exposed now. Anyone that enters into this
homework will *automatically* be able to see people who are not really
serious! You will see those amongst you who are just in the "talk
school" of mysticism. They are just interested in talking "about" it.
They are not ready yet to, as Theravadaji says, "go into war." They are
still hiding. They are playing games of hide and seek. "Bhagwan, you
can't see me! I'm hiding behind my philosophy, my language, my
terminology, my *seva.* I'm hiding." It's really interesting that you
think nobody can see you.

Children are like that. Have you noticed that little children will
hide from you right in broad daylight! I have a little grandson, and
when I go over to his house, he will hide from me. "Baba, you can't
find me!" He just has his head bent, butt sticking up in the air! He

---

[2]Unless otherwise indicated, all references to "Maharaj Ji," refer
to Maharaj Charan Singh Ji, Bhagwan Ra Afrika's Guru.

cannot see *me* and, therefore, thinks I cannot see *him*. But *that* is the way a child is. I am simply saying that it is time for those of you who have been playing this childish little game to stop. Yes, I can *see* you! It's in broad daylight. It's all over with, and there is *no* need to do it.

Let us go ahead and get real and *be* all that we have an opportunity to be. Why be anything less? When you have a chance to become a mystic, *why* be content with just talking about it? Why? When you have a chance to *become* a Buddha, why go on just wanting me to tell you stories *about* the Buddha? Why? You have an opportunity to become a Buddha, to become a Mahavira. It is like food: Why be content with just talking about food, when it is much better to eat it? So I am calling you, and if it is only a handful, great! I am all right! I am not into numbers because numbers are not important. If it is just a handful of us, great because we will no longer be a "talking-head" school of mysticism. We already have plenty of those places. Many of you have *come* from places like that! We are going to go ahead and become a sangat, we are going to become *mystics*. Is there anybody in here interested in becoming a mystic? Good, then I think that we are now going to do this—not just look the part, not just have some "terminology"—we are going to do this! So it starts here, now.

I know many of you are very knowledgeable. You are educated people. As I told Bilal, over the years some of the most educated people in the 'hood have come through this place, to this Path. That is truly the case, so I cannot complain. I am really, really satisfied with that. I am happy with that, and I know that we can now really go to another whole level. I have been waiting, so let's go to work. I know you are educated, and you all study. But you do not have real, authentic knowledge, and I want you to get some *real* knowledge.

You know about the Bible and the Gita and all of those scriptures. You can hold your own. In fact, anybody who comes through this door (and has not been a part of this thing), you would just blow those people through the water! They cannot stand up to you. I know you all are ferocious, much sharper than the ordinary Christian, the ordinary Muslim. You yourself become surprised sometimes. Sardarji the Conqueror was telling me that he was talking to some people at his job, and they were looking at him like he was a Buddha. He says, "I don't understand why. I don't even *know* anything." He discovered that people are responding to him like he is a scholar. Strange! And how (and when) did he become a scholar, he wondered? Just the little, peripheral knowledge that you get here at the House is profound.

Sat Ra Heru, the therapist, is having a different experience than a lot of people because he is a practitioner in the business of "deep" thinking. It is what he does for a living. That was the thing that initially attracted him. He said, "I have been to school and studied all of this stuff!" He *saw* that, "I don't know *anything*! My God! Just the psychological depth of the House is incredible!" Guys have come through here and then gone out and *trained* psychiatrists. They would get dizzy because they have understood Freud. They have enough of a background. The pathology of ego may not impact you too much because you do not *know* anything about psychotherapy and psychoanalysis, but a therapist would understand it and it would just blow them away. It is just that clear. You are blessed by all of the traditions. I am saying that you are *ready* now; *let's go*. You have a little knowledge, and it is time to get some *big* knowledge! Right? I do not want you to be mistaken! *All* that you have been getting is "little" knowledge, and it is now time for the "big" knowledge: the knowledge of *thyself* and *who* you are (spiritually).

Ra shekum maat.

CHAPTER TWO
THE ORIGIN AND ANATOMY OF EGO

This is the first in a series of five workshops where we will be discussing managing *ego*. Actually, that is a misnomer because ego is the very thing which must manage itself. It is almost like asking a criminal to catch himself. Because there is a limitation in the language we can use to communicate, for lack of a better phrase, we will call this "managing" ego. However, I want you to remember that when talking about managing ego, the mystics are talking about becoming "egoless." It is not so much about a big ego managing a little ego as it is about becoming completely egoless.

Actually, when we begin to discuss the topic of ego and all of its ramifications, we enter into the very heart of mysticism, the very core. The attainment of a state called "egolessness" is the objective that underlies the ambitions of all spiritual traditions. We will be dealing, then, with the nucleus of all that is meant when we talk about meditation, when we talk about spiritual development, and so forth. As a result of that, it will necessarily cause us to revisit a lot of old things, but in a very different light. So, in some respects, this is a kind of summary series in the sense that it will cause us to revisit a host of prior topics that we have been discussing throughout all of the last workshops—nay, throughout all of the last ten or fifteen years.

It will be a little difficult to talk about this subject simply because there are dimensions that are wordless. Egolessness is not something you can really talk about. It does not lend itself to any kind of "linguistic" captivity. It is very hard to reduce that experience to words. Yet we have had a little luck in the past, and we simply pray and hope that we remain fortunate enough to try to gain some insight into this whole business about "ego."

You have to come to a different level of understanding of what is meant by the word ego. Normally, when we talk about egotism, to what are we referring? When we say that somebody has a big ego or is ego-tripping or is very egotistical, what is the normal connotation of the word "ego" as we use it, the colloquial use of the word? "Very self-centered." Right? Some other meanings would be "full of themselves," "arrogant," and so forth. Yet, these are really byproducts of ego. They are not ego proper. These are the *derivatives* of the state called ego. Egotism is not simply a reference to a person's arrogance, their self-centeredness, or their being full of pomposity, even though they may be pompous and all of these other things. Egotism is not that—and that is bad enough—I am that saying egotism is worse than those things. It is much worse than being arrogant. It is much worse than being pompous. It is much worse than being simply self-centered. It is worse than being a megalomaniac. It is worse than all of these things, because it is the *mother* of them. It gives birth to all of these negative, repulsive traits that we find in each other. It behooves us, therefore, to go deep into this subject of the nature and anatomy of ego, its origin or genesis.

Remember, we will be going into an area that will be painful for some of us, because to traverse this path leading toward the origin of our egos, we will be coming across many things in ourselves of which we may not have been aware. We will be pointing out, for all of those who have eyes to see, certain dimensions in ourselves that are not particularly flattering, so it will be a little difficult.

Emma: *I just want to say one thing. You have talked about this before in the anger seminar and, from what I can remember, you were saying that the ego is really those false feelings of separateness from God. People have isolated themselves in their minds or even nominated themselves as God and their whole life proceeds from that assumption.*

Already you have started this deep stuff! You couldn't wait? But you are absolutely right. That is a very good working definition which we will use for egotism.

So, Emma, let us begin first with a definition of "ego." Ego is that mind process, as the flyer says, which separates man-consciousness from God-consciousness. Ego is the *felt* experience of being separate, isolated or *individuated* from that which is the source of our being. It is a kind of "spiritual amnesia." How did it begin? Much has to be understood to appreciate our predicament.

THE BEGINNING

In the beginning, or before the beginning, because we really cannot even talk about "time," since there was no time at the stage when all that exists was simply in a state of absolute, total *oneness*. You will find that the common thread which runs through all of the great traditions—whether it is Buddhism, Hinduism, Islam,

Christianity, Judaism, Zoroastrianism, any of the great traditions—is that there is only *one* God; there is only *one* consciousness. The whole objective of all of the great traditions is to bring its adherents into the realization and experience of this oneness. Some will approach it this way, some will approach it that way, but they all are trying to attain the same fundamental goal: the rediscovery or the recapture of the experience of oneness. God, Allah, whatever you call it—it does not really matter—that which is the ground of existence prior to manifestation, existed in an unmanifested, undifferentiated state, with no form and no distinction.

The words of all the scriptures have said, "In the beginning there was nothing." Now, that's interesting. Remember, by "nothing" they do not mean nothing, zero. There is a hyphen in between: *no-thing*. There was no distinction. There was no individuation. There was no duality. There was no hot, no cold; no wet, no dry; no tall, no small; no near, no far; no black, no white. There was no dialectic, no duality—simply oneness, undifferentiated and unmanifested. The soul was merged into the ocean of God. There was no experience of being an individual soul at all! There was only the experience of oneness. The Sikh and Radha Soami mystics call that state *Sach Khand*. The authors of the Kabbalah called it *Ain Soph*. The ancient Afrikans called it the state of being in *Amen*. The Buddhists call it *nirvana*. Different words have been used throughout time by different cultures to refer to this state of nothingness, no-thingness.

It is hard for the mind to even imagine this, because our minds can only think in terms of dialectics. Our minds can only think in terms of dualism. Our minds, our intellect cannot think of something being cold without simultaneously having the concept of something that is hot. So, it is hard for us to even imagine that there was something before there was anything; that there was nothing before there was anything; and that things came out of this nothingness, this *potentia*, as one philosopher called it. Simply potentia existed, and in that sea of potentia, in that *nunn*, as the ancestors called it, in those "waters" as some of the early Christian fathers and mothers called it, in that "ocean," the wave rose which gave birth to the first differentiations. This wave of the will of God, this "Word" of God, this *Logos*, this *Shabd*, this *Nam*, this "Sound," caused the creation to come into being.

I am just going over this casually with you, because you have to understand some of the cosmology of the phenomena that gave birth to the experience of your individualism. Out of this unmanifested, undifferentiated sea of potentia, there arose the so-called "soul." Later you will appreciate why I say "so-called." In any case, this was the first descent of consciousness, down through all of its lower manifestations in existence. In the parlance of the mystics, it was the *descent* of the soul from God down into creation.

There was not yet even a "creation" at the first separation. In fact, the souls did not even know they were *separate*. They were separate, but they did not know it! They had no concept of this. There was still this feeling—this experience of oneness—even though in reality, they had become separate. This was the stage right beneath that state of total, existential oneness.

Then, the *force* of creation moved again and the soul descended further into creation, and at this next level, it became aware of its own *individuation*. It became aware of its own separatism. Now, remember, this was still a very high state. There was still no time, no space, no causality. There was still no mind, no senses, no body. It was "nothingness": the state where the soul first becomes aware of its own individuation. The state that the Sikh and Radha Soami mystics call the level of *Sohang*, the *Bhanwar Gupha* region; the second and third *Sephiroth* of the Kabbalah system. Here, the soul's experience of its own individuation came into being, and that was the first illusion of ego—*maya*, as the Hindus call it. What is "maya"? Maya fundamentally means "illusion," and the *maha maya*, the "great maya," is the illusion that you are separate from God. All other illusions arise from, and are rooted in, this one fundamental illusion. At this fourth level, looking up from the bottom, we come into the experience of our own individualism for the first time: *Sohang*—I am.

Next, the soul descends further into creation, to the *Daswan Dwar* region, sometimes called *Par Brahm*—"beyond the Creator." The soul (consciousness) then descends further into the creation. Now, it picks up a mind and the experience of time and space. It is covered now, and that sense of separation becomes more intense. It then descends a bit further to the *Anda* region and picks up the *astral body*, a body of sensory systems, and the ability to perceive only "dualistically." With each further descent of the soul into creation, the intensification of the experience of separation goes on increasing. Finally, we find ourselves (consciousness) at the physical level, the *Pind* region, encased in a physical body, at the maximum level of maya, where we experience our so-called individuation and separateness.

We will revisit some of this as we continue the rest of the workshops, but I wanted to start out by setting the tone, setting the stage so that you can begin to understand and appreciate the metaphysical origin of the experience of egotism. Again, for most of us, this is not going to be easily accessible, because we are talking about things that, by definition, cannot be comprehended at our lower level of awareness. Let us reverse the direction and try to approach this subject at a level we can understand, which is the "psycho-social" origin of ego. I will try as best I can to help you visualize this.

BIRTH

I want you to understand that it all begins with this thing called "birth." It is simply an illusion because, how can that (pure consciousness) which has never been in time or space be born? If birth is a reality, then death—its opposite—is also a reality. That which we are, in essence, never was born; therefore, how can it die? What, then, is born in us? It is ego. "Birth" and "death" refer to this experience of egotism, this experience of separateness.

The Zen Masters have always put the question to us: "What was your original face like before your grandmother was born? What did you look like?" The inference is that, that which you are at the deepest levels, *existed* even before your physical mother existed! There is something in you that is very elemental. Something in you has been floating around since *before* time immemorial which simply coalesced in the form of a body. However, that which you are preexisted this physical body. Before this body was even born, part of it was in my father since he was a little boy. Part of it was in my mother since she was a little girl. They had not even met and I was in *potentia*, and so it was with all of us. I want you to understand that we have to use the words "birth" and "death" very carefully.

As we begin to look at the evolution of ego, let us consider the time of your pre-birth, when you were still in your mother's womb, as a state of egolessness, as an experience of egolessness. Because when you were in the womb, you were one with your mother. You had no sense of individuation. There was no sense of "I," no sense of "me" at all. You were in a state of "unconscious" oneness. Some psychologists say that we all unconsciously seek to *psychologically* re-experience this oneness we experienced in our mother's womb, to re-experience that thing they call "oceanic bliss." You were not conscious of this oneness, but we will use this as a symbol of egolessness. This is something which is accessible to our imagination. You can imagine how the child in his mother's womb is just a part of that whole milieu, with no individuation. It has not yet come into this "outer" world. It is *unmanifested*. The whole development of this ego begins after birth.

THE SEVEN STAGES OF EGO

The mystics have talked about seven fundamental stages in the psychological evolution of ego. We must understand that our ego is a very important thing. It is very important that we have ego. Now, I know this is striking you as odd, because I just said a few minutes ago that the objective of the great traditions is to become egoless! All of our effort on the Spiritual Path is to attain this state of egolessness! Yet, on the other hand, I am telling you that ego is absolutely necessary! It has a useful function. It is imperative that you have ego! I have already warned you that we would be traveling in a dimension that is not always logical. It is "cosmo logical," and you have to come up a notch.

You have to be able to think "holistically." You have to cease making separations between day and night and understand that they are simply different parts of the same reality. You have to cease making distinctions between good and evil and understand that good and evil are simply different dimensions of one reality. You have to see that fear and love are linked together, and that it is the same energy. You have to move to the very highest parts of your intelligence. After all, that is the function of intelligence: to help us understand this mystery we call "life."

Ego has a legitimate function. It is like this. Consider ego like a toothache. We have all had a toothache. Painful, isn't it? However, think about it: If you have never had a toothache, you cannot enjoy *not* having a toothache! It is not possible! Do you see my point? So, you must have ego in order to really experience egolessness, and this is a very strange concept at first. If you do not have a strong, mature ego, it is very unlikely that you will ever achieve a state of egolessness. Now, I know this is strange to you, but I have to tell you my perception of the truth. I will leave it to you to judge. The problem, you see, is that most of us have *weak* egos. I know I'm getting into trouble now!

Our egos are not yet *mature* enough to transform into the experience of egolessness. I want you to see why I make this statement.

Please keep in mind that, in order to attain the final stage of egolessness, we must mature through all of the stages of ego. In order to appreciate not having a toothache, you must have a toothache. In order to appreciate food, you must have hunger—the opposite experience. In order to appreciate higher dimensions of consciousness, you must have the experience of this lower dimension of consciousness. In order to appreciate heaven, you must have the experience of this hell. It is mandatory. *Ais dhammo sanatano*: That is the law. Let us begin.

STAGE ONE: THE BODY-SELF

The first phase in the development of the experience of separateness is the emergence of the "body-self." When the child comes into "the world," it still does not have a *full* experience of being physically separate from its mother. Isn't that interesting? Mothers, you all know that better than a lot of us men because you are right in the mix of it, and it works both ways. The woman does not know that the baby is no longer a part of her. She still has this feeling of oneness, and that feeling lingers literally all of the mother's life in connection with her children. That child always feels "one" with her, because it is hard for a female to break that experience. This psychological and emotional umbilical cord remains connected because she, too, has had an experience of "oneness."

When the child comes out of its mother's womb, the body-ego is still very weak. The child really does not have a sense of separation. The full sense of separation begins only in its later stages of development. The first fifteen months or so of a child's life are all related to its coming into a *subjective* state of physical, individual separation from its parents, the mother in particular. But they very often still do not know the difference between the inside and the outside of their bodies! There is fuzziness there. Their experience has not yet been broken up into a subject and an object. There is as yet no subject-object faculty developed in them. This, then, is the first stage in the development of the experience of ego.

Some people stay locked in this first stage all of their lives. Once they finally are able to establish a sense of individuation physically, when they are finally able to *feel* physically separate and that the body is the foundation of their identity, they never move beyond that point. They go on the rest of their lives feeling that "I am only the body." Have you ever noticed that there are those people whose whole life revolves around this physical body, and all of their energy is expended on this "I am the body" type of philosophy? These are individuals whose egos never developed beyond the first stage.

Emma: *Do you mean people who are vain, very much into themselves?*

No, I mean people who are basically "materialistic," and they are stuck in the body-self, the body-ego, the first stage of development. When the identification of who you are is locked into your body image, and it never emerges beyond that, you will simply remain on a level of materialism: food and sex. All your actions, everything you think and do will be centered around this body, because this is *who* you think you are! This is all you think you are. You did not go any further in the developmental stages of ego. Hopefully, this will become a little clearer as we continue. As usual, the first workshop is the hardest, because we have to introduce so much new material.

STAGE TWO:
THE DEVELOPMENT OF SELF-IDENTITY

The next stage in the evolution and the development of our egos is that stage where we begin to develop a "self-identity." We have already discovered that we are no longer in our mother's womb. We have finally discovered that there is a difference between "inside" and "outside." We now begin to put together an "identity," in the sense that we develop an identity which has "continuity." We need to somehow be assured that the self which existed yesterday is the same self that exists today, and will be the same self that exists tomorrow. You will see little children, for instance, get in front of the mirror and look at themselves and just smile. They are reassuring themselves that "I am still here. I am the same one that was here yesterday. This is *me.*" The experience of "me" gets developed—the "me" that is distinct from others and has continuity. In fact, the feeling when this stage of ego development is complete, is that this "me" will always exist! You will find that there are many of us on these Spiritual Paths and in religion who, under the delusion that it is this second stage of ego development which we mistakenly define as the "soul"—but is really the "me"—that will live forever! This is the "me" that wants to go to heaven! This is the thing that wants to avoid hell. This is the thing that wants to become enlightened! This is the sense of "self" that wants to obtain buddhahood. This self is impermanent! This self will die. It has no existence beyond this physical body. It has arisen out of it. It is nothing but a collection of the experiences that have occurred to this physical body, and it too shall pass.

Sharon: *You mentioned not moving past the physical body, and that what we call the soul is really the "me," because people mistakenly use the word "soul"—whether as religious organizations or individuals—then what is a soul?*

That is a very good question, and I hope Pam will answer that for you right after I finish! Let me develop it a little for her, because the reality, sister, is that most of us have no idea what our souls are! We really do not. We have no authentic, "conscious" experience of being a spirit! Our conscious experience is of being a body, and a collection of the history that is connected to that body. This is what constitutes our feeling of me (self). When you say "me," this is what you are referring to: your body, its history and your name. A very important component in self-identity is name. The child now knows his name, and when you ask him, "Who are you," you get the name. They become very identified with their name and things of that nature. This "me" starts developing, and when we are stuck at this level of ego development, our whole ambition is the perpetuation of this historical "me."

When the body dies, we still think this "me" will survive the body and go to heaven! Anyone who is aware of this can easily exploit us spiritually because we want this "me" thing to live forever, and this "me" thing does not live forever. It is false. It is pseudo, and it will not survive the death of this body. Very often it does not even survive the life of this body! But it surely will not go beyond the life of this body. So, if you have been imagining yourself (the "me") up in heaven, you might as well drop this nonsense, because that which you think you are does not have a chance of going to heaven! That is not the part of you which can be in heaven at all. That part of you which you are calling "me" will be left right here, and this is what creates the deep fear of death in all of us. Somehow, intuitively, *deep down inside*, you know this "me" is not going to survive, but you are hoping that the priest is right. You are hoping that the mullah, the Imam, the rabbi is right. They will tell us, "Oh, don't worry about it, Bhagwan, you will be right there on the right-hand side of Christ." Or, "You will be right there sitting next to the Buddha." Yet, something deep down inside of us recoils; we have doubts and our death becomes a terrifying thought.

Remember, at some point in time, "you" (the "me") will not be anymore! Yes, the world will be here. Birds will go on chirping. Sunrises will go on happening and the sunsets will still be beautiful and the seasons will still rotate. Waves will still crash against the seashore, but "you" (the "me") will not be here to experience it at all. You will be no more. All of those whom you love will still be here, but you will not be here.

Whenever our minds begin to reflect on this truth—and this is one of the noble truths of the Buddha—that this ego, this "me" thing, this body is of the nature that it will grow old, get sick and die, seeing this, we become terrified. You have an identity that is only made up of your body-self and your self-identity. That is all the ego you have. However, this physical body will get sick. The body-ego is of the nature that it will become ill and it will die. This is reality! It will grow old and die. The relationships which you are in also will end, because they are impermanent. When one begins to reflect on these kinds of truths, it fills one with a certain terror, because there will be no "me" after this body is gone! No "me" that is going to any paradise at all. This is hard to accept! We will come back again throughout the course of these workshops and explore these things in a little more detail.

Let us continue looking at the unfolding of ego from the initial state of egolessness in our mother's womb to full-blown ego. Remember, I have said already that unless there is a full unfoldment of ego, we will not be able to return to this experience of egolessness. There is a kind of egolessness in the womb that is unconscious. It is egolessness, but it is *unconscious* egolessness; therefore, you can't experience it. There is no toothache, but you do not experience the bliss of no toothache, because you have yet to have a toothache. The unfoldment of ego is the way existence gives you a toothache. So, when you reencounter egolessness beyond the levels of egotism, you can appreciate that state.

STAGE THREE: THE EXTENSION OF EGO

What happens next in our evolution as egos—and, remember, we are adding on to this experience of separateness, deepening it as we go through this process—is what we call the "extension" of ego. The ego begins to extend itself. Here, the key words are "me" and "mine." The "mine" mind-set emerges. As the ego begins to extend itself, it begins to incorporate other elements into the definition of identity, into the experience of "self": "This is *my* gun. This is *my* dolly. This is *my* toy." You can see clearly when children enter this stage of ego development, because they start becoming very, very attached. Very, very persistent. Very, very "selfish," as we parents call it. We will tell the children, "Don't be so selfish! Share." "Oh, no! Hell, no, I don't want to share! It's mine!" Even though nobody else picks it up, the child doesn't want to play with the toy! They are not interested in it anymore! That is not the point. The point is, "That's *my* toy, and this other little boy or other little girl can't have it. I am not interested in using it, but it is mine! It is a part of me. It belongs to *me*." We now start entering into the world of attachment.

What is "attachment" and what makes attachment so difficult? Attachment is nothing but the extension of your sense of identity onto other things and people. You incorporate them into your own definition of who you are, and cling to them just as you did when you were three years old! Please notice it! Many of us have never developed our ego beyond this third stage, and now it is, "That's *my* car" or "This is *my* TV. You don't watch this TV unless I tell you to! This is mine!"; or "This is *my* house! You get out!" Just listen to your day-to-day language. Whenever somebody does something to that thing you call "mine," look how agitated you become! "You are messing with my stuff!" This is *your* stuff! It is the stuff that you are *made* out of now. In addition to your personal histories and all of those other things, you now add your possessions to your definition of "self."

In fact, this stage is where very serious conflicts in personal relationships begin to develop. Very serious trouble begins here. You are getting deep into the *dukkha* now. You are getting deep into suffering. Remember, these are the doors through which your suffering comes. These are the doors through which dukkha enters your life. These are the doors through which misery consumes you. The more we have the more we want; and the more we want, the more we are possessed by those very things! *That* is misery! "Mine!" We create more distance between us and other people, and the gap goes on increasing.

Remember, everything that you call "mine" will ultimately be taken from you or you will be taken from it! *Ais dhammo sanatano*: That is the law. That's how it is. "My house." Before you bought the house, someone else was calling it *their* house. In any event, sooner or later, either you will die or you will lose the house, one or the other. It is just a temporary thing. Yes, we can use these things, of course, but we do not "own" them. And, worse, they are not extensions of us, and it is at this third developmental stage that we now take on an additional *kosha*, an additional covering, an additional layer over our pure consciousness which begins to create in us the feeling of being the things we possess, the things we call "mine." Whenever that which is "mine" is threatened, I feel threatened. Strange, isn't it?

Vernita: *Bhagwan, how should we refer to our things, then? I mean, since we are really not our cars, how should we refer to them?*

You have no choice. We have to use this language, it is colloquial; but behind it, there should be some understanding. There is no language in which we can accurately speak. Understanding is the key! As we go through this series, you will find that the faculty in us, the quality that has been given to us for the transcendence of this ego formation is intelligence. It is *understanding*. We all have been endowed with the capacity to understand, even though it is dormant, even though it has just been lying there undeveloped for lifetimes, through innumerable births. Nonetheless, it exists in you, and the whole aim and objective of meditation and growth on the Spiritual Path are to trigger and revitalize this enormous capacity to understand. It is this understanding that transforms all of these wrong views. We need not worry too much about our lexicon, because what else can we do? The Masters have always said that, ". . . Once you have spoken, you have already distorted truth."

I am reminded of a story about St. John, the great mystic who, after becoming an old man, was asked on one occasion to give a discourse on the beautiful teachings of Christianity and the historical Christ, to speak to an audience and give them some kind of idea of what it means to become a Christ. Remember, Jesus' name was not "Christ." "Christ" was the state of consciousness he was in. They wanted St. John to speak on the dynamics of becoming a "Christ."

St. John took what seemed like forever to get up out of his seat and make his way through the crowd, and there he stood before them and he said, "Love God." Now, the people who had put this thing together said, "Man, we have been standing out here for hours in this hot sun. Some have come a long way and brought food and stuff and they have heard about you. You had better get up or we will have a riot on our hands! You have to say something." John said, "Well, if I say more, then I will begin to lie. Then, I am going to be destroying it; I am going to be corrupting it. I have already said as much of the truth as can be said and it took me a long time. What do you think I was sitting there for? I was trying to be as accurate, as precise in my language as possible." He said, "The only word that I found in the entire vocabulary available to me, to mankind, was this word 'love.' Now, you want me to go and start lying to them." The man said, "Say some more." John said, "Love and all things will be added unto you. Beyond here I will not go any further." The point is that words fail us. There must be the understanding.

As I mentioned earlier, at this third stage of ego development, the stage where we have begun the extension of our ego, we begin to add to our experience of being a "self" the experience of things being "mine." Remember, there was a time when you didn't feel anything was yours! I know you cannot remember it, because it is buried. Yet, there was a time in each and every one of our lives when we did not have this experience of anything being "ours," and we were blissful, absolutely blissful. All of your problems begin to escalate with the manifestation of this stage of egoness. Life starts going downhill from there!

The vast majority of mankind and womankind hardly ever goes beyond this stage! Their whole life is spent trying to perpetuate and maintain the existence of their ego extension. Every time one of those extensions end or is damaged, they experience pain and suffering. "My car broke down." Now, you are not going to sleep for two weeks! You lie awake all night and can't even sleep because, "My transmission went out. I'm in misery!" You are not a transmission, but in this state of ego development you can make no distinction between yourself and your transmission! There is no distinction between you and your car, and you just suffer. But it is in the nature of transmissions to go out. It is inevitable!

STAGE FOUR: THE CREATIVE STAGE OF EGO

The fourth developmental stage we come to in the evolution of our egos is what we can call the development of self-creativity, the "creative ego." You might not have been able to see this in your own development. How many of you still have small children? If I were you, I would get out a notebook and I would study that child, because that child can be a Koran to you. It can be a Bible to you. It can be a great scripture. It can give you more knowledge than the Vedas and all of the *sutras* put together! If they are still younger than seven, you really have hit pay dirt and, for those of you who do not have any children younger than seven, start over! You messed up, because you should have watched your first set! So make two or three more children and maybe you can see. No? Then you had better pay close attention to me!

You will see the child eventually hit a stage of ego development where its emphasis is on "doing" something. This is the stage where they become the "doer." They do not want you to do anything for them! "I can carry it myself! I want to do this myself." They want to do stuff themselves. They do not want any help. "Don't put my shoes on! I want to dress myself." "Don't comb my hair anymore. I am a big girl. I want to do it myself!" They want to become doers. They want to express their own creativity because they now have a stronger self, a stronger sense of identity. They have made their extensions and have discovered their own creative power and want to demonstrate it in their lives. And when you interfere with this, you get a strong reaction from them. Is that right? They do not want you to interfere with their power! They become capable of doing their "own thing," and they love doing it.

Sometimes when learning language, they will just go on asking you questions: *Mommy, where is Daddy?* "Daddy is at work." *Mommy, where is Daddy?* "Daddy is at work. I just told you!" They will ask you ten times. They are not interested in your answer, they are just practicing saying, *Mommy, where is Daddy?* They are enjoying their mastery over the ability to speak. There is nothing behind the question! Do you understand? They are learning. You will see little boys take off and just run. You will say, "What are you running for?" They are not running for any reason! They are not going anywhere in particular; they are just practicing running! Sometimes they will hum "roo, roo." They are humming about nothing, they are just practicing doing their humming. They like to *do* stuff, and when we interfere with the normal development of the creative ego, we set up some big problems. We have to learn how to "channel" this. This is all very insightful, especially for those of us who are parents.

It is also insightful for those of us who are in a relationship with another human being, period. As husbands and wives we need to understand all these stages, because you may be married to somebody who has never developed their ego beyond the first level of identification with the body. They may be stuck there. That means all you can do is have sex with them and give them something to eat! Now, if you cut down on that, you are going to be in trouble! You are going to have hell to pay! You are talking about abstract stuff, such as retirement and traveling, but this person is not interested in traveling. This person is not interested in seeing what is going on in the world or world issues. This person says, "Where is the food? Where is the sex? Do something for me, do something for my body! Give me some food and some sex, some pleasurable experiences." And that is it! You have to be aware of all of this. Try to understand how all these things impact on your relationships with people.

Resuming our discussion, the fourth developmental stage in the evolution of our ego is where we come into the discovery of our power to create, and we become "doers." As I stated earlier, there may be those of us who are stuck in this stage. Like that little child, we go on just talking nonsense! It has no meaning. We are just practicing talking. We are going to church asking, "What happened to Jesus? How did Jesus do this? How did Buddha do this?" You are not interested in any answers; you are just talking! You are practicing formulating questions, just like you did when you were four years old: "How did the world come into being? How do I meditate?" You are not going to do any meditation! You have no intention whatsoever! You are practicing talking! You are practicing asking questions. You are just doing stuff. You are just doing shit, with no aim, and no rhyme or reason. Where are you going? You don't know. Now, you are breaking your neck running! Where are you going? "I don't know, but I'm running." Where are *you* going? What are *you* doing?

Ask yourself, "What am I trying to do with my life?" Really think about it: *What are you trying to do with your life?* Have you ever thought about what you are actually trying to do with your life? Every day you get up and rush around, doing this and that; you have so much to do. Yes, I understand, but what is the point? What are you trying to *consciously* and *deliberately* do with your life? Most of us do not have a clue! We are just doing shit and hoping for the best. Is that right? Do you bear witness? So this fourth stage is the stage where all of our emphasis is simply on doing. It is doing with no goals, no clear-cut understanding of why you are doing anything, with no particular or deliberate plan at all. You are just doing shit.

STAGE FIVE:
THE DEVELOPMENT OF SELF-IMAGE

I want you to get this because we have already talked so much about it. Still, I cannot miss the opportunity to talk to you about it again. It is this fifth stage of ego development where we develop our "self-image." I want to remind all of us again of what is involved in this. This is the stage where all of our arrogance begins to seep in. Remember, we have talked so much about self-esteem and all of that. We have talked so much about our arrogating to ourselves qualities and virtues that we do not even possess, etc. All of that is beginning to take place as we enter into this fifth developmental stage where we now are formulating our image of ourselves. God alone knows what we put into that image of ourselves! What constitutes the image that we form of ourselves?

This is usually the stage of "feedback." Our parents, siblings, friends and associates begin to give us feedback. They begin to comment on that package we have put together, that persona, that ego, that thing we have created for ourselves. When it interacts with other people, they give us feedback. They say, "Oh, Bhagwan, you're this," or "Bhagwan, you're that." And you begin to start forming an "image" of yourself. Other people become like the mirrors you look into in order to get a glimpse of who you are. That glimpse becomes your persona, and you start trying to act it out. Someone who does not know who *they* are has told you something that you have bought as being absolutely true about yourself! Is that right? They said, "Bhai Rani Ra, you are so and so. You're like this, you're like that." Now, you buy that; you *internalize* it.

Very often, as children enter this stage of ego development, and begin to formulate images of themselves, is when most "abuse" takes place. Some parent has said, "Oh, you're no good," or "Oh, you're very smart. You're better than everybody else." Because your mommy and daddy told you how much better you were than the neighbor's child, you internalized that crap, and that arrogance has followed you throughout your life. Now, you are walking around and actually having this built-in feeling that you are "better" than other people because your parents have put it into your head. You have actually formed your image of yourself based on that. You have set yourself up for all kinds of heartaches and heartbreaks, because the reality is that nobody is better than anybody! If anything, we might be a little worse than other people, but we are certainly not better.

STAGE SIX:
THE DEVELOPMENT OF THE RATIONAL SELF

At the sixth stage in the evolution of our egos, we begin to develop a "rational" dimension to our egos. We begin to think and to accumulate knowledge. We become "reflective." Unlike that doer who is just doing stuff, we *do*, but we are reflecting on what we are doing. We may still not know where we are going, but we are reflecting, we are pausing and examining things. We are able to see into things. We are able to penetrate a little of this veil. We have a little more control now. We are a bit more deliberate. We become rational. We become the "thinking" ego. However, *very* few people get to this stage.

Philosophers, teachers, professors, writers, great men and women of intellect, have at least developed enough ego to do those things. All of the great contributions to civilization have come from these sixth-stage developed egos. A person in the first stage of ego development cannot be a philosopher or a teacher. As I have just said, this person is only trying to get some food and some sex. They are not interested in teaching anybody anything. We cannot make computers. Yes, we can buy them and plug them in, but there is no way we can figure out how to make them. We are not even interested in math and circuitry and binary things. "I'm trying to find out where the party is." Our egos are too immature to be interested in that stuff. Only those egos who have matured can do these things—and, remember, this is a kind of *spiritual* maturity. You can think of these as levels of ego maturation, and the rational ego as another level of ego we have to mature to. Yet, there are people who are stuck at this level as well, and they never go beyond it.

Again, at the sixth level of ego maturation, we now have matured to a point where as egos, we become reflective. The rational ego can now look back and examine its self-image and edit it. You have to be very mature to do that. If your degree of ego development has not gone beyond the fifth stage, where you have only formulated your image of yourself, and you have not been able to mature to the next level, you cannot *critique* yourself. You cannot truly *see* into yourself.

When you get angry, you cannot handle your anger, because you cannot pause and try to see into the nature of your anger. When you are correctly practicing effective management of your anger, you will find that if you look deeply into the nature of your anger, into all of the subtle and underlying aspects of it, that anger will transform itself into compassion. Now, somebody has done something to you and you are full of rage, you are angry—but you do not have enough maturity to go deeply into it. You cannot go into it because your "image" is saying, "Somebody has done something wrong to me. That person is no good; they are bad. I'm perfect, and I have given them no reason!" You must understand all of the nonsense that we say to ourselves, all the defensiveness we go through. We are trying to protect the self-image we have formulated of ourselves to such an extent that we cannot evaluate or investigate it.

Something has come into you, this anger has come into you. It is on your porch, it is in your "house." You should investigate it! If there is a noise downstairs, shouldn't you find out what's going on? You may have to call the police or you may have to use that baseball bat or something, but you need to investigate! Yet, when this anger comes into you, you do not investigate it. You do not pause to see, "Wow, why am I having this kind of reaction to what this person said?" You do not look at it: "What is going on in me? What is there deep inside of me that has caused me to get so angry about this little thing? They didn't say 'Good morning' to me, and I am furious!" Why? Go into that? What is in you that is the root cause of this kind of overreaction?

In order to be able to do that, you need to have some degree of ego maturity. You need to go into that, because you are looking for something that may be "wrong" in you, something that may be "weak" in you. However, you also know what is "right" in you. It is not that you only know what is wrong with you; you also know what is right with you! You know those areas that you are strong in, those areas that are your good qualities. You are very aware of those things. Some people's problem is that they do not know what is wrong with them, nor do they know what is right with them! Now, they are in very bad shape! They do not know their weaknesses, nor do they know their strengths. There is not enough ego maturity to see these things. So, at the sixth stage of ego development, for the first time we begin to develop some capacity for "insight," the ability to look into ourselves and see. And, remember, we're looking into ourselves not to judge, not to condemn, but to understand: "I want to understand what in me is generating this kind of reaction."

The same should be done not only with anger, but also with our fears. When we become full of fear, the normal instinct is to flee, to escape. Your instincts will say, "No, no, turn away!" because something "foreign" is inside of you. Something "dangerous" is going on inside of you. Therefore, look into the nature of your fear. What is causing you to have this frightening, fearful reaction? When you look deeply into fear, this looking transforms fear into "security." Strange! Very strange, but this is the power of understanding, sister, that you mentioned earlier. This is how we are to use our understanding, to *know* and to be able to explore all of the stuff that is going on in our subjectivity. By exploring them, we are able to transform them, because life is dialectic. It is dualistic: fear and love, which are polar opposites. You can all transform any fear into security. Please make a note of that! In every area of your life where you experience fear, if you can become *mature* enough to turn your insight inward and investigate it, explore it, you will be able to convert that fear into security. In every area of your life where there is still a lot of anger, if you are able to become mature enough to turn your seeing inward and explore the *nature* of your anger at that person, it will transform that anger into compassion.

Remember, there is a distinction between *compassion* and *sympathy*. Very often *your* sympathy is a lower-stage ego trip: "Poor thing. Look at him. I feel so sorry for him." That's not compassion. That is arrogance! You are tripping. You secretly feel, "Oh, I'm better than that person. Poor person!" You are looking down on them, but compassion is something you can have even for people who have injured you, who have done something that you perceive as being wrong. If you can look into your perception of somebody having done something wrong to you that has caused you this anguish and this hurt, and if you can look deep into the nature of your own anger, the *understanding* that will emerge will transform your reaction from one of anger to one of pure compassion. When you understand that, "They did not know what they were doing," and that, "They are as ignorant as I am," it becomes a very different experience. This is the secret. That is what the Buddhists have called the *buddhi* (intelligence). The word *buddha* comes from this: one who has awakened this capacity to understand.

STAGE SEVEN: THE STRIVING EGO

The seventh stage in the formation and development of our egos has to do with our striving, our "intent." Once the ego has matured to these higher levels, we begin to seek answers to the question I was asking you earlier: *What are you trying to do with your life?* You begin to strive, to live life meaningfully. You no longer are so immature that you are just running around doing shit, just for the sake of doing shit. Do you understand? You become much more "on purpose." You are trying to find some meaning in life. You are pondering the questions "Who am I?" and "What am I trying to do with my life?" You are now tackling this search for meaning full-time. Your ego becomes pure intelligence. You have understood that this body is going to go, and you have understood that all of its relationships are temporal, transient. Now, out of that understanding, you are trying to find some way to live that is reflective of all the knowledge and experience you have gained.

Very often when we enter our forties, we go through a "mid-life crisis." That crisis develops among people who have at least developed a certain degree of ego maturity where they are pausing and asking questions: "Do I want to spend the next twenty-five years with this man (or this woman), or on this job?" They begin to question all of that because they have become more mature and can see, "This is crap, this is a joke. I'm just going through motions. I am not doing this anymore!" Something in them starts insisting on more.

QUESTIONS AND ANSWERS

I think rather than go to the next level of the exploration of the origin and evolution of our egos, we will pause now to take any additional questions and explore any of the stages that have already been discussed. I want to do this as thoroughly as possible because of the complexity of the subject we are discussing. Remember, it is *transcending* this ego that is the goal of the Spiritual Path. Everything revolves around dealing with our egos. All of your misery and all of your suffering are rooted in and related to this ego, so it is a worthy topic.

Sharon: *Looking at the final stage, of turning back, in a sense reversing itself—or releasing the lower stages of ego because that's what I would take it as—would you say at that point the "Self" would then be turning back to its natural state, the state of enlightenment?*

Yes, in fact, you have just said it. From the seventh stage, you now return to egolessness—after you have exhausted all of your striving—but you first have to be mature enough to be striving. When we hit this striving stage, we must now *exhaust* ourselves. We are now diligently searching. We are not playing anymore! Before you were playing with this search. Now, you are serious! You become like a Buddha. You are in the forest. You are meditating. You are doing yoga. You are going all over this world, searching every nook, every corner, everywhere you hear about something that will help you solve this problem you are having as a mature ego. You exhaust this striving and, in the process of exhausting it, like Buddha, you sit under the *bo* tree and you become enlightened. It is like when fruit becomes ripe, like fruit your striving "ripens" and falls of its own. But, remember, there is nowhere to cheat! I have to remind you, because we cheat as much as we can! Right? You cannot cheat. You must absolutely *exhaust* that level of ego.

Allen: *That was one of my questions. I notice there are certain stages and you said that this happens in your forties. That means a brother like myself, twenty-seven years old, may still be in the "mine" stage of the ego and is thinking that he is the rational self, and that's why I'm feeling this pain. I am just asking, does it have to be a certain age?*

Remember, you said this just now! Normally, ego does develop chronologically, but not always. Hence, you can find young people, teenagers, who are very mature. It depends on what you brought into this creation. It depends on what you were in your previous birth. So, it is a kind of question that can only be answered on a one-on-one basis. However, as a rule—and there are always exceptions to rules—this occurs in chronological stages. These stages are not pigeonholes, and sometimes two of these developmental stages will coalesce, and you will be working on two things at once. It is really kind of individualistic. That is why one has to explore one's self. All mystics since time immemorial have said, "Know thyself," because you want to know where *you* are. This is when you begin to get good insight. You become aware that, "My God, I am still so immature. I have been living my whole life at the level of *mine*. I'm still caught up in *mine*. I'm still caught up in *me*. Oh, God, I'm still caught up in my *body!*"

Sometimes something from the outside has to shake us up so that we become aware of this, because those who are asleep, by definition, cannot wake themselves up. *An object at rest will remain at rest unless acted upon by an outside force.* This is a law of nature. And so it is with our minds. Hence, the need for a Buddha, a Jesus, a Muhammad, a Moses, a Ptah Hotep, a Kabir, a Dadu, a Lao-tzu. These people have to come, and they have to speak to us in such a way that it makes us wake up a little bit. The greatest benefit that can occur to any human being, in any lifetime, is to come into contact with the teachings of these great men and women. Because, unless we are able to encounter the teachings of these great Masters, we will simply remain asleep.

When they asked Buddha, who are you, what are you, Buddha simply said, "I'm neither male nor female. I'm not a Brahmin or a *kshatriya*. I'm not Indian. I'm not white." Then, what are you, Buddha? "I am simply awakened." There exists a different species of human beings, the "Awakened Ones." All of us have the capacity to be a Buddha. Please make no mistake about that. In all of us therein lies this capacity to become "awakened."

We begin first, though, by expanding our egos, by becoming more and more mature until we can get to this point where we are really striving. This striving is playing the game of life (*lila*). Play it all the way out, and then a point will come, brother, where the ego realizes it has gone as far as it can go. Then the ego does what? It *submits*. It surrenders. It is beautiful! It lets go, and in that letting go and submission, *egolessness* comes into being. This "submitting to the will of God" is what ultimately dissolves the ego. It is just like the sticks that we use to make a fire. We rub them together to get the fire going, and then we throw the sticks into the fire. It is like a boat that we take across the sea. Once we cross, we do not carry the boat on our heads. We leave it moored. It has done its job. Similarly, the ego has done its job when it has exhausted itself.

Then you come to the experience of your powerlessness. Right now you think you have power! You think you, as an *individual ego*, are in control! You are way down in the scale of your ego maturity! You are still caught up somewhere down in the third stage where you think you are the doer. The little four-year-old child thinks it can do everything: "Mommy, let me carry up the TV set. I can carry it"; or Mommy, let me drive the car." The boy is four years old. How is he going to drive? Can you drive? "Yes, Mommy, I can drive!" You know exactly what I am talking about, because as children we have also gone through this stage, and we see our own children go through this stage. Yet, many of us emerged into chronological adulthood and we are still trapped in that stage, which I call "magical thinking." You still think you can leap tall buildings in a single bound and all of this other stuff. That means your ego is not mature.

Sharon: *Going back to the soul, would the soul then equal the mind?*

No, but I am very glad you asked that question. At the next workshop we will begin to go into that. We say "my soul," or "That's my body." Anything that can be "mine" cannot be "me." Yes, the soul is a certain level of your reality, but the essence of what you are is beyond the soul! The mystics have used the word "spirit," but that is not a good word either. Again, we could say "my spirit." You are that about which you cannot say, "I am this" or "I am that." What the Hindus say is *neti, neti*—not this, not this. Go on eliminating. Are you the body? No. Are you the senses? No. Are you the mind? No. Are you the intellect? No. You are that which exists at the end of the process of neti, neti—not this, not that.

Sharon: *A nothingness?*

Yes, a nothingness! You catch on fast! The closest you can come is to say, "I am nothingness." That is about as accurate as you can be with words and concepts.

LEVELS OF CONSCIOUSNESS

Sharon: *At the beginning of the stages you started off by mentioning the egolessness within the mother's womb, and you* *finished by talking about the return to egolessness. My question is this: When a person begins the stage at birth, or even prior to birth, and they become stuck, for example, at the second stage which is self-identity, would that not make them closer to the beginning stage of egolessness than if they were to continue on? Or would it be necessary for the person to continue on in the stage of ego development to complete the cycle from "egolessness" to "egolessness"?*

Yes, they would have to continue, because otherwise they would be moving backward! And, remember, the experience of egolessness within our mother's womb is fundamentally an *unconscious* one. The experience of egolessness on the other side of the cycle is *fully conscious*. It is the difference between a rock buddhahood and the buddhahood of Gautama. It is the difference between the state of "Christos" of a Jesus and the state of "Christos" in a piece of wood. Now, fundamentally, both are without mind; the Jesus, the Buddha, no mind, but there is *consciousness*. In the womb, there is also no mind, but there is *unconsciousness*! So, the difference is in the "self-consciousness" of the two identical states of egolessness.

Patanjali, the codifier of the *Yoga Sutras*, the yoga system of India, talked about the categories, if you will, of consciousness. One of them, the lowest, is what he has called *sushupti*. Sushupti is deep, dreamless sleep where one is in an absolute state of peace; where there is a return to the unmanifested state; where mind drops out; and where all senses drop out. You exist in that deep state of sushupti, but you are *unconscious* of your existence. Because you are not conscious in this state of sushupti, you do not have a *conscious experience* of the bliss!

Above sushupti, there is *swapna*, then *jagrat* and, finally, the state called the *turiya*, the fourth state, which is "superconsciousness." The state of superconsciousness is just like sushupti. They are the same in the sense that there is no mind. Remember, when I say "no mind," I mean there is no experience of *time* or *space*: there is only the experience of the *eternal now*—the present. This "present" the mystics talk about is different from our ordinary understanding of what it means to be in the "present moment." For us, the present moment is so fleeting because it is simply the transition of the past instantly into the future. It is the *flow* of time, and the time that it stops in the present is so short, a nanosecond—it is really just a flash. However, the present that the mystics talk about is eternal. One loses the experience of past, present and future! Time is not experienced in that dimension! So, the experience in the state of superconsciousness is the *same* as it is in the unconscious state of sushupti. The only difference is that you are aware of it. The difference is in awareness! So it is with egolessness.

After the maturation of ego in the state of striving to the point of surrender, you are conscious of this egolessness, this "nothingness" and oneness. So, you cannot go backward. To go backward is to become only more unconscious! To move forward is to become increasingly more conscious. That is really what is happening, isn't it? Even as the ego is maturing, there are increasing degrees of awareness.

Notice also that there are shifts in identification! At the first stage of body-ego, one identifies one's self entirely with this physical body, and those who have become locked into a total identification with their bodies as the dominant core of their being, suffer very much. They have become identified with this body, which itself is subject to constant change. It is fragile. It is but a bubble. The least little thing can burst it. People who are totally identified with their body usually live in a great state of fear because this body can go at any time! It gets sick. It hurts. There are so many things about that level of identity which make happiness, and our experience of happiness, very vulnerable, very temporary, at best. As one moves up in the cycle of the evolution of ego, the basis of identification shifts, and this process of evolution continues. After the seventh stage, the basis of one's identification with one's mind-body drops entirely. This is what constitutes, technically, the real emergence onto a Spiritual Path, when one has the experience of "no mindness."

Bauji Ra: *I guess I am asking the same question, because you said the concept of "me" drops after death, right? That concept drops? Okay, is it ego when we say I want to obtain this and I want to obtain that? If that is the only thing we can relate to, how can we experience blissfulness? If the ego is the source through which we experience things and we drop the ego, how can we experience bliss?*

What will be there to experience bliss if not the ego? The Self. The Self is really the core of all experiences, even now.

Bauji Ra: *But we have to experience ego to even get to Self, right?*

Yes, to get to a *pure* consciousness. The difference, Bauji Ra, is only in terms of consciousness. That is why we call ego an "illusion," because the reality is that you were never separated from the totality of existence! That never has occurred. It has *always* been the case that we are one with that which exists! It was never the case that we are separate. This experience of separation is purely a mental phenomenon! It is like a person who is sitting in a chair at home and falls asleep. While asleep they begin to dream that they are somewhere in Paris, and that they are being chased by thugs and are about to be robbed; they are undergoing all kinds of terror! In their dream, they are just wishing and praying that they can escape and go home and, suddenly, they wake up and find that they were at home all the time! They were never in Paris.

So, it is all in the mind, and it exists in the mind because of ignorance! As long as we are ignorant of our fundamental oneness, we will have this experience of ego, this experience of separateness. But this ego, this experience you call "me," is simply your personal history—the "you" (body-self) that has been perpetuated through a fixed period of time. It had a beginning and it will definitely come to an end. The thing that you *think* you are (the "me"), the contents of your historical experiences as a body (the ego) is empty, what the Buddha called *shunyata*, just one of the five *skandhas*. It is unreal! It does not exist independent of the body.

This is why Jesus said, ". . . Take no thought for thyself, what ye shall eat or what ye shall drink, nor for thy body, what ye shall wear." (Matthew 6:25) Jesus referred to it as the "self," because that is what we call ourselves, right? Take no thought for thyself, what you shall eat, what you shall wear. Do not worry about that. Why? Because this ego is not ultimately substantial. It does not *really* exist, because it (you) is not separate or different from the one and only Being—God!

However, this is not a kind of conclusion you can reach by simply sitting in your arm chair. This knowledge has to be developed through the surrender of the ego, by the ego *dying while living*. This is the most difficult thing to accomplish, because this ego is the thing which does not want to die. The ego is the only *barrier* between you and the experience of your reality. When the mystics and saints talk about your having to "kill" this ego, they mean you have to cut off your own head, so to speak.

What they are trying to indicate to us is that we have to somehow, through an effort of deep understanding, see this: *that which you are calling "me" is an illusion*! This thing that stands behind "me" has had many egos! The ego you were in your last lifetime is very different from the ego you are now. This is not the first time you have had a body and the experiences which go with that. This has happened billions of time; egos come and egos go. We are like the sky in which clouds arise and scatter, but the sky remains clear and empty. The clouds just drift across the sky. So it is with the experience of our consciousness. It is your consciousness that is experiencing the ego, and egos come and egos go.

Our effort is to keep "me" the same. Even psychologically, we try to not change! Have you ever noticed that? You are doing your best not to change! Look at the insanity of it. Everything we are made of will change, but we go on clinging to this "image" we have created of ourselves that is passe; that is historically no longer the case. However, change is the nature of all things.

You are not the same physical person you were ten years ago. Nor are you the same ego you were ten years ago, but you try to cling to it. Now, the realities of your life mandate that you make certain adaptations, certain changes, but you cannot change. You are still clinging to the "me" that existed ten years ago: "Not me, I don't do these kinds of things. I never did it. I will never let a person do this to me." Now, that is the "old" you. The "new" you is going to have to adapt. If you refuse, then you will come into conflict with reality, because you are trying to maintain and perpetuate an ego (self-image) that is no longer appropriate for the reality of your situation and circumstances.

I do not even know if we can talk intelligently about the state of egolessness, but if I can say anything about it, it is that this state of egolessness is really the *capacity* to be anything. You are no longer limited! You can move in any dimension of your being, and be *aware*. Not only would you be aware, but you would have freedom. At this level, you have no freedom to be other than what you are! You really do not *want* to be anything other than what you are! That is what you are clinging to. You think, "If I stop being the historical Bauji Ra, the psychological Bauji Ra, this 'me,' then what's going to happen?" There is great fear. But there are many situations in life for which the identity you are clinging to is totally inappropriate. It will not work.

One of the things that happens in meditation—and this is always the most frightening thing—is one is able to separate one's self-awareness from one's continuous identification with the physical body.

The body serves as the primary basis of generating your sense of identity, and you are overwhelmed with a deep sense of fear, because you feel like you are about to die! In some sense, you are right! *That* ego, that you, *will* die! It becomes a very frightening experience. The mystics say that you can either die willingly while living or you can die the death of a coward, but you are going to die one way or the other! There is no escaping that. This "me" will come to an end. It is something pseudo, temporary, transient. Yet, look how much your sense of who you are is restricted to your male or female body. And where is the ego of your prior birth? It did not survive and this ego, too, shall die.

Pam: *You say that as the individual progresses from one stage of evolution to the next, they become more mature. When you get to the seventh stage, would that be the stage where the person starts to want to find out what their "dharma" is, what their life's purpose is? If that is the stage, would the person's level of ego naturally start to diminish because they are submitting more?*

No, no. It does not diminish. It gets stronger because you need a very strong ego to surrender! It is a very different thing. People who have weak egos cannot submit. It takes *maximum* intelligence. Only intelligent people can surrender, because the more intelligent you are, the more you realize how little you know! When you are very intelligent, you realize you don't know anything; hence, the surrendering. However, if your intelligence is small, you have the illusion that your knowledge is much and it now becomes difficult to surrender. It is *very* difficult. Only a very well developed, a very strong, mature ego can surrender. *Never* is it the case where a weak ego can surrender. It is just the reverse.

Pam: *This is part two of my question. You titled the seventh stage "intent" and "ego maturation" and, since I have been recently fascinated by the whole idea of "desire" and "intent" and how they are related, I was wondering if when you are trying to move toward stage seven and are trying to find out what it is you want to do in life, how you want to contribute, isn't that ego?*

Of course, that is what we are saying. The seventh developmental stage of our egos is characterized by the coming into presence in our lives of something that begins to *strive*. There is a will. There is intent. One begins for the first time to talk about the purpose of one's life. In lower states of ego development, there is no purpose. One of the things which characterizes these lower stages of ego is that there is no purpose. They are not "purpose-oriented" at all. At the seventh stage, you begin to see the emergence of goals, and the emergence of purpose behind the actions. "Intent" simply means "will." It is time to *will* your life along a certain pattern. You are trying to *do* something with your life. You are trying to figure out *what* you are doing with your life.

Pam: *That's still a little different from that earlier stage where you are in the "me," and you might be desiring enlightenment. Isn't that a different stage?*

The "me" cannot, by definition, become "enlightened." Enlightenment is the exact opposite experience of the "me." Actually, Pam, they are sometimes all-inclusive. You can be working on different parts of ego development. I do not mean to say that these are exclusive processes. These are just add-ons, if you will, on top of our basic ego structure. Certainly, if one is in the so-called simple state, the "primitive" state of ego development, where the identification of one's separateness is of being essentially a body, or essentially this "me" with this personal history, you will not find in the actions of an individual at that level any kind of spiritual goals or purpose in the sense that we are talking about. They are not *serious* about enlightenment. They are not really trying to do anything with their lives other than have more food, sex and things of that nature; just strictly living on a very materialistic level. They only *pretend* to be interested in spirituality. It is good for their "image." Now, remember, I am not condemning that. I am simply saying that this is just a fact. We all go through this.

I want you to begin to see your ego a little differently, because you always hear about how you have to "drop" the ego, how you have to get out of the ego. However, I want you to understand that you must first have an ego! How can you drop something you do not have? Most of us are in such bad shape, how will we drop it? So, the ego has to first *be*. Thank God for that, because if we have never had a toothache, how can we experience the bliss of not having a toothache? If you have not had a full experience of the ego, you will not be able to appreciate a state of egolessness, just as the embryo in the mother's womb cannot have the experience of the bliss of being in a state of egolessness.

In the garden of Eden, Adam and Eve were separated from God, but they did not know it. Hence, it had no value until they ate from the "tree of knowledge" that gave them essentially the knowledge of being separate, and they entered into this whole drama. Yet, ego has a purpose because, unless you have knowledge of your separation from God, how will you appreciate and experience your oneness? It is almost like the old question of evil and good—why they exist. If there was no evil, how would you experience goodness? It is not possible. It is just like asking the question, why do I need hunger in order to eat? It does not make sense. It is nonsensical. If there was no hunger, you would not eat! You cannot just go on eating if there is no hunger, or can you? I know some of you have tried, out of habit!

Sharon: *Looking back at all the information on ego—your karma and things—when does the cycle end? I mean, this constantly being created through different lifetimes—when does it all end? I know the ultimate thing is to become "one."*

The final cessation of the experience of individuality is what the Buddhists call *nirvana*. The word is beautiful because "nirvana" means something like blowing out a flame. The flame is blown out, but where has it gone? Back to nowhere, back into nothingness. The experience of ego, or individuality, ends when you become one with God. That is why the mystics say, as long as *you* are, then you cannot, by definition, have the experience of God. Only *one* can exist, either God or you, but not two. Never two.

Those who have experienced the ending of their ego have talked very strangely. Jesus said, "I and my father are one. If you have seen me, you have seen God." (John 10:30) That is big talk! That is why they wind up being crucified! Muslim mystics who have attained that state exclaim, *Ana-ul-Huq*!: "I am truth; I am God!" Not that I am the body or I am the body's history, or I am the contents of my mind. Nor do I feel that I am my likes or my dislikes. I am neither male nor female. I am not black or white. I am not American or European. All of that is gone! Who am I? *I am God*! I am this totality, this nothingness. *That* is who I am.

Sharon: *In that last statement you said that the feeling is "I am God." So, looking at individuals in the flesh, if I exclaim that I am God and someone else is still working their way to that—*

There would be no "someone else." That is the difference in the experience! There *is* no one else! The experience is just *oneness*. Remember when we talked about what one experiences as one moves through these higher levels of consciousness, where we talked about the level of Pind and the astral region? As we move deeper and deeper into the interiority of our being, I mentioned that our identification goes on shifting. That whole process becomes reversed.

First of all, we realize that we are more than just the "body," that we have a reality which is not the body. That is one of the first experiences we have in meditation. That is why meditation is so indispensable for the dissolution of the ego, for the attaiting of the egoless experience. Without meditation, this is not going to happen! Meditation delivers the first taste of this expanded understanding of who you are. While sitting in meditation, after a certain period of concentration has been achieved, one loses the experience of the body altogether! For the first time you realize, *I am that which functions through this body, but I am not just this body.* You begin to really come into a very different relationship with this body.

As you go deeper into concentration, deeper into the practice of meditation, you similarly begin to feel a distance between all of these things, and you are able to find the "gap" between your thoughts. Normally, right now you do not even experience a gap between your thoughts. All you experience is a constant flow of thoughts running through your mind, continuously. You have never experienced the gap where there is no thought! Once you experience that, you realize you are not the contents of your mind! What you are doing is moving deeper and deeper inside. You go on eliminating: *I am neti, neti*: I am not this; I am not that. You are not just eliminating *intellectually*; you are having the *experience* of the elimination. Then you go back further and further to a state of "nothingness."

That is what is meant when a thing is said to be in a state of "potentia": you can take *any* form. One of the characteristics of God is that God can take any form. It is not limited, not locked, not trapped, not attached. That which we call God can be a tree, a rock, a stick, a human being, a bird, a microbe. It has that freedom. That is also our intrinsic capability, to be anything. But the problem with our ego is that we can only be this little "me"; hence, we miss the true breadth and depth of our being.

Now, specifically addressing your question, after you have transcended the level of identification with the body, with the emotions, with the mind and its contents, with time and space, you come finally to the final frontier of the experience: the experience of individuation. You have transcended all the other lower levels of identification, but you still feel that you are an *individual* soul and that there are other souls! As you take the next step, you lose even the experience of the individuation! That is when the drop has merged back into the ocean. When the drop merges into the ocean, you no longer experience being a drop! "Drop consciousness" is gone, and is replaced by "oceanic consciousness."

Sharon: *Well, then, I would be everybody else.*

There would be no "everybody else."

Vernita: *You would be back with the source.*

You know what the mystics would say? Everybody in here would look just like you. Every movement *they* made would be in perfect synchroneity with *your* will and intent.

Sharon: *Just like the same flow?*

Yes. There would only be you. It is difficult to really encapsulate the experience in words and concepts, but I am just trying to give you a general idea. It is not accurate, because we cannot be accurate! It is certainly very different, but *that* is the experience of egolessness! Remember, the experience of egolessness is the absence of the experience of separateness. There is no more separation. There is no more "other." There is no more "me." There is no more duplicity. There is no more duality. That whole experience is gone.

Vernita: *When you spoke of a drop going back into the ocean, wouldn't you say the ocean was like the Creator? She would be one with the Creator again, and since she is a part of Him, that individuality doesn't really exist anymore?*

It never did. It was an *illusion*. It was a dream. **Vernita:** *Because all of this is in the mind of the Creator? All of this is an illusion, right?*

So we say. The reality is that it is "inscrutable."

Sharon: *I know I have not realized my oneness with others, so who am I really talking to, "you" or myself?*

That question should also be asked as to whom you are praying. Who do we pray to?

Sharon: *Basically, I am praying to myself?*

I know it sounds crazy, but you have to understand that as you go through this stage of ego dissolution, it will look just like madness. In reality you *are* losing your mind! There is not much difference between "breakthrough" and "breakdown." There is only a difference in direction. Otherwise, it is just alike. One of the old Zen masters would sit in meditation with his eyes closed and "go in," and when he came out of meditation the first thing he would say was, "What happened to all the people and where did all the mountains go? Where are all the trees? Where is all that stuff? It is all gone. There is only *me!*" That is the feeling had by all. The poets have had much better luck than we have had in their attempts to make this experience respond to the use of language, and their efforts are really just incredible when you think about it. The library is full of the poetry of these great men and women who have had a taste of this "oneness," and have been able to give expression to it with words.

I particularly like one of the sutras of the Buddha. I am very fond of quoting this Buddha when it comes to talking about ego and its dissolution, because that was his whole thing. Buddhism is the path of the cultivation of *intelligence* to a very, very high degree. Now, intelligence is only one of the paths, only one of the yogas. There are others. There is *bhakti* yoga for those who are more emotionally oriented, and so forth. Buddhism is one of the best expressions of what we call *jnana* (*gyan*) yoga, the use of understanding.

One of the pinnacles of the Buddha's teachings is reflected in what is called the "heart sutra," the *Prajnaparamita Hridayam Sutra,* which was given to Sariputta, who was one of his chief most disciples. He gave a special discourse to Sariputta. Buddha gave discourses to his entire *sangha*, but to Sariputta he gave a private discourse on his teachings. He called it the heart sutra because it goes to the heart of the teachings. *Prajnaparamita* means the "perfection of wisdom," and in those teachings the Buddha tells Sariputta that: The reality is this state (oneness) cannot even be attained! It is not a state that can be attained at all! Why? It need not be attained, because it is *already* the case! One simply *realizes* it. It is a very different thing. There is no yoga or "methodology" at all, because all methodologies are for various stages of ego development. Now, that is the truth. *Ais dhammo sanatano.*

Sharon: *I was just thinking of something when you mentioned there is nothing to be attained because it is already in existence. It made me think, because I know in a lot of cases religions speak of going somewhere, such as a heaven or hell. Would that be an illusion of ego, because there would not be a place to go?*

Yes. There is no place to go. There is no "home." There is no movement. Consciousness does not move; only that which exists in time, space and causality moves. Time-space exists in consciousness! Consciousness is just the opposite; it does not move! That is one of the beauties of the insights of the Dravidians of India. There is a kind of mysticism that is comprehensible only through a deep comprehension of science. One of the concepts in physics and things of that nature is that of space and time. The idea is that things *exist* in space and move according to a flow of time. Actually, the reality is that time and space do not exist independently; they exist in consciousness! The "world" exists in us, not us in the world! So, we (as consciousness) do not ever move through time and space! We are having an experience from a stationary point that is *not* located in space.

Sharon: *So, you are saying it is a flow?*

I am saying that the creation is literally flowing before your eyes, but you yourself are not moving! There is nowhere to go! There is no heaven, no hell to go *to*! You are *already* one with God. That has *always* been the case; you must simply realize it! If you did move, you would still be *in* God wherever you went, because God is equally present everywhere (omnipresent).

Enough for today. Ra shekum maat.

CHAPTER THREE
THE TRANSEGOIC STAGES

This is session two of five sessions where we will be exploring the nature and management of ego. As I pointed out last time, transcending the ego is the very core of all that we are trying to accomplish on the Spiritual Path. We talked a little about the pre-egoic stages and the egoic stages, and today we will be talking about the "transegoic" stages. I want to remind you that the ego is the very last covering we will shed on our way back to oneness with the Creator. So, ego will be with us for a long time.

Remember, we defined ego as fundamentally the experience of being "separate" from that which exists. The child is separate in the mother's womb, but it has no awareness of its separateness. That whole birthing process, that whole entrance into the world is nothing more than the increasing awareness of the individual separateness. It is a stage and that stage has to be fully gone through.

We have to understand ego in a very different light. The problem for most of us is that we have "ego deficiency disorder." I know that sounds strange, but if you have been following me and have understood, you will understand that, just as there is a pre-egoic stage within the womb of our mother where there is yet no ego—the potential for ego is there, but the child in the mother's womb has no awareness of its separation—there is also a transegoic stage. We really must try to understand this whole evolution from the pre-egoic stage through the egoic stage to the transegoic stage. With that understanding, we are able to ground ourselves solidly on the Path.

You have to understand that it is your ego which is on the Spiritual Path. It is out of ego that you pursue meditation. It is out of ego that you even pursue God. Without ego, you will make no movement whatsoever. We talked about disciplining certain negative states of mind on the Path. You have to understand that the ego, this feeling of separateness (the *primordial* ego), exists even before we get a mind. When we talk about disciplining the mind and dealing with the perversions of mind—anger, lust, greed, attachment and vanity—all of these are rooted in ego. Therefore, ego is *always* the last one to go.

A few things more have to be understood when we talk about the subject of ego because of its immense importance for those of us who are on the Spiritual Path. Ego will not, in any way, be affected by a change in your "philosophy." Now, you can change your philosophy all you want! You can go from Hinduism to Islam, from Islam to Christianity, from Christianity to Judaism, from Judaism to Taoism—it makes no difference. The ego will remain unaffected! You will *still* suffer! You will *still* experience the limitations of your ego, because these kinds of changes are only at the level of mind.

You can change the way you think, but this is meaningless because the ego *precedes* even the process of thinking! It is more *integral* to your being. I want this to be clarified because, very often, the assumption by those who enter onto a Spiritual Path is that if you change your thinking, your opinions, your world view and your religion you will do something to your ego. You will do nothing to your ego! You cannot *think* yourself out of an egoic stage. Hence, the necessity for meditation. I am always going to be emphasizing this, because one of the major characteristics of the *spiritually immature* ego is that it does not wish to yield itself to the process called "meditation." Meditation is the only thing which dissolves the experience of being an ego. There is no other way to dissolve the experience of being an ego whatsoever!

I want to stress this because there is a stage in ego development where one gets caught up in what I call "talk religion," "talk mysticism," "talk philosophy," where the whole emphasis is on talking! The whole emphasis is on acquiring different ways to express your opinions about these matters. "Talk religion" does nothing to ego. "Talk mysticism" has no effect on ego at all. Yet, talk religion and talk mysticism are stages that the ego has to go through. After all, you have to start somewhere! However, I want you to clearly understand that an authentic Spiritual Path always begins *beyond* the realm of talk.

I do not want you to become "spiritually" comfortable because we have discussed so many profound things. I have given you enough data to enable you to engage in "talk mysticism" for the next millennium! But I do *not* want you to become stuck in talk mysticism or talk religion, because you will have really made no progress. You will simply have changed your opinion. We have to always bear this in mind when we talk about ego management. What we are really talking about is meditation, the "process" which dissolves the experience of being separate from that which exists (God).

RECAPITULATION OF SESSION ONE
STAGE ONE

If you recall, one of the things I discussed in detail the last time we were together was the different stages of evolution that our egos go through. We talked about how the first stage of the development of ego involves the ego identifying itself with the *body*. That is, the ego takes a form, does it not? The form the ego takes is first at the level of the body. Very often, our sense of who we are is inimically linked to this body and the feeling is that, "I am the body." This is the very first and most primitive stage in the evolution of our egos. What happens is that most of us seldom evolve beyond this first stage, and throughout our life our identification is with this physical body.

What is the downside of the identification with the physical body? As long as your feeling that "I am this body" persists, your *dukkha* will be tremendous. Your suffering will be tremendous, because this body will go. This body is on its way out of here. This body is of the nature to grow old. This body is of the nature to become ill. This body will perish and all relationships connected with it will also come to an end. Because we are so identified with this body, we have the *illusion* that we will die. The fear of death becomes our greatest fear in life. We are all afraid of the fact that we are going to die. This is *reality:* this ego is going to perish! So, the very first stage in the evolution of this feeling of separateness that I have called "ego" is association with a form, which is the physical body.

STAGE TWO

We talked a lot about the second stage. Who took good notes? What was the second stage in the evolution of the ego? The "self-identity" stage. We acquire a name and the ego becomes a little stronger. I have associated who I am with this body and I have now also acquired a name, an identity. You will notice that a small child starts responding to its name and putting together the first foundation of a persona. It starts developing the continuity of identity. The acquisition of identity includes your name, your relationships—this is my mother, this is my brother, etc.—and how you earn your living, along with other things. Again, many of us never move beyond that.

STAGE THREE

We also talked quite a bit about the third stage in the evolution of the ego, the stage we have called the "extension of ego," where we now have extended and incorporated other things and people into the basis of our identity. This is the stage where attachments are formed. This is the stage where "my" and "mine" emerge. We now have the concept of "mine," of things belonging to us. For sure, the vast majority of us never emerge from that stage.

Every time something that is "mine" perishes, something in me dies. It is almost as if *I* have died. Now, I am bound to lose my child or my wife, and when that happens, because I have incorporated my child and my wife into my basic identity, something in me dies. I have incorporated my house into my identity, so when the house burns down, notice how I suffer. I have incorporated my job, the way I earn my living, into my identity. When I get fired from my corporate position, I am so dejected that I hurl myself off a bridge. I have incorporated my wealth into my identity, so when I experience financial ruin, I blow my brains out. It is as if I have died, because I have extended my identity to incorporate other people and things. Since the nature of the creation is constant change—things are coming into being, things are going out of being—I experience this kind of horrible chaos all of the time. I experience tremendous insecurity! What is "insecurity?" Have you ever thought about it? Why do you feel so insecure?

June: *Not being in control?*

Right. You are not in control, but you are not in control of something that is vital to you, isn't that right? This feeling of security and insecurity begins to come into play at the third evolutionary stage in the development of ego. When we have not evolved beyond that, we have no experience of security whatsoever. Can you imagine a life like that, where you are constantly in a state of anxiety? It is not a pleasant experience. The whole effort is to control, as June has pointed out. When you are in a state of insecurity and anxiety, you will automatically seek to control things. How will you control the world? How will you control life? Is this possible? You can't even control yourself! How are you going to control all of the variables of life?

Not being able to achieve this degree of control, you just mentally suffer.

For example, you have plenty of money for today, but you cannot enjoy it; you are so busy thinking about tomorrow and how to control *it* that you cannot enjoy the *now*. We cannot live in the present and, remember, life can only happen in the present. There is no such thing as living "down the line." I notice that we all push our happiness off to somewhere in the near or distant future. You are planning on being happy in the future. Why? Because you do not know how to be happy in the now, and that is the only place where happiness can occur.

This loss of the ability to experience security goes a long way in shaping our miseries. As I said earlier, most of us never mature beyond this third stage in the evolution and development of ego. This sounds very strange, I know, because most of you who have been studying mysticism, spirituality, philosophy, new age thought and things of that nature, have heard so much talk about the fact that the ego is the greatest barrier in the individual quest for God-realization and enlightenment. Of course, that is true, but you have never understood ego! You have been trying to *drop* your ego, but I am telling you that you do not have *enough* ego to drop! Your problem is not ego; it is lack of ego! There is no maturity. As you examine these primary stages in the evolution of ego which, incidentally, take place before the age of seven, you can really see where you are spiritually. Most of us, *spiritually*, are still six or seven years old! It is amazing!

STAGE FOUR

The fourth stage in the evolution and development of the ego was what, my brother? The "creative" stage. We start feeling that we are "doers." Self-esteem starts developing. You now begin to have the experience of "pride." How old were you when you started feeling "proud"? At what age did your arrogance seep in? Have you ever noticed it or thought about it? Have you looked into yourself? Most often we define ego as this exaggerated arrogance, this false basis of pride, this arrogation to ourselves of qualities and characteristics which, in reality, we do not possess. That whole process of arrogating to ourselves qualities and characteristics which make up the foundation of our identity and our arrogance began when we were children.

"Esteem" comes from the same root word as estimation; it is your "estimation" of yourself. When a child is in that stage, its whole preoccupation is on "doing." They want to show you that they can "do" things. Our pride is fundamentally rooted in our desire to show people we can "do" stuff: "Look at me, I can do stuff." We hardly ever grow out of that: "Look at me, I can make money! Look at me, I am very cultured." The whole point is for somebody to look at me because I can do something "good." It is childish! It starts when we are three or four years old: "Mommy, Mommy! Look at what I did." Mommy is, perhaps, not around anymore, and you are now simply saying, "Whoa, look at me. Look at what I did, world!"

The tragedy is that you have become trapped in this syndrome and, now, everything you do is done to get the *attention* of the world. There is nothing intrinsic in it. You are not going to school because you want knowledge; you are going to school because you want status. You want the Ph.D., the recognition and the honor; you do not want any knowledge! You are three years old and still want people to hang your scribblings on the refrigerator door! The ego has not matured beyond the point where it lives for the *commentary* of others. Millions of people are locked into living for the commentary of others. It is as childish now as it was thirty or forty years ago. Their sense of identity has not matured beyond that, and their whole life is wasted like this. I want you to look deeply into this and see how this "drama" is playing out in your own intrapsychic realms.

STAGE FIVE

What was the fifth? "Self-image." After you get the feedback from people—"Oh, baby, this is a pretty picture"—and they hang it on the refrigerator, you then begin to come to some conclusions about yourself. You start to form an image of yourself. Now, if Mommy did not put the picture on the refrigerator or praise you, you would still come to a conclusion about yourself. Whether the parents praise you or not makes no difference: As a child, you are still going to come to some *conclusions* about yourself. Those conclusions about yourself form the foundation of the image that you will develop, your "ego-image."

Look deeply into the image you have created of yourself. How do you see yourself? I know you are afraid of these kinds of questions, because they will force you to grow up! Look into it if you have the courage. From where did you get this image of yourself? Can you locate a source other than the commentary of other people? What do you know about yourself *independent* of the commentaries of other people; that has not been told to you by someone else? Do you know anything about yourself that does not fall into this category? Is your entire image of who *you* are made up of the commentaries and remarks of your parents and other people during your formative years? "Oh, Bhagwan, he is such a good little boy." Now, am I still walking around fifty years later thinking I am Mama's "good little boy"? Are you still thinking you are Daddy's "little girl" after all these years? Some of us are clinging to images of ourselves that have no correlation to our reality whatsoever! Perhaps the person who made the commentary about you when you were four or five years old was mistaken. Maybe they called *you* stupid because, perhaps, *they* were stupid. That is possible, isn't it? They said, "You are my son and I'm stupid; therefore, you cannot be anything but stupid." They passed that down to you, and you then incorporated that into your ego formation. You came out of your early childhood with the image that, "I'm a stupid so-and-so." With that conclusion, you forgot all about going to college. You forgot all about pursuing those areas in life that require intelligence. Why? Because you had become convinced somewhere in your early developmental stages that you were not intelligent. Or, you were convinced that, "I'm not pretty," or "I'm not handsome," or "I'm not athletic." Maybe you have been convinced that you are athletic and you are not, or that you are pretty and you are not! It goes both ways! The point is, we have this image of ourselves and our whole lifestyle emerges out of that image, an image we formed when we were probably six or seven years old! You must investigate it and come to a certain knowledge about yourself that is not "other-based"—what Buddha called *vipashyana*, looking into yourself.

STAGE SIX

After the development of our image of ourselves comes the development of the "rational" side, the sixth stage in the evolution of the ego. We now begin to develop this rational dimension, and hardly anyone ever goes beyond this. We can *think* and we now start to have the experience that we are *always* right! Because we can use logic and reasoning and do deductive and inductive thinking, there is no way we can believe we are wrong! We begin to actually have the feeling that we "know" something. This feeling that we have knowledge occurs only in the sixth developmental stage of ego. Beneath these, you do not feel that you know anything; hence, your dependency on others. At the sixth stage, you will say, "Girl, I don't care what you think! I *know* I look good." You are starting to gain some knowledge and you are freed from dependency on the commentaries and opinions of others. You now have your own epistemology. You have your own system for the acquisition of knowledge that transcends the commentary of others, and you feel it is infallible; therefore, you cannot be told anything!

Now, no one can tell you *anything*, because this ability to generate a sense of knowledge is so full of *maya*, so full of delusion, that it is hard for you to believe you do not know anything! It is as difficult as believing that "you," as you see yourself, do not exist. To understand at this stage that you do not know anything is impossible! Hence, most of us at this level can only learn the "hard way," from experience. There is no other way, because you cannot be told anything!

When children reach this stage, it is very difficult to tell them anything: "The fire is hot!"; "No, the fire is not hot, Mommy." You argue and try to convince them, but does it do any good? They have to stick their hand into the fire. "Son, don't shoot that dope!"; "No, no. I'm not going to get addicted. I'm going to just hit this pipe a little bit. I'm not capable of becoming a drug addict. I know what I'm doing!" Then, the boy hits the pipe and he is strung out. It is the same with the girl who thinks she is ready to be a mother: "I'm grown!" She is thirteen years old, but she *thinks* she is grown! "I'm ready to have a baby. I know what I'm doing!" But they have to go out into life and have the experience.

We all can identify with this. Look at how many things we have done in our lives under the spell of certainty, under the illusion that we actually *knew* what we were doing. Be honest! Look into it. What has been the outcome of those things? Remember, it was preceded by the feeling that, "I know what I'm doing! I have thought about it and reasoned it out." The problem, of course, with knowledge which is based on reasoning, is that deductive and inductive logic are always based on data; and since you can never have all of the data, your conclusion reached on that data will always be incomplete! Thus, the wide margin of error. There is no way for your biocomputer to have conscious access to *all* of the data from your many prior lifetimes. So, you work with the little data of this lifetime, perform some deductive or inductive reasoning, come to a conclusion, have the euphoric experience of "certainty" and act upon it, only to find out that there was an area of data of which you were unaware—and whoop! There it is!

However, it is too late, because the law of *karma* mandates that you must undergo the consequences of those actions! Yes, you married the wrong woman, or you married the wrong man. Your calculations were off, but the suffering has to be gone through: *Ais dhammo sanatano*. This is the law. This is the way it is. Then, the dukkha is there. Most of the suffering we are undergoing as a result of these "miscalculations" is related to this illusion that our "rational thinking" produces certain knowledge. This is the sixth stage in the evolution of our ego. It is more mature than the "body-ego," of course, but it is still subject to putting us at risk for the experience of dukkha, misery.

STAGE SEVEN

The seventh stage in the development of ego is where we become mature enough to reflect on our lives. We begin to *probe* and go deep into things. Our lives are becoming more "intentional" now. We are beginning to live more deliberately. Before, you were not living deliberately, you were just doing shit! You are just going wherever the wind blows you! Your living is not on purpose. It is not conscious. You are like a pile of dust that is swirled and blown in all directions by the wind, totally at the mercy of the variables around you. Your life is "accidental." Everything is an accident. You will meet someone and fall in love by accident!

You have learned so much as you traveled through all of these lower evolutionary stages. You begin to now try to answer the question, "What am I trying to do with my life?" Ultimately, these kinds of questions come into your mind. Are any of us who have not evolved beyond the lower stages of ego concerned with what we are doing with our lives? Not at all! Those people are not concerned with what they are going to do with their lives; they are just out here. If they are locked into the first level where their identification is fully with the body, they are strictly into what they are going to eat and when they are going to have sex. That is it! They have no *real* ambition in life. Real ambition occurs only at the seventh developmental stage of ego. Egos beneath this level have only one ambition: to fulfill their *animalistic* needs. As we mature as egos, we begin to look at this phenomenon called "life" and ask ourselves these deeper questions. This is the "homework" I asked you to reflect on last time. You need not volunteer your answers. We are not going to examine them, because these are very private answers, but it is homework that you should do. You have to answer these deeper questions. Are you going to live your life at the level of soliciting praise from the world? Do you want the world to put your little life on the refrigerator door with magnets? Is that what you are doing? "Look at me, look at how knowledgeable I am. Look at how educated I am. Look at how spiritual I am." Is that what you are going to do with your life, waste it soliciting the praise of the world? Are you stuck somewhere in the third developmental stage where you are just trying to have the feeling of pride? That is where little children are: They want to stimulate their experience of pride. They want to feel as much pride as possible. Is that what you are doing? What are you trying to do with your life? You have to work on this in order to know the answer. This is *mature* ego work.

The spiritual search usually begins after we start to do this kind of introspection. You are looking at your life: "I'm going to die. I want to know if there is a God and, if so, how do I discover it? How do I experience it?" You have now also seen the impermanence of relationships. All of these questions arise as the ego matures. The immature ego is not concerned with these matters at all! This seventh stage is where we begin to look for answers. That is why from the beginning I have said we have to go through all of these developmental stages until we get to that level of ego maturity where we can begin to reflect on and ponder these things. We are now in a position to move into the transegoic states, where we *transcend* the ego.

THE TRANSEGOIC STAGES

Today, I wanted to start to talk a bit about the transegoic stages and what they look like. Actually, now that you know the various stages through which your ego is developing, you can see that the transegoic states are really a reversal of the whole process! The first transegoic stage is where you are coming out of this experience of separateness, where you are transcending the experience of being separate. Remember, ego is fundamentally the experience of your being separate. I want you to understand how this relates to *you*. I do not want you to think of this as some kind of abstract metaphysical or philosophical thing. No!

THE EXPERIENCE OF LOVE

When you are suffering from the experience of separateness, it makes the experience of love impossible. This sounds strange to you, because you think you have been loving people. Some of you actually think you have been in love! I know it is going to come as a shock when I suggest to you that you have not ever been in love! You are still caught in the lower realms of your ego. Your ego is not *mature* enough to have the experience of love. What you have been experiencing is *attachment*. What you have been experiencing is the "my" and "mine" phenomenon: "My husband." He has been a part of your identity, and this is not love; this is attachment! This is stage-three egotism!

All of the seven prior evolutionary stages have one common characteristic: they are all selfish! All of the relationships in which we are involved at these lower evolutionary stages of the ego are rooted in selfishness, in our own interests. They are *self-aggrandizing*, aren't they? Look into it! This is *not* love. The experience of love cannot happen until we are able to move beyond the ego.

When I say that love becomes possible only when we transcend the ego, why do I say it? Because love is essentially an *experience of oneness* with another human being—oneness, not duality. It is an "us" experience. There is no clear demarcation between you and the beloved. It is "identification" in the true sense of the word. You become one with the other individual. This is not possible unless you are able to start transcending your ego.

That is why all mystics, saints and sages, with no exception, throughout recorded time, have not differed by one hair on the proposition that love is the *highest* spiritual experience on the Path. You have been thinking, "Oh, Bhagwan, what about those lights and sounds and going into the higher regions?" That is *your* concept, because that is what *your* ego wants! Why do the mystics say that the capacity to experience love is the highest spiritual experience available to human consciousness? Because it causes you to *transcend* this feeling of separateness, and that is replaced with the experience of oneness.

When you get to about the sixth or seventh stage in the maturation of your ego, the *potential* to transcend the ego starts to manifest itself. Even at these levels of ego, you begin to approach this thing called "love" a little differently. You begin to "intuit" something. Remember, there is another way of knowing other than through knowledge and reasoning—intuition. The one thing that you begin to intuit as it relates to this love, this experience of transcending the ego, is what the mystics call "glimpses" of love. *That* is what this Path is all about. It is not about supernatural power. It is not about *siddhis*. It is not about reading people's minds and all of that. This thing is strictly about *love*! This is the whole point of it all.

We begin to intuit certain insights and look deeper into our relationships. Before we had these insights, we would be saying things like, "I love you." This is meaningless, because to love another person means you have to be able to identify with the person. There has to be a oneness, and that oneness can only arise out of a deep *understanding*. Hence, you can never have love where there is no understanding! It never has happened and never will happen! To love someone, you must have the willingness and intention to love them, but willingness and intention by themselves are not enough. You can say, "I want to love you." Okay, you are on safe grounds. That is okay. That is permitted. Bomani, you can tell Florida, "You know, Florida, I want to love you." Okay. There is nothing wrong with that. So far, so good. But if you declare "I love you," you have to be able to demonstrate a deep understanding of this woman.

Love means that you understand the person, that you understand their suffering and pain. When this understanding is coupled with your willingness, you are now able to relieve the suffering of another human being. Love is the intent and capacity to relieve the suffering of another human being. That kind of understanding brings you to a level of oneness. You can get in "tune." You actually *feel* their suffering. There is no longer any distinction. Their suffering *is* your suffering. It is very different, and that requires the ability to merge.

If you are in the lower realms of your ego, you cannot merge with anybody! By definition, you are separate. Ego means you have "contracted." You have recoiled. You have pulled back. You have isolated yourself from others. Two egos cannot relate. It is wrong to use the word "relationship" with two egos. That is not possible. How can egoistic people be in a relationship? There is nothing with which to relate. They will never come near each other at all and no love is experienced. I want you to bear this in mind as we begin to look at this transegoic experience that the mystics have called the experience of "love."

MEDITATION: THE PREREQUISITE
FOR TRANSCENDING THE EGO

The first thing we must do is learn how to meditate. Remember, I said "talk religion" and "talk mysticism" will have no impact on the transcendence of ego. I must emphasize this over and over. You say, "Oh, I think I will go to *satsang*. Bhagwan will be there and he will be doing some good talking." I know you feel like that! That is why you are here! That is why I have to remind you that talk is *not* going to do it. The talk is simply to motivate you, to somehow try to seduce you into doing meditation. Meditation is where it is at. *Everything* is locked into meditation.

We know that the first developmental stage of ego is the body-ego, this feeling that "I am the body." We have to transcend that; but you cannot read a book to transcend the experience of being the body! You cannot read any *sutras*, the Koran, the Bible, the Gita, or the Tao Te Ching. No book on the planet will enable you to transcend this experience that you are the body. You can come to as many of these satsangs as you like and you will still leave here feeling that you are the body! I do not care how "elevated" the discussion is: Only one thing can enable you to transcend the experience of being a physical body, and that is meditation.

We have already talked a lot about this, so in your memory you can pull those files up and review the whole meditation process as we go through this subject to see how they correlate with each other. For instance, the whole purpose in adopting an *asana* and in controlling the thinking process is to create a loss of awareness of the body! In order to lose body awareness, you have to turn your awareness somewhere else. In the turning of your awareness, you will lose this experience of only being the body, and will then transcend the first restriction on the transegoic experience of love, of nonseparateness. You have to give up this identity with the body, and that is done through a process of meditation. You have to clearly understand this. Once that is done, does it mean that those who have transcended the body, transcended the ego and all of its stages, will not have the experience of being the body? Of course not, because the body is *included* in a higher experience. However, your experience is of *only* being the body! The mystics are having a very different experience.

We know that the second stage in the evolution of the ego is self-identity, the name. We have to now go through a process of spiritual practice—not talk mysticism, not talk religion—that goes beyond our identification with our personal history. All of the thinking that you have been doing about this "me" is the problem. We cannot make spiritual progress because this me is in the way! But this me, itself, is the thing that eventually comes to the Path. Ego has its place, do not misunderstand; but the idea is to *transcend* it. In meditation the objective is to withdraw our attention from the physical body and, thereby, transcend the *experience* of simply being a physical body.

As our self-identity has expanded, similarly, we now have to transcend the psychological limitations that we have imposed upon ourselves in the form of these additions. This, too, is involved with the process of meditation because you are having the experience of "me" through thinking! Whenever thinking shuts down, you lose the experience of me. Every day we all travel in a cycle of consciousness. We move from this wakeful level where we are *thinking* about me, and we drop a little lower into the state of dreams, where now we are *dreaming* about me.

There is a third level—*sushupti* the mystics call it—we drop to where there is no thought about "me," but that which you are still exists! When you are in that state of consciousness where there are no dreams occurring, do you cease to exist? Does *being* cease? You act like you are guessing! Don't you know whether you exist? *You* are still there. That which you are remains, even in this deep state, but notice there is no me. "Me" is an experience that accompanies your thinking. Drop thinking, and you will have no experience of me; you will simply *be*.

You have contracted yourself into this tiny little history. This "me" is a period, a dot; it is something very small. It is the smallest form into which you can contract yourself, because you are infinite. Do you know how many of these "me" you have been since time immemorial? You have had billions of me, billions of lives and billions of relationships and careers. Yet, you are clinging to this little identity in this little lifetime, this little seventy years on this little speck of mud called "earth," which is drifting aimlessly amidst the appalling immensity of the physical universe! You are defining yourself as this? It is madness! Only through meditation are we able to shut down this thinking process. We lose the experience of *me*, and we become nothing but pure *existence*. It is very profound, and you have to look at and understand all of the restrictions in your life. They are based only on "me": "You know, Bhagwan, I can't do that, because I am like this!" Look at how many things you have eliminated from your life which you have not even *attempted* to do because you have restricted your abilities based on your definition of "me." Is this not madness? "I can't do this because this is how I am. I am doing this and I am going to keep on doing it, because that's how I am." Nonsense! We must transcend that which, in turn, will cause us to transcend this second stage. Every time we drop one of these coverings, we are increasing this feeling of *nonseparateness*. We are coming closer to a state of maximum Self-realization.

The third stage is when we have extended our ego to the stage of "mine." Again, when we shut down the thinking process, is there anything that is "yours?" When you are not thinking, are you having any experience of owning anything? What gives you the experience of owning something? Thinking! What gives you the experience of loss or gain? Thinking! What happens, then, when we are able to shut down the thinking process that is going on in consciousness and which serves as the foundation of this ego-experiencing phenomenon? We lose the experience of *mine*, and everything becomes *ours*!

Another way of looking at it is that the experience of *only* owning those things connected to the ego becomes reversed, it expands! You will see that not only do you own this or that, you own the *whole world*! You will now respect the other person's property as much as you respect yours! These higher spiritual beings seem to be as concerned about your stuff as you are! You are not concerned about *their* stuff, and you are trying to figure out why in the world are they concerned about *my* stuff. They are more *spiritually* developed than you, because you are still contracted. You are still limited to this "me" and "mine" type of thinking! When we shut down thinking we realize, as the mystic poets say, that "we are all interconnected," that "what happens to one happens to all of us," and all distinctions drop out.

In ancient times, when people were a little closer to this natural state of spirituality, they lived more in that kind of communal spirit. It was as if the children belonged to everybody in the community. There was none of this, "That is not my kid. I don't have anything to do with that. I am not getting involved!" That did not exist, because the child belonged to the whole community. However, we have become so contracted into our tiny egos that, even within our own family, we have siblings who are struggling and we simply say, "Hell, that is *their* problem. It is not *my* problem!"

America is a manifestation of this egotistical contraction to its maximum degree. Here, you can step over people bleeding in the street and feel nothing! That should be a moral indictment. The fact that you can walk past another person who is suffering and feel nothing should scare the hell out of you! Yes, you will feel "sorry" for them, but I am not talking about sympathy; I am talking about feeling, about *compassion!* Compassion and sympathy are two very different phenomena. Sympathy has to do with you "ego-tripping": "Oh, look at that poor bum. How unfortunate!" You look down on them in order to create sympathy. Compassion is something else; you cannot even call it thinking. Compassion just breaks your heart.

The hero is a person whose faculty of compassion was functioning at the time of their heroic deed. The hero is that person who, perhaps not thinking, walked across a bridge and saw a child in the water, drowning. Before he could even think about it, the compassion faculty kicked in, linked him with the drowning child, and he simply jumped into the river to save the child. And when you ask these heros why they say, "I don't know what happened! I can only tell you that if that child had died, *I* would have died. It was like *me* dying." There was no distinction; the link had been made. The separation was gone and the heroism occurred automatically.

The reason there are so few of us who are "heroic" is because we have no compassion for others. You will not jump off a bridge to save anybody! So, the process of meditation shuts down the thinking process to such an extent that we can transcend the limitations of those conditions related to our egos—the contraction that we call "mine" and "my"—and we are able to have, at a minimum, the experience of compassion, which is a derivative of love.

The next stage of ego, "self-esteem," is doing something simply for the purpose of praise, of pride. It is performing actions for the purpose of generating or acquiring other people's praise. This is deep. Much of our actions are based on the soliciting of other people's praise. Be honest with yourself! Look into yourself and see how much of what you do is simply based on your desire for other people's praise and recognition! See the horror of it all. It causes you to live a "pretended" life. Your life is pseudo, it is false. It is a pretense; hence, the lack of fulfillment and meaning. You do not feel *fulfilled* because you are not living in relationship to yourself! You are living on the terms of your "public." You are a politician. You are looking for votes in the form of these praises and your life has simply become a pretense, a fraud, false! The immature egos can live like that, because they do not want anything anyway. However, if we have the desire, we can transcend this.

When we "shut down" the mind—when we learn how to live without thinking—the stage of ego based on praise from other people, of the experience of continuous pride in our actions, this feeling that "I am the doer" ceases. I know this sounds strange to you, because you have been thinking that every action you do is done as a result of your *thinking*, and I am now telling you something that is probably radically different from your experience! I am telling you that not one single action of yours is flowing from anything you think. Your thinking is an *illusion*! The actions are going to flow anyhow! Fate and your cognizance of it have no connection whatsoever! But the fear in the immature ego is that, "Oh, Bhagwan, if I stop thinking and stuff like that, I am going to become immobile." No! That is nonsense. Destiny and the law of karma will mandate that you act! You have no option! Things happen. It is like when the spring comes and the grass grows by itself; the grass need not *do* anything.

It is your ego that is giving you the feeling that, "If I don't do it, it won't get done!" That is your ego! You are sitting in a universe that is in motion, a universe that is the cause of your well-being. Nevertheless, because you think you are alone, that you have to *do* everything, this kind of thinking is a great source of your suffering! It is you against the world, you against the universe: "There is nobody on my side! God has abandoned me! No one is helping me! If I don't do it, it won't get done!" This is a *horrible* way to live your life. You have simply contracted your well-being into the domain of your childish effort to do things by yourself! What can *you* do? You cannot change one damned thing. You are powerless and you know it! That is what is causing you so much anxiety! On the one hand, you are trying to do everything and on the other hand, you *know* you don't have any power to do anything! Now you are in this dilemma of effort, powerlessness and anxiety. You are headed for a psychiatric institution! You are headed for Prozac, for sexual promiscuousness, for alcohol or drugs and/or food addiction. You have put yourself in an impossible situation. This illusion that you are the "doer" becomes transcended as you go through the transegoic stages.

By learning how to live in a *state* of meditation, you will have the experience that you are not the doer. I said "the experience," not read a book and say you are not the doer! That is not the same thing. This only happens when you have learned to carry your meditation with you throughout your day-to-day activities—when you are in a state of *constant* meditation. The problem is that we do not really understand meditation. You are thinking that meditation is a few hours you set aside in the morning to perform a practice. This is not what I call meditation, though it is part of it. *Meditation is a perpetual state of mind.* It is moment-to-moment.

Unless you can live in this moment-to-moment state of meditation, you cannot lose the experience of being the *doer* and, therefore, be relieved of all of the suffering which you are undergoing because you think you have to do *everything.* Move through the day not caught up in thinking, and you will see. By perpetuating the state of meditation—disciplining the mind, shutting down the thinking process—you will simply see this truth. Remember, "meditation" simply means "to see." The word for meditation translated from the Sanskrit, *dhyan*, means to see. It is also called *viveka*, discrimination, the ability to distinguish the "real" from that which is "unreal."

Freed of your ideologies, your ideas, and your beliefs, you can see clearly into life. When you can see clearly into life, you will see that you are not the doer at all, that in reality you do nothing, that life is truly a *gift*, in the truest sense. What are you doing to breathe? Nothing! What are you doing to metabolize your food? Nothing! What are you consciously doing to split your cells? Nothing! This "non-doing" is true across the board, but because of your ignorance of this process (which extends beyond your physiology), you actually think you are *doing* something and you do not know how to *let go*. In Taoism, the great gift that Lao-tzu gave us is how to let go and just "flow in the *Tao*"; there is nothing to do. It is beautiful! Unless you are able to achieve, through a process of meditation, the requisite degree of disciplining of the thinking process, you cannot lose the experience of being the doer, and until you are able to do so, your dukkha will go on increasing.

The next level of ego is self-image. This *false* image that you have created of yourself becomes transcended through meditation. Through meditation, the *identity* of who you feel you are *evolves*.

What creates your image of yourself? It is your thinking! Who are you when you cease to think? When you are in a state of sushupti, are you male or female? You will have no experience of being either. Are you black or white? All of this drops away. Are you "good" or "bad" in a state of sushupti? No. It is all gone. That is what Buddha meant when he said, "gata . . . Tathagata": Gone . . . all gone. The image that you have been dragging around and perpetuating, all of that stuff is gone!

What makes it even worse is the fact that some of us are so immature we think we are the same person we were ten years ago! You are not even the same person you were ten minutes ago, or ten seconds ago, for that matter! You have an image you formed of yourself when you were a teenager and you are still clinging to the dammed thing, and cannot move forward! You will see people trapped in the seventies, with stacked heels, big hats—"Super Fly"! They are still caught up in the image that they formed of themselves when they were in high school! You can see tragic old men and women who are still clinging to the images they had of themselves when they were twenty or thirty years old!

I saw a guy from our old neighborhood who used to be a "player." I remember him as a little boy in the seventies. He had a 1970 Cadillac! I will never forget it! It was green with a white convertible top, and he used to always have his top down. He was a handsome, older brother. Even then he had a little gray beard and a little gray in his hair and he used to wear a tam. I guess it was popular to be a "French" Negro then! He was at that age, forty or forty-five, where he could still attract women who were a little older or a little younger. He was living in the best of both worlds. The brother was smooth and had class! I was going down Kostner (a Westside street) a few days ago and I saw this brother sitting in an old beat up Pontiac, but it was a convertible and he had the top down, he still had his tam on and he was still leaning, twenty-five years later! He is still clinging to an image of himself that is gone, that is no longer relevant to reality!

We all do that. You are still clinging to your bullshit! You are messing up your whole life. Some of us are still clinging to that "persona" we developed in high school of being "cool": "You know, I'm cool. Yeah, I get 'high,' man. I'm the man!" You are not seventeen anymore! This is not high school! You are still getting up saying, "What you got on a bottle?" You are not fifteen anymore! That is not cool! That is nowhere, but you are preoccupied with getting high! This is nonsense! This is a thirteen or fourteen year old's behavior, and you are still clinging to that. "Well, this is how I am. You know, I like my drink." Through a process of meditation we are able to shut down this mind in such a way that we are able to stop the thinking which gives support to the manifestation and perpetuation of these false images of ourselves. The mystics say that we have developed only a false image of ourselves, because it is not based on our *own* investigation. It is based on hearsay and feedback from people who do not even know *themselves*. Investigate your image. Have some courage and look into it! You say you have courage and are brave; here is a real opportunity to use your courage! See the falseness of this image you have of yourself and become free! It is a *silly* thing. Meditation does that. It shuts down that whole thinking process which maintains your false image and liberates you from your captivity to it.

THE ROLE OF THE GURU

The destruction of our false images is why these Gurus and mystics are so dangerous and why they have been killed. They did not kill Jesus just to be killing him, or boiling Mansur just to be boiling Mansur. They were not burning the Dadus and Tukarams just to be doing something. These people are dangerous because they are going to destroy your ego, your self-image, and that is going to hurt you! You want to cling to your bullshit and with the Guru, you cannot do that. That is why many disciples will turn against the Guru, and it is understandable. It makes sense, because the Guru is going to anger you and tear your ego up! He is going to be a death unto you. That is what we need, because we do not have the maturity to let go of these images of ourselves.

This is why so many of us seek solace in a dead Guru. With a Jesus you are absolutely safe; Jesus is not here, and you can get away with your nonsense. You can say anything in the name of the Buddha, because the Buddha is not here. The living Masters are always dangerous because they will challenge your bullshit. Be reminded that when we talk about ego, there is some risk you undertake in coming to these workshops. I will have to point out—over and over—on behalf of these great Gurus, that you really have to drop your bullshit. You are full of bullshit! It may be "holy" bullshit, but it is bullshit nevertheless! No "talk mysticism!" No "talk religion!" That is *not* going to get it. You are going to have to drop all of that if you want what you came here to get.

THE DEVELOPMENT OF WISDOM

The most amazing thing which will happen through the process of meditation as you shut down the thinking process, is you will *simultaneously* open up other faculties which were laying dormant, obscured by the thinking process. One of them is the *intuitive* faculty. Again, you have been feeling that you can only have knowledge through thinking, in spite of the fact that with all of your thinking, you are still messing up your life! "To be or not to be? Is she the right one or is she not the right one? Is he the right one? Should I marry or should I not marry?" With all of that, you are still messing up because you do not have the capacity to have any authentic knowledge at this rational level. You are clinging to your pondering as if you have some knowledge, as if you can "do" something to know anything at the mental level. Through the process of meditation and shutting down this thinking process, the intuitive faculty *automatically* opens and pure knowledge descends. You do not have to think; it is just there! Wisdom is there and you know *exactly* what to do, and you have also become spiritually strong enough to do it.

To do that which is correct will require you to transcend the lower stages of your ego. There is a state of ego that is totally linked with the body and only seeks comfort, and the right thing might be "uncomfortable" to the body. You are not mature enough to set aside the discomfort to the physical body in order to act out of your highest intelligence. "Bhagwan, the meditation hurts." Okay, it hurts! What is the problem? Why do you keep telling me this? I know it hurts! I am not stupid. Do you want to act out of your intelligence or do you want to act out of your body? *You* choose. If you want a path that is going to please your body, I do not have one for you. Go to the storefront church. They specialize in giving you paths that appease your body! I do not deal in that. It is going to hurt, yes! Discipline it. Go through the pain! Have some intelligence! "Bhagwan, should I marry this man?" Hell, no! Do not marry him. You are going to ruin your life. "But I am so in *love*." No! You are not in love; you are *attached*. You are in *lust*. You are identified with some lower portion of your body.

You are so egotistically disordered that you cannot even be alone. You are psychologically weak and are only suffering from loneliness, but you are calling that "love." Girl, get your shit together! You do not want to hear that, but that is the right answer! You cannot stand this yet, but this is the truth. You are too weak and cannot be alone. If you cannot be alone, you cannot be with anybody else! You are moving into a relationship because you are lonely or you feel you are "inadequate." Psychologically, you are too *immature* to be happy alone, so you need someone else to help you to be happy. You are still an infant in the ego hierarchy. You are still too "little" for adult relationships. You need to work on yourself and you are not going to like that!

As we peel off the rational limitations on consciousness, we are able to see *truth* for the first time! It is this truth that sets you free from all of these unnecessary degrees of suffering, and that is only possible through meditation. Remember, I said that only through meditation—not through talk mysticism, not through satsang—are you able to transcend the rational limitations on consciousness. There is no other way to have infallible knowledge, knowledge that is never wrong and that can never be taken away. As we peel away each of these egoic limitations, our experience of being separate goes on diminishing, and our experience of oneness, of totality, goes on increasing. With meditation, *oneness* will manifest in our outward lives as an increasing display of *love*.

Vernita was asking me, "What kind of man are you? What did you do your last time around?" She is always asking me, "Bhagwan, can you go inside and do all of these things?" Vernita is right; these are the right questions. But you need not be wholly dependent upon my remarks. Watch how I *love*. If you do not see any demonstration of love from me, know that I am a fraud and know that about anybody, because anyone who has made *any* spiritual progress will *always* demonstrate love, compassion, understanding and gentleness. You cannot have it any other way. Some fool will come in here today and say, "Bhagwan, you know, I have read this and I have read that. I have been on the Path and I have been really seeking." However, I am looking and saying, who have you been in love with? Where is your love? There is no evidence of any love in your life! What nonsense are you talking? The life and living which is truly based on higher knowledge will *always* become more and more loving, not less.

Some will say, "I have read the Bhagavad-Gita. I know all about karma." If you know about karma, demonstrate that knowledge by being more loving! You know about karma and you are still eating meat? You do not know *anything* about karma! You know about karma and you are still shooting dope and drinking alcohol? You are a fool, lost in the lower dimensions of your ego! You are *arrogating* to yourself knowledge that you do not have and probably will not have for a long time! Your knowledge is always reflected in your living, with no exception. Meditation is a process which not only allows us to attain knowledge, but also enables us to apply that knowledge to our life and day-to-day living.

Through the process of meditation, we have already learned how to discipline our body and our body is not running our lives anymore; we are running this body. If I tell this body to sit in that corner for two hours, this body had better sit in that corner for two hours! It is not ruling *me*; I am ruling *it*! However, your body rules you. If your body does not want to sit, you simply do not sit! This order has to be reversed.

DISCOVERING OUR DHARMA
THROUGH MEDITATION

The seventh stage is when the ego starts developing a "will," an intent. It starts trying to *deliberately* do something. It starts trying to live on purpose. I watch your faces whenever I put the question out there: *What are you trying to do with your life?* I am aware that you do not know the answer. You really do not have a clue about what you are trying to do with your life! That is why you come here! You are hoping and asking, "Bhagwan, can you give me a hint about what I am trying to do with my life?" When we go inside through meditation, the first thing we discover is our *dharma*. We find our purpose!

You came into this world with a tremendous gift and you do not even know what it is. Therefore, nothing can be more tragic than your ignorance of your gift! You do not know what you have in yourself. You do not know *who* you are and this is sad. The Creator has put something unique and magnificent in you, and you do not know what it is! You are living the life of a clown, of a buffoon and of a fool. Buried deep within you is this immense gift that the Lord has put there and you are wasting this gift! Meditation takes us inside and we are able to see what that gift is. This is perhaps the most transforming experience you will have in meditation: You find that which you *are* and then you *live* it. For the very first time, your life has meaning.

Out of their compassion, these mystics come, because they know who we are. They have no "need" to teach us. They could just kick back and enjoy the bliss of their own enlightenment, but they come out of that blissful state because they have seen that "thing" in us. They help us find our gift, our dharma. Once we discover our dharma, our lives are never the same. When you are acting out of your talent, you lose the experience of time and space. To lose track of time is called the "present": time stops.

I remember at Harrison High School—Big Emma and Bilal might also remember—there was a teacher named Mrs. Martin, who was my home room teacher. Because Mrs. Martin was an *authentic* teacher, she had a teacher's eye and could see deeply into her students. Most teachers do not have the capacity to see deeply into their students; hence, their inability to effectively teach. I can remember one day while "cutting" classes, I was sitting out on the fire escape, smoking a "joint" and having a little wine. At the time, I had already been absent sixty-five days! Mrs. Martin somehow, from across the expanse of a parking lot, saw me sitting on the fire escape and she raised that powerful finger in the air and beckoned to me.

The reason she had such an effect on me was because I really loved Mrs. Martin. Mrs. Martin was not a Hollywood beauty, and I was sensitive to the fact that she must have suffered immensely in her life. She had very Negroid features, what you might call an "ugly" woman, not at all attractive. The children would make fun of her. I identified with her suffering and I loved her. I still would not go to her class, but I loved her! So, when she beckoned for me, that finger was enough and I sat my wine down, pinched my "roach" (reefer), and began to cross the parking lot to see what was going on with Mrs. Martin.

As I got closer to Mrs. Martin, I could see that she was kind of distressed. I could see the tracks of her tears, that the woman had been crying. Perhaps somebody had stolen something from her or done something to her car. My mind was racing, trying to figure out, what is going on here? As I was thinking, I was becoming angrier and angrier, because if someone has been "messing" with Mrs. Martin, we are going to change some situations up in here today! I always came to school *prepared* to change situations. I had my "change the situation people" with me, so I was capable of changing situations that day! Whatever the problem was, I was ready and capable of handling it! I was getting in that mood, because I had come up there that day looking for something to do. I was looking for some *seva*! I discovered that the cause of her anguish was *me*! I was the cause of her tears! She talked to me all of what was about five minutes. She spoke "love" to me. For those of you who haven't had the experience of having love spoken to you, it is impossible for me to tell you what that is like! She pleaded with me to relieve her of her agony and her suffering by making something of myself, to not waste my intelligence. I promised her I would not. I said, "Mrs. Martin, I won't do that." I got back into high school, went to night school, went on and did my thing. She spoke to something deep within me. She was the first to speak to me of my dharma.

I can remember graduating from Roosevelt University the first time and taking my little philosophy degree back to Harrison, finding Mrs. Martin, laying it at her feet and touching her feet. Her love was education par excellence. Those college professors taught me *nothing* about me. This woman taught me about *me*! For me, she is a Guru. If this is what a great secular teacher can do, can you imagine what these great buddhas did? What a Buddha did for a Sariputta or a Mahakasyapa, or what a Kabir did for a Charan Das? What Krishna did for Arjuna was to remind him of who he was.

This is the problem: *You do not know who you are*! Maharaj Ji used to say that we are kings and queens and are living lives of paupers and beggars! This is not right! Meditation is the way to discover thy *true* self, and the question, what are you trying to do with your life, will be clearly answered for the first time.

Ra shekum maat.

Chapter Four
The Transcendence of Ego
Through Spiritual Practice

This is session three of five sessions where we have been discussing the anatomy and evolution of ego. The purpose of this ego series is to help us understand the essence of what spirituality is all about. We all know that the *only* barrier on the Path has always been defined as the *ego*. All saints, sages and seers have made the same statement. The idea is that the more you investigate the nature of your ego, the more understanding that investigation will generate. It is out of this understanding that your meditation becomes rooted. Let us begin.

We want to move into the deeper dimensions of the anatomy and evolution of the ego. We previously talked about some of the preliminary stages. I now want to bring your attention to a few things as we continue to discuss the evolution of the ego. We know that this whole Path is only made difficult because we are egocentric. We are almost "autistic" in a sense. This whole maturation of ego is nothing more than a decline or decrease in the experience of being separate. Remember, I defined ego, fundamentally, as the experience of being separate. Therefore, as one's ego matures, the experience of separateness decreases, so there is a kind of *expansion* of identity taking place.

It takes a little while to become accustomed to this, because we have been thinking just the reverse. We have been thinking that as the ego matures, we experience more separation. No, it is just the reverse. As your ego matures, there is an actual *decline* in this felt experience of being separate. Hence, the mystics emphasize and focus on the fact that the ego has to be *transcended* by going through the various stages of development. I want you to begin to appreciate this a bit more. Let us enter a little more into the metaphysics of this thing.

The Pre-egocentric Stage

There is a state that is even pre-ego, the "pre-egocentric" state. That is a state where there is not even an ego yet. The person is totally unconscious of their separation. This should not be confused with the "transegoic" state that the mystics talk about, just as deep, dreamless sleep where there is no mind activity going on should not be confused with *samadhi,* where there is also no mind activity going on. They are opposite poles of the experience of consciousness. This is almost like a *zero* state, you are just autistic, totally turned in. You are *pre-egocentric*. We can almost call that the "bio-centric" stage in the development of ego. By bio-centric, I mean that the consciousness is totally structured around the senses. There has been no differentiation yet in order to produce the egocentric. It is pre-egoic and there are only the senses and sense perception, the "sensorial motor" experience, if you will.

You have to ponder this, because I am challenging you to dig deep and investigate the nature of your ego. You will see where you are. If you are having trouble on this Path, if you are having trouble bringing your life into alignment with the teachings, if you are struggling in your meditation, it is because your ego is immature! You are having these problems because you are too "compacted," too contracted to do *sadhana.* It is understanding that will liberate you from this situation.

Here, at the pre-egoic stage, consciousness is still bio-centric. It is still identified with biology, the senses—tasting, smelling, feeling—that is it. There is not even a "formal" concept of self. You do not even know you *exist.* You do not even know you are in space and time. You are in a stage of subconsciousness or unconsciousness. It is existence with no awareness of existence, just merged into the bio-center. You are breathing in the intrauterine stage in your mother's womb, of course. All of the functions are going on in the body: blood is being circulated, food is being digested, etc. You are "fused" to the biology of being, and that is it. However, as the progress continues, you now technically begin to become an ego. We are talking about the actual evolution of the experience of separateness that I have defined as "ego."

THE PHYSIO-CENTRIC STAGE

The next stage is where you become "physio-centric." For the first time, there is the experience of being a physical body. At about the fourth to sixth month after birth, we sort of "hatch" in the sense that we become aware of the physical body. It is interesting, because even at this stage, there is no *distinction* between your body and anybody else's body! There is no way to differentiate between the inside and the outside. If we observe closely, we will see that a child in that state cannot distinguish its body from anybody else's body. It has no experience of "subjectivity" at all. It is just fused with all that is physical. That becomes the shell, the husk, the first form that this ego takes as it experiences being separate. The only way you are going to understand this is to investigate it. I am simply giving you a structure, something to look at.

What do I mean by "bio-centric" and "physio-centric"? I mean that this is the center, the gravity of your identity. Your sense of self is *centered* around this experience. It is interesting to note that as we are phasing through each of these hierarchal stages of ego, it is generating in us a whole set of what we call "needs." As our identity begins to expand, it also creates in us a felt sense of what our needs are. People in the bio-centric stage are totally closed in. Thus, you will not see them moving toward any needs. You have to do everything for them because they are caught up in themselves. But at the physio-centric stage, you will begin to see the emergence of needs that correspond to that level of identity. What are the needs when the spirit has reached the second stage in the evolution of the ego? The needs are all physical: sex and food. That is it.

You can see that many of us are still physio-centric! Our identities are still centered in this body, because all we are concerned about is sex and food! Every exposure to reality that we are having is, "How can I have sex with this?" or "How can I eat it?" That is it. It constitutes your whole world view. Just as each of these centers of identity is accompanied by a set of personal needs based upon that stage, you will also see a kind of *morality* that accompanies each of these stages. The individual who is still physio-centric has a certain kind of morality, but their morality is "me and the hell with the rest!" In fact, there is no "rest." At the physio-centric stage, you are so *focused* in on yourself that you do not really have the experience of others. It is a strange state. Your entire sense of identity is simply locked into your physical aspect of existence. You can now begin to see how very difficult it will be for us in life when we become stuck in this stage of physio-centric development.

THE UNFOLDMENT OF SPIRIT

I have to pause here and try to make you understand some things, because as I told you when we began to investigate the nature of the ego, it will require your best intellect, your deepest understanding. We are entering into very subtle territory, so you will have to be able to *concentrate*. If you cannot concentrate, you are not going to be able to follow the train of thinking. Very often, the mystics did not even discuss all of these things with us until there was a certain degree of progress made, because if you could not concentrate, you could not follow their train of thought, and that made it very difficult to understand these kinds of things. You will just have to bear with me as we try to go through this thing.

There are a few more things I must explain in order for you to begin to appreciate this model. Remember, this is just a "model." I am trying to give you some sense of it. These stages are not "isolated" from each other; they sometimes overlap. The reality, of course, is that as we expand and make progress, as we evolve from a lower stage in ego development to a higher stage, we automatically *enfold* the lower into the higher. Do you follow me? You do not lose the lower experience; it is incorporated into the next stage. There is this constant evolving and integrating of what you have evolved *from*. This is very important to understand. When a person gets to the physio-centric stage and their sense of identity has now evolved to the level of the body, they do not cease their relationship with the bio-centric level. That is folded in. At the physical level, you are still partially identified with your senses. What is going on here is a kind of *expansion*: spirit is *unfolding*. Maybe we should talk about evolution in a wider sense of the word, because I want you to understand more about this stage. Let me pause and make sure you really appreciate the unfolding aspect of spirit, because it is critical in order to understand evolution even as it applies to the ego. We will come back to this in a moment.

There are a couple of ways to look at things from a cosmic point of view. You can look at the *evolution* of spirit or you can look at the *descent* of spirit into creation. As we explore the descent of spirit, what we begin to see is something like this: This infinite spirit begins to "condense" itself or "contract" itself, and at the first level of contraction, it begins to manifest itself into what we call a "subject and object" relationship. I am trying to make this as easy as possible. I know it is a little difficult, but those of you who have understood the *Metu Neter*, please try to follow me. We are talking about the *descent* of spirit, meaning that spirit is continuously *pouring* itself out into creation. Maybe it will be easier if I start from the bottom and leave spirit at the top.

When spirit manifests itself into creation, it starts in the lowest form, matter. Spirit and matter are not different; matter is simply a lower manifestation. Spirit exists in matter, but at its lowest manifestation; hence, the lifelessness. For example, a rock appears to be lifeless. The spirit in the rock is there, but it is not dynamic, is it? It is contracted into its lowest possible state. After that state, the next is cellular. Atoms enfold into molecules, molecules enfold into cells and cells enfold into organisms. This is high school biology. You can see that the next evolution is moving toward the full expression of spirit. At the cellular level, there is a little bit more spirit manifesting, and it is reflected in the manifestation of life in the form of vegetation. In plants, we see a little more because it is a higher organization of spirit than what you would see in a rock. What is the next one above the vegetative state? Insects. You see a little more of the presence of spirit in creation.

Remember, all mystics and saints have said that God is in the creation. Thus, that which we call "God" is in a rock! It is immanent in the creation and, if a rock is a part of creation, then spirit is in the rock! It is just that spirit is so contracted, so unmanifested in the rock that you cannot see it. So, as spirit progressively unfolds, we begin to see *life*. What we call "existence" is nothing but the drama of the unfolding of spirit from the lowest to the highest stages. After insects come birds and fish. Those of us who have studied Darwinian theories of evolution now have a schematic to follow. First, you will see marine life, then birds, reptiles, etc. and, finally, animals and mammals. When we are exploring the maturation and evolution of the ego, we are starting at the human level. When humans start out, the first stage is bio-centric, which is really nothing but this entire lower complex.

The next stage, as stated earlier, is the physio-centric. Again, you can begin to see how each level includes the previous level, because the cellular level includes the material level, does it not? Molecules include atoms and cells include atoms and molecules. You can see this building process occurring. I want you to understand that, if we are talking about the *ascent* of consciousness back to the level of spirit, what we are really talking about is the *unfoldment* of spirit. If we are talking about the *descent* of spirit into creation, we are talking about the *contraction* of spirit into smaller and smaller or lower and lower stages of life.

Let us return to our analysis of the evolution of ego. You will have to work with all of this because this is *deep* stuff that we are moving into. We talked first about the zero state, the bio-centric, where you are separate; you exist, but you do not know it. Now, we are talking about the physio-centric stage in ego development where you now know that you exist, but it is only at a physical level and it is not distinguishable. The child cannot really distinguish its body from anybody else's because it does not yet have much of a sense of identity.

THE EMOTIO-CENTRIC STAGE

The next stage in the development of the ego is where we become "emotio-centric." That is when our identity now shifts to being more than the body. It includes the bio-centric fusion that we previously experienced with the senses. You then pick up the experience of being a body, and next move to a level where you begin to realize that you also have feelings and emotions, and you now become identified with your emotions: "I am happy," or "I am unhappy." Your emotions become the *center* of your identity, whereas before it was "I am hungry," or "I am hurt," or "I am in pain." Do you see how the blanks after the "I am" statements continue to evolve? Remember, your sense of identity is with whatever you fill in the blanks after the "I am" statements. At the emotio-centric level, you are listing all of your emotions, because that is what you most identify with: You are *essentially* your emotions.

Remember, when I say emotio-centric, I mean that you are "locked" into the experience of *your* emotions—you cannot experience other people's emotions at all! For example, if a child in that state wants to play, it thinks everybody should be playing. If it is sad, it thinks everybody should be sad. Sometimes, if we are stuck in this stage and we are in a good mood, we figure the whole world should be in a good mood. If I am satisfied with this, everybody should be satisfied. Do you begin to now see how we project our own emotional state onto everybody else? We cannot experience any differentiation at all. That is what I mean by "centric": You are *centered* at that level. The ego has moved to this emotional-centric state in its development where it is now essentially identified with its emotions. It is still centric; it is still contracted; it still has no sense of the "other." It does not even experience the other. What you must understand is that, at these stages, there is no experience of the other at all. It is all "you" (selfish).

Don't we become stuck at this level? Some of us are still locked into this level where we are centered in our emotions, and that is our fundamental sense of identity. We are so centered on how *we* feel that we cannot even experience the feelings of other people! Others are not an issue. When you do something, are you concerned about what other people feel? Hell, no! You are only concerned about how *you* feel, and you act only out of that concern. You never for a moment pause to consider the feelings of other people. Those are people whose egos are still stuck in this lower level of development where they are emotio-centric and totally locked into their own feelings. It does not matter what the "feeling" is. If you are locked into a feeling of fear, for example, that is how you react. There is no experience of the other's fear, love, pain, etc.

THE PSYCHO-CENTRIC STAGE

A little more evolution takes place and you become "psycho-centric." Now you start to develop a *concept* of yourself. Before the mind got to this stage of ego development, you had "images" of yourself and you had "symbols" representing yourself, such as your name. You can clearly see this happen with children when they begin to recognize their name, or you will see children walk in front of a mirror and look at themselves and just smile, because they recognize their image. Sometimes you will see grown women walking pass a mirror, pausing and looking at themselves! They will stop to stare into any glass that reflects their image and check themselves out. They are still unable to have a sense of "seeing" themselves beyond their physical images.

However, at the psycho-centric stage in the development of ego, for the first time you start thinking in terms of concepts. It is still centric because now you think everybody is like you! You have finally developed beyond your first image of yourself—and we are not even going to argue about whether this image is correct or not—to the point where you are now able to *conceptualize* your own self. Yet, you are still centric and still do not experience the other.

It is strange how so many of us have not gone beyond this stage either. We are very, very psycho-centric. Everybody is like "me." Think about it. In your relationships, can you really experience the other person's uniqueness and individuality? No! You can only "see" the other through your own eyes and all of your effort is to make the other person become like you! This is violent, isn't it? It is disrespectful, but you want your employer, your neighbor, the whole world to be like you! This is immaturity! This is childish! It is appropriate when you are five or six years old. It is totally inappropriate when you are forty something years old and pushing it. This is the kind of perspective out of which a person who is psycho-centric, who is still at a lower stage in the maturation of their ego, functions. What do their needs consist of? What needs do they have at this stage? Their greatest need is for everybody to "do what I tell them to do." That is what they feel they need.

THE "NEEDS" OF THE EGO

What you should be doing here is writing down what *your* needs are. I want you to start thinking about this as we go through this discussion today. Start becoming very, very conscious of your needs. What are the things that you feel you need? Let us pause for a moment because I don't want you to play games with yourself. I want you to investigate where *you* are. What are the things that you need? Some might say, "I need some money," or "I need a man," or "I need a job." What are *your* needs. Be honest! Write them down. The greatest barrier in the maturation of ego is lying to yourself! The more you lie to yourself, the more you actually regress. Lying to yourself will cause you to regress to a bio-centric state! Tell yourself the truth! What are the things that you have been saying you need? Are you all ashamed to write them down? Tell the truth! What have people been saying that they need? Let us put them on the board. Rick, you need some paper, right?

Bhai Rani: *We are always saying that we need some money.*

Yes, one of the things most of us say we need is some money. So, that is number one. I want you to prioritize them. Become very conscious of what you have been thinking you need, because that is what you have been obsessing about. That is what you have been staying up all night trying to figure out: "How am I going to get what I need?" You have a list, look at it. Let us zero in on *your* needs because you are investigating *your* ego, right? The whole idea is to investigate *our* egos; we are not worried about what the other person's ego looks like right now. Let us first start with where *we* are. What are the things that *you* need? Prioritize them: give me number one, number two; write them outside the margin, if necessary. You might have only listed them spontaneously, but I now need you to prioritize them. What is your "number one" need?

One of the things you will see is that this "need" thing is kind of foolish, isn't it? Right now, you need this and the next minute, that priority will shift, right? That is all right, because over time you will be able to track the movements and you will see your patterns. You will see what keeps popping up in the number one slot, and you will start adding up all of the number ones and get an even deeper insight into yourself. But you must write down your needs. No cheating, Florida! Don't tell Bomani what he needs, such as "you need your wife"! Don't be influencing him! Bomani, you are going to have to move over here!

As we move through this model in the evolutionary stages of ego, you will see, as I have already told you, that it has a "needs" side. Each stage will display specific needs of the self when it is at that stage. Let's say that a person's number one need is for money, as Bhai Rani said, because there are also certain cultural factors here, right? In Western cultures, for instance, we know that we are fundamentally materialistic. Reality is that which you can see, taste, touch, feel and smell. That is it! If you cannot experience it at the level of the senses, it is not real. The means by which we can manipulate our so-called material "reality" is to have some money, because most of us equate money with reality. What is it that you want the money for? Let us go deep. You say that your number one need is for some money. Why do you need the money? What are the needs you have for which only money can provide? Let us go into it. Don't become ashamed now!

June: *It might make your "dukkha" a little easier to bear!*

Bhai Rani: *Pay some bills. Have some peace of mind, some consistency.*

Pay some bills and get some pressure off of you, right? A little more money will give you greater peace of mind? It will give you a small sense of security, right? What else do we need money for?

Mensa: *Food and clothing.*

That's right, food and clothing, entertainment, shelter, and so forth—basic stuff. If money is your number one need, I want you to explore that. Whatever your number one is, explore that, go deeply into that. The fundamental thing you will begin to see is that your needs can all be fitted into this model. For instance, at the physio-centric level, the greatest need is for security: food, shelter, clothing, things that are totally related to the body. That is what people at that level need, because their sense of identity is primarily centered in their bodies.

They are physio-centric people, and they are dangerous people to deal with because they can only think in terms of sex, food—survival! Their morality is based on the reasoning that, if it leads to them having more sex or more food, it is all right! "Whatever results in my getting this stuff is right!" Their sense of morality is very different. If they need some sex and they go out and rape someone, they do not understand why they are being charged, why they are being locked up. They are just getting themselves some sex! If you had some food in your house and they broke in and got themselves some food, they cannot see what they did that was wrong! So, their sense of "morality" is also confined to where they are centered. *Your* sense of morality is also related to where *your* ego is centered!

At the psycho-centric level in the development of our ego, as I said before, we have formed a concept of ourselves, and our whole thing is we feel everybody is just like us. Not only do we *feel* that everybody is just like us, our morality is that everybody *should* be like us: My wife should be like me; my husband should be like me; my children should be just like me; my neighbors should all be like me. The only moral stance the psycho-centric person is able to take is that everybody should be like them. This is their sense of morality, but it is still egocentric, isn't it? These are only different derivatives of egocentricism.

The way to see it from the back side is to make that list of your needs. From that list of your needs, I can see what *dominant* stage you are in, because sometimes you may become psycho-centric or you may become emotio-centric, but your dominant center may be physio-centric. You are primarily functioning out of that sense of identity. You may slip back and forth, but this is your anchor, what Gaurdijeff called your *chief* characteristic.

I want you to please notice that as you evolve, as your ego matures, the locus of your identity goes on *shifting*. Where before, you were totally identified with your biology, you now become identified with your body, which is a little better, and includes the biological. From there, you move to the emotio-centric level, where your identity has now shifted to your likes and dislikes as well as other feelings, but it also includes all of the lower stages. They have become *integrated* and enfolded into the higher stage and made a part of it if the integration has been healthy. However, sometimes we do not make "healthy" integrations, and one part of the identity moves up and another part is "held back." That becomes a "complex," which means that some of you are stuck in the lower stages, and it creates a kind of "leak" in your spirit! But we will talk about that once you have understood all of this.

THE SOCIO-CENTRIC/ETHNO-CENTRIC STAGE

As I said before, the next level is what I call the "socio-centric." The socio-centric stage in the development of ego is very often expressed as "ethno-centric." The identity moves and it is at this level that, for the first time, you really begin to experience the "other"; you are able to see things from the other person's perspective. It is only now beginning to happen. Since you now have developed conceptual abilities, one of the things that happens is your identity begins to be "associated" with others in the sense they may be members of your same sex or race: "I am black." When your identity is centered in your race, your "blackness," it means that your ego has reached the ethno-centric stage. "I am black," meaning that I am a part of this group—not white, not Chinese, not Mexican. There is still that split, but at the ethno-centric level, our identity *expands* to the point where we now identify ourselves with others who "look" like us.

The ego has now become identified with its race, its tribe or its gender: "I am a man. I belong to a community of men. I can identify with them. I am a man, not a woman." Women are now the enemy! Why? Because whomever is not in your group, your moral stance towards them is, "screw them"! Your care, concern or compassion, which was previously restricted to yourself at the lower stages, now becomes spread across your socio-economic, gender or racial grouping, doesn't it? The same concern and care you had for yourself at the prior stages is now shared: "You are like me, Keebah. You belong to my group. I can now care about you just as I care about myself." You become "incorporated" into my identity and, therefore, I can expand some of my own egocentric concerns to include you, but no one else! Anybody outside of our group is "the enemy; let's get them." Tribalism develops out of this kind of thinking. Your Afrikan-centered movement is stuck here in this stage of ego development. I am not condemning it, I am simply trying to make you understand that this is not the final stage of maturity, but it is on its way.

Sometimes it is the family. We all see people who are caught up in their families: "My wife and my kids," and the hell with everybody else on the planet! That is their actual attitude; "I don't give a damn about what happens to anybody else! I am only concerned about what happens to *my* wife and *my* kids." Remember, this does not include brothers and sisters, only the nuclear family! Some people are simply locked into an identification with their nuclear family, and they cannot "experience" anything outside of that. They cannot confer any concern on anything that is outside of that immediate group. Period! A person can also become socio-centric about religion: "I am a Christian and we Christians should stick together. Let's kill all of these Muslims!" Or, "I am a Muslim. Let's stick together, Muslims, and kill these Christians!" It is still the same thing. The point I want to make is that when the ego reaches the socio-centric or ethno-centric stage in its evolution and development, it is now able to *expand* its identification beyond its body, emotions and lower parts to locate its identity in this larger context, but it still includes all of the lower ones.

One of the most significant things I want to point out is that, at the socio-centric or ethno-centric stage of ego development, what you will see emerging are *roles*. Usually, at this stage the ego becomes stuck in roles: "I'm a father," and that is it. There is a dominant role that you become stuck in. What dominant role are *you* stuck in? I need you to investigate that. "I'm a daddy"; "I'm a mother." Some people's dominant role is the type of work they do: "I'm a doctor"; "I'm a therapist"; "I'm a cop"; or "I'm a teacher." If you ask them to tell you something about themselves, they will say, "Oh, I'm a doctor and I have this wife." Notice how people define who they are. Listen closely with your third ear, and you will begin to see the components of their identities. So, what is the dominant role that *you* are stuck in, that you have become identified with? Your dominant role may be, "I'm a wife." Your ego is identified, located and locked into this one role: a wife. You can now be nothing else, because you have *contracted* yourself into this one role. You have crippled yourself, limited yourself; your spirit has been "hobbled."

THE RATIO-CENTRIC STAGE

The next stage in the development of our ego is what I call the "ratio-centric." At the ratio-centric stage we are able to do all of this so-called "sophisticated" thinking and reasoning, and we become identified with our "knowledge": "I know this and I cannot be moved!" We start having the feeling of being "right," which is based on our knowledge, limited though it is, and we cling to that and cannot move. It is a higher stage of ego development and includes all of the others, but if you are stuck at this level, you cannot see the merits of another person's arguments at all. You only see *your* knowledge: "I know this and this is the case. This is how it is. Case closed!" You become very inflexible, because you think *your* knowledge is the sum total of *all* knowledge! You are still egocentric, therefore, if it does not mesh with your knowledge, it really does not count! The other person is simply wrong!

THE HUMAN-CENTRIC STAGE

The next stage in the evolution and expansion of this original pre-egocentric state can only be called "human-centric." Now, your identity has expanded to the entire human family. You are able to clearly see the other. This is the birth of democracy. This is a higher moral stance. The need at this level, as the self expands, is for harmony, for cooperation and all of those kinds of things. From this level, a better world can come into being. The human-centric level is more "global-centered," or world-centered. Not only are you concerned about your peace of mind, you are also concerned about your neighbor's peace of mind. At the lower stages, you are only concerned with *your* peace of mind and *your* enlightenment. You are only concerned with *your* spiritual growth. You are not able to incorporate the totality of humanness or humanity into your world view. That occurs at this higher stage in the maturation of ego.

THE ECO-CENTRIC STAGE

The seventh stage is what I call the "eco-centric stage." By eco-centric, I mean that now the identification process *expands* to include all sentient beings. Where before your concern was restricted to other *human* beings, you are now concerned about *all* beings: rats, roaches, dogs, cats. Your identity becomes "fused" with nature, and you are now as concerned about the comfort of a tree as you are about yourself. Your ego now expands to include all sentient beings as well as nature.

When the ego has finally matured to this point, we are now ready for the Spiritual Path, for some spiritual training. Now, we can do some meditation, some sadhana. When the gift of initiation, the gift of the opportunity to meditate has been given to us and we have not yet evolved or are mature enough to take advantage of it, it is because we are stuck somewhere beneath this stage in the development of our egos.

The way to see where you are is to look at your "needs" list that I have asked you to write down. What are the things that you think you need? Where are they related in this schematic? Do you need other people's recognition? Okay. You are located in the socio-centric stage of ego development, and you need other people's validation or praise. That is your need, and anything that does not result in your being praised, you cannot do it. You will flatly refuse to do it because there is no praise involved. Look honestly at *your* needs and you will begin to actually see where you are located in the scheme of things.

THE RELATIONSHIP BETWEEN EGO DEVELOPMENT AND SUFFERING

Let us now begin to close our discussion with some specific things. One of the things I want to emphasize is there is a definite relationship between the suffering you are experiencing and where you are in terms of your ego development. The reality is this: *The world is not the cause of your suffering.* This is a misnomer, a misunderstanding. It is not the "world" and the people and the circumstances in the world that are causing your misery or that are the basis of your *dukkha*. The truth of the matter is that your dukkha is caused by how *you* are *perceiving*, interacting, relating and orientating to the *world*! And this is determined by where you are in terms of your ego development! If your ego stage is still low and immature, you will know it because your suffering will be great!

We see this all of the time. People are just suffering, and when we look "objectively" at the person who is suffering, we become amazed: "What is this person's pain about?" Somebody is suffering immensely over what appears to be little, nonsensical stuff. Somebody has broken a limb on the tree in their back yard, and this person is just torn to pieces because their neighbor does not respect their property! You will see people who have millions of dollars, Bhai Rani Ra, and they are just suffering!

As we begin to look deeper, we come to the understanding that suffering cannot be based on having money or not having money. It cannot be based on any of the conditions to which we have been ascribing our suffering. The suffering can only be based on *us*, and in a very specific way: our level of ego maturity. This is the key insight you will gain the more you understand your ego. All of the suffering that we experience is due to our ego developmental stages, with no exceptions. Remember, the bottom line is how to *transcend* this thing, how to come out of it. This is not a game or "Mysticism 101." There is no grade at the end of the course. The idea is to come out of this state and ease your suffering.

The reality is that we should all be in an absolute state of bliss! If we are not experiencing uninterrupted, moment-to-moment bliss, we are out of *maat*, out of order, and the problem is with us and not "those people" with whom we are in a relationship. I am emphasizing this because I invariably come into contact with so much of what can only be called "imaginary" suffering, in the sense that the person is causing their own pain; what I call "pinching" yourself. Again, this is dictated by the level to which our egos have been able to evolve.

Bear in mind that the "payoff" of doing homework and investigating the nature of your ego is that, with increased understanding, you will be able to relieve the suffering you are experiencing. If you can see that your *suffering* is the direct result of *your* being stuck in a stage of ego development where you expect the whole world to mimic *your* desires, you will simply drop that expectation, and in the dropping of that expectation, the relief. You will then mature, and with maturity comes a decline or decrease in suffering. The only way we can mature is to "consciously" participate in the process of ego maturation, *i.e.* meditation.

THE EXPERIENCE OF ONENESS

We were talking about the ego being, fundamentally, this sense of feeling separate from that which exists; that this ego is fundamentally the absence of the experience of oneness. What exactly is the experience of "oneness"? When the mystics, saints and sages are talking about the growth in consciousness where one is capable of having the experience of oneness, what do they mean by that? Because, if we have been so mistaken about the nature of ego, and so mistaken about so many other aspects of what we thought constitutes "spirituality," perhaps we are also mistaken about the nature of this experience of oneness. Have you thought about it? Let's have some suggestions from you.

Sharon: *Just from my knowledge of it, I would say no separation.*

Yes, but that is a tautology. We know this is what oneness means by definition. I want you to fill in the blank for me.

Sharon: *It is like you are everything and everything is you. You are there; you are it. There is nothing that you are not.*

Mensa: *It is like being on the same page. You make no distinctions between you and anyone else. We are all the same.*

Pam: *An experience of aloneness. When you look outside, you don't see any differentiation.*

We are moving there, because these are popular definitions of the experience of oneness. Let us now see if we can get a *satori*, a glimpse, or gain a deeper insight into this.

When this oneness which is prior to all experience "differentiates" itself, we know that it differentiates itself into a subject and an object. The feeling inside of us is that this is our subjectivity and we move into this side of our being. Then when we have the experience of objects, we have many different things that go into this objective experience of reality. Reality becomes composed of many different objects and events, and so forth. The mystics have said that this is an "illusion," that there is truly no distinction between the subject and the object: The two events occur simultaneously! When you are *seeing* something, there is *something* to be *seen* and they both occur simultaneously! They are one, one in terms of time and space, one in essence! Let's back up a bit.

We talked about the physio-centric stage in the development of ego and the fact that all of our experience is with our body as the *reference* point, because at that level, our *identification* is with the body. As we move into the transegoic stages, as we go further out in the expansion of ego, we begin to have the experience of our body being the same as any other object! It is very different. It is like that bottle over there; "you" experience the bottle. There is the subject in here (inside the body) that is having the "sensorial" experience of the thing that we have collectively agreed to call "bottle," out there! So, our experience is a "dichotomy" between me, the observer insider, and that which is being observed, the bottle outside. The first movement out of this lower stage of body-ego occurs when we begin to *experience* our body as any other object out there! The experience is that my "self" is something "interior" to my body. You actually experience your body as you experience any other object.

Remember, Al, we were talking about the fact that, as we move through these stages of the shifting of identities from lower to higher centers of ego organization, there is a kind of "dying out" process? We talked about the fact that each experience is then *enfolded* into the next highest stage. One of the interesting things is that, when we move into the spiritual side of this whole thing, and through meditation we actually begin to make some *authentic* progress, one of the first experiences in this transegoic stage is that you begin to have the experience of your body as an object which is occurring in your consciousness.

THE WITNESSING SELF

At the transegoic stage, what has been called the "witness" state begins to descend in you. There is an observing Self. At the next level beyond the seventh, you begin to move into a center where you become identified with the witnessing. There is something in you that *witnesses*. Notice that it witnesses your *subjectivity* as well as the *object* of your subjectivity! There is something in consciousness that actually witnesses the ego, and you become identified with that! That is the next shift of the locus, the center of identity. You become identified with the witness, the observing self, what Ramana Maharshi called the "I" of the "I," the "I" of the ego! There is an "I" behind the ego, a "sense of identity" that is transcendental to the sense of identity which comes with your ego identification. Remember, your sense of identification at the lower ego stages has been with the objects that you experience! As we now move into the higher dimensions, the locus of identity shifts to the witnessing Self, the observing Self. It takes a little while, and you have to feel for that. Let us see if we can talk through the experience of what this is like.

Please bear in mind that this is not the experience itself! We are just trying to talk ourselves into some kind of sense of what the experience is like when you are identified with and abide in the witnessing center in consciousness. You have the experience of all that goes on outside, and the body is just like any other object in your awareness! You simply watch it! You see all of the ego's wringing of hands, all of its complaining, all of its reactions, and "you" simply watch "it" like you watch other people's body-egos. There is a part deep inside of you that simply watches *you!*

When you meditate, you get a sense of this. Remember, the "commentator" that says, "Oh, you are not meditating right. Boy, your mind is really running"? What is saying that? Where is that coming from? It is not even involved in the repetition, the *japa.* There is something in you that says, "Oh, I am really focused now. I have got good concentration." How do you know when you are focused? From where is that arising in consciousness? It is the *witness*, and there are about *ten levels* of this witness; it has depth! Even at the lowest level you can feel it, because it is the thing that is *commentating.* If you meditate, you know exactly what I am talking about. The witness is experienced when the attention has been liberated from the mind and its identification with the body.

There is a witness in you that actually "hears" yourself talking to yourself, what we call "thinking." It hears the thinking that is going on in your mind, but itself is not involved in any of that; it is simply observing. *Tat tvam asi*: Thou art that. This is where the identity shifts to next, where you become localized and centered, and that is the basis of your transegoic identity. You begin to understand that "I am this witnessing Self." It is the Self with a capital S, the *higher Self.* There have been many different terminologies for it. When we are able to feel this and get into this state, we then begin to experience all of the things that previously served as the basis of our identities as *objects*, no longer as subjects! Let us look at some of this experience.

Remember, we talked about the bio-centric stage where the awareness and identity are simply rooted in the impulses and processes occurring in the body. You have to kind of turn some of your attention back onto yourself to move through this exercise with me. Let's say perceptions, the whole sensory thing—hearing, for example. There is something that witnesses hearing, that hears what is heard, but itself is not the ears or the sense of hearing. You *witness* this whole process, but you are not a part of it! The part of you that is feeling, touching, tasting, smelling and seeing becomes an *object* that you experience from the witnessing point.

QUESTIONS AND ANSWERS

Now, let us go back and review what we have said thus far, and next week we will pick up from there. You will know where we will be moving: into the nondual. It is very hard to understand nonduality, because our intellects can only understand through contrast and we are now moving into a different phase. So, let us wrap it up with any questions or comments that you might have on anything we have discussed thus far.

Andrew: *Is the subject the same as the witness?*

The subject becomes an object! This whole package of subject and object itself becomes an object. What I am trying to get you to see is that your *subjectivity* itself becomes an *object* that you witness! Let me try to give you a different way of seeing this, because it is a little tedious and, perhaps, you will not get it with the first couple of stabs. Let us say the mind, for example. Normally, the mind is the subject and the world is the object. As you move into the next level, you actually witness your mind as an object! I do not know if you can understand how radical this shift in consciousness is, but you actually *objectively* witness your mind! There is no longer any dichotomy between the subject (mind) and the object (world). It is a very strange experience.

Sharon: *I think I understand what you are saying, because I have experienced that, but it seems like you are dying when that happens. What I am saying is you are dying to the lower level, because it is changing. It is like a shift.*

If you are having the experience of dying, you are regressing; you are moving in the other direction. If you are having the experience I am speaking of, you are more alive. It is not like a shift either, because the lower level remains absolutely the same. It is a different experience. What "changes" in you shifts, but "you" do not change the lower experience. Water is still water, wet and delicious.

Sharon: *I know that doesn't change. Let me specify. What I am saying is that within myself, I would shift because of the process.*

There is no "Self." It is a hard thing to understand, but I am saying that what you have been calling the "Self" is an illusion! In reality there *is* no thing called Self. It is deep! We are putting it out here to have something to work on until the next workshop, but I want you to get started, because we are moving to an entirely different level. *Self* is just an *illusion* in consciousness. It is almost like a mantra that you have to repeat and focus on. What is the "Self"? Have you ever gone in search of your Self? Look inside yourself and find the Self. Look outside yourself. Is the Self the body? There was a time when you thought the Self was only your physical body! Probe a little deeper and you will find that it is not the Self, because the Self is interior to the body, isn't it? Look a little deeper, and you will feel that the Self is your emotions! No, probe a little deeper and you will find that the Self is not the emotions. You say, surely the Self is my mind, my thoughts. No, probe a little deeper and you will see that it is not the mind! My soul? No. Push a little deeper. It is a very different experience.

Bhai Rani: *So, the witness is not the spirit? The witness is just there? I know it is not attached to anything; it is simply there and it sees and hears and it has no title.*

It is just there, and it has *always* been there. You are talking like a mystic, Bhai Rani Ra!

June: *It is not God?*

You can call it "God." Some people call it God.

Dorothy: *So, the books that say the Self is the soul are wrong? I gathered that from some of the books.*

It is just a problem with terminology.

Rick: *I am thinking in terms of the Self as being nonexistence, and if a person would look in the mirror they would not see the Self, they would see an image. You can never see the Self. It is like your sight is seeing what is on the outside. You can see outwardly, but you cannot see inwardly.*

Right. That is the point. Absolutely! Rick, you may as well come up here! You can see outwardly but you cannot see inwardly. The Self can never be a subject of your perception. That which can be perceived, by definition, is not the Self, because the Self is that which stands outside of that. Are you with me? Meditate on this! The Self does the perceiving, but it is even wrong to say that. *Tat tvam asi*: Thou art that. This is the area that we will now move into, where Self has always existed, never was created, never came into being. It is totally outside of time and space. It was not at the beginning; it was before the beginning. It descends, then unfolds and returns to its original identity. Rick, are you ready? Rick will answer all of my questions. Go ahead and formulate the question.

Sharon: *Let me see if I can. When a person is saying, "I am this" or "I am that," they are perceiving themselves. If the Self cannot be perceived, but the Self is doing the perceiving, would the person then at some point in time stop saying, "I am"? They would no longer identify themselves with "I am this" or "I am that," because they would come to the realization that they are neither. From my understanding, the Self would actually do it.*

We have gotten her today! We will let you suffer with that! You can tussle with it all the way home. Besides, you are riding home with *this* man (Sat Ra)? But you are right, keep moving in that direction.

Pam: *Bhagwan, are you saying that the Self just is? If that is so, is the witnessing Self in me the same as it is in you? There is only one? What is confusing me now is when you are talking about the ten levels of commentary, one commenting on the other—what is that?*

Right. The Self just *is*, but there is no "me" or "you." The experience of the many drops out. The ten levels of commentary are the stages leading toward that. Those are the transegoic stages which we will go into next time. I want you to begin to understand that the whole thing is about a shift in the locus of identity away from the lower self, because the Self is not a subject. The Self with which we identify is an object. It is very difficult to explain, because of the language that we are forced to use, and I am cognizant of this. The mystics have said that the only way to truly understand this is to go through the meditation process, because we are entering into a realm that is denied the logician.

You cannot go there with your rational mind, because this is *beyond* your rational mind! We are now entering into the "transrational" zone and this is where your rational mind stops. It is like trying to figure out the sound of one hand clapping. Your rational mind cannot go beyond that! It can only imagine the sound of two hands clapping. One hand clap? You cannot reason it. We are going to talk about it in "rational" language, but it is not going to be very accurate. It is certainly going to be topsy-turvy. It is going to require a lot of paradigm shifts and so on. Nonetheless, I want you to at least understand that there is a level of reality which you cannot understand with your mind, and we are moving into that now: the experience of *oneness*. It is the experience of being a mountain, of being a bird, of being one with the plants, the experience of being one with your thoughts, one with the words that even run through your thoughts. This whole thing is nothing like what we have been thinking.

This oneness, if you look at it from a temporal perspective, is the "simultaneity" of experience. Whenever the subject arises, the object simultaneously arises. It is not like there is the subject that exists independent of the object. You come into being simultaneously as the object comes into being, and this whole view of you coming into being along with the object coming into being, is nothing but something that is occurring in the "witnessing Self."

San Ra: *With just that understanding of where you are, you can move yourself to a higher level?*

Yes. That is the whole point. You see, all somatic evolution is done by nature. There is nothing you can do to accelerate the growth of the body. That is built in, but the *inner* evolution—there is external evolution and internal evolution, the inner evolution of consciousness—*can* be accelerated, and the way to accelerate it is through meditation and introspection. So, you are absolutely right, San Ra, this is "conscious" evolution as opposed to "unconscious" evolution, and this is all based on your turning inward and investigating it. Sometimes whether you even can investigate it is dependent upon what stage you are at "egoically."

Albert: *It seems that the problem usually comes when you are dominant in one of those stages. Do you also have to have the willingness to want to transcend that stage?*

You have to actually *give up* the identity. What we are talking about are movements and shifts in the basis of your identity; therefore, in order to go to the next stage, you have to give up the identity with the stage beneath that one. As long as you are simply identified with roles or gender and you cannot give that up, you cannot get to the next stage. For example, if you are locked into an ethno-centric definition of identity and are trying to "remain black," you cannot go to a higher level. It is not going to work. You have *contracted* the range of your identification into only the color of your skin and that is a limited manifestation of spirit. The reality is that spirit is *immanent* in creation, and evolution is nothing but the unfoldment of this spirit, which is without *form*. The spirit is more than just matter, so how can you limit the ultimate identification of spirit to it? You are absolutely right, Al, and it is a tremendous insight. The mystics say that you have to actually "die while living." You have to die to that "old" identity (self) in order to rise to a "new" level of identity (Self). This is what makes spiritual growth so painful. Yet, if one understands that one is giving up an old identity and is thus moving to a higher state of identification, it becomes a little easier.

It is interesting that in the ancient Afrikan systems of spiritual development, one of the first stages in the initiation process was to get the student to *shift* their sense of *who* they were. The process would start by your seeing yourself as *Ausar*; you would actually sit and visualize yourself as Ausar. The way you would do that would be to "visually" put the crown (the miter that Horus and all of the pharaohs wore) on your head, and visualize yourself as being Ausar. Many different techniques have been suggested by the different schools of thought, but the one thing they all agree on is that you must *let go* of these lower levels of identity.

Andrew: *Would you consider someone who, let's say, has a preference to marrying within their own race, as being in a state of egotism?*

Everything is egotism, it just depends upon what level you are on! If you think it is actually "morally" wrong to marry outside of your race or class, it really means that your "identification" is still at the socio-centric or ethno-centric level and you do not consider other people who do not look like you. *That* is the problem: White people are centered in their own Euro-centricity; you are centered in your Afro-centricity. The fact that both are centered in their respective ethno-centric stances mandates conflict. It is only those individuals who can transcend the socio-centric or ethno-centric stance that can enter into a "human-centric relationship." Highly developed spiritual people are *always*, without exception, human-centric.

Bomani: *Would it be possible for a person to jump through those stages? I mean, one day he might want to shoot his neighbor because of what the neighbor did to him, and the next day almost wreck his car trying to avoid hitting a cat that was crossing the street.*

Can you drift back and forth? Well, yes, in some sense you can, but you will find that one state is dominant. The other thing is that, in terms of evolution, you cannot skip stages; you cannot go from bio-centric to eco-centric. You cannot leap over all of those stages in between. You have to grow, but as you grow, you can move in any of the other lower stages. For instance, if I am at a humanistic level, I can certainly act in all of the others, but I cannot go beyond where I am. We have freedom to move in all of the lower forms of ego; we just cannot go beyond the topmost one.

MYSTICISM VERSUS "IDEALISM"

Albert: *I want to ask about the psychologist Maslow, who said that from his hierarchy, according to his theory, there are three people who actually reached that peak of self-actualization. I believe it was Abraham Lincoln, Einstein and Martin Luther King, Jr. Would you* *consider King as being in that higher state, because he wanted to integrate everything? He was for all—black, white, whatever.*

He was in this model. His ego had matured to a level which made him capable of living at that level of selflessness. Maslow called his model "self-actualization," but the reality is that there is a "Self" in us that is never "actualized." This is where we get the whole concept of a "false self"! Most of us are normally functioning out of this false self. This false self exists in us because we have lied to ourselves. We do not tell ourselves the truth. We are not able to go deep into that, so we never actualize this deeper Self inside of us.

The other thing you have to remember about Maslow is that he never meditated, as few of these psychologists do, so what they have is a lot of ideology. They have no "methodology" by which you can verify whether or not they are telling you the real deal. This is what distinguishes *mysticism* from mere *idealism*. In mysticism, the Master says, here is the technique, and you can verify whether or not what I am telling you is the truth. Buddha said, here is a technique; experiment and see whether or not what I am saying is the case. Maslow, Jung, Asaggioli, Freud, Fromm—all the way down the line—had no methodologies. That is why, very often, the hard-core "materialists" discount them. They will say, you are talking nonsense; there is only matter. The reality is that there is *nobody* inside to actualize! They will say that the self is nothing but the results of the chemistry in the brain. They are not able to think in terms of quadratic reality.

I know we are getting a little off the subject, but reality really exists in quadrants. There is the individual "I," which is interior, and there is the external physical body, the objective world. What I simply mean by this statement is that, as a scientist, I can hook you up to machines and I can look at, measure and quantify the activity of your brain. I can tell when the neural transmitters are firing, the synapsis and all of that. Nevertheless, by looking at all of this objective data, I cannot for the life of me tell what is going on inside your mind! You do not know what the person is "thinking," because all you can see are the "objective" correlatives of the thinking that is going on, how thoughts manifest themselves in objective, empirical phenomena. Yes, I would be able to see that your serotonin level is high, but I would not know if it is because you are depressed or upset or daydreaming!

Then, you have to look into the other quadrants, such as cultural, because reality manifests itself in all of these. It is never isolated. What happens to you "interiorly" is reflected in your behavior, in your moral stances and in your functionality. It is across the spectrum. When we are talking about "full" actualization, we have to talk about the whole thing. That is a subject worthy of deep investigation, particularly for those who are going to be working in the field of mind and things of that nature. However, the point I really wanted to stress is that without meditation, you cannot access any of this "inner potentia," and that is the problem these therapists and theorists have: They do not *meditate*, so their knowledge is limited.

Sharon: *I just wanted to ask a question based on what you were stating before about not being able to objectively see into the other person's level of consciousness. You stated that if you can go into it with the mind, you are still dealing with the mind. Does that mean that the person who is not meditating cannot deal in that area?*

You can still deal in that area, but it will not be very effective, in the sense that you will not be able to move the individual to a higher level, because there is nothing in you to do so.

Sharon: *So, it wasn't about going into the mind of the other person through meditation?*

Not so much through meditation. But even if you have not reached that point in your own spiritual development where you can intuit the contents in the other person's mind, you will be very willing to enter into a "dialogical" relationship with the person, meaning that you will ask them what is going on, you will seek to understand what is going on in the other person's mind. You will begin to function "intersubjectively." You will not simply base your conclusions on the measurements of their EKGs and the level of chemicals in their brain! The *only* way to access a person's "subjectivity" is through dialogue, and that is something we never do even in our ordinary relationships. We look at the other person and can clearly see that something is wrong, that something is out of whack, but we do not try to *understand* what is going on with the person. We look at the *outer* appearance, reach conclusions and react to those conclusions, and this is never satisfactory. We must have a dialogue with them and interpret what they tell us. We certainly cannot skip this by simply hooking them up to an EKG machine and think that, as a result, we know anything about their subjective thinking.

Sharon: *In reference to the statement you just made when you mentioned that people who are highly spiritual are human-centric, are you saying also that they have egotism and, if so, can they ever in this lifetime drop it?*

You cannot function in this world without ego. We will go into that later when we come to the higher transegoic level, the "nondual." The point is not to be limited to ego. It is hard to understand that you cannot make any spiritual progress without ego. An *enlightened* person is not *less* spiritual because they function in ego. Is that hard to understand?

Sharon: *I was kind of thinking that, because of reading about enlightenment, if a person attains total enlightenment, the ego has totally evolved and has diminished.*

It is just the reverse! The ego has *expanded* to include everything, and as the ego expands, it is almost like an inverted pyramid—it begins to incorporate into its own identity the *totality* of things. Remember, ego is the feeling of separateness, so when we talk about dropping the ego, what we are really talking about is dropping the experience of being separate as it relates to your identity. Expansion is the opposite of contraction, and that is "enlightenment": the identity becomes *total.* Hence, those sages and saints who have reached that level make the statement, *Anuk Ausar!; Aham Brahmasmi!*: "I am God!" The same sense of certitude is there as it is in your sense of identity where you feel, "I am my body," or "I am my likes and dislikes." The *whole* has become *you*, and the experience of the *other* drops out! We are on the other side now. The ego is still there, but ego in the sense of separateness is gone. It is now the "I" that is called "God."

The thing to remember is that, even when spirit descends into matter, the whole of spirit is there! Spirit has been present at every stage in its own unfoldment. It is never a case where it is not there, so when it evolves all the way back up, it includes everything! There is nothing outside of that. It is a difficult thing to understand. Maybe it will become easier when we begin to examine what the transegoic stage looks like where the expansion becomes greater, and the experience of separateness becomes less.

Throughout these discussions I want you to really stay focused on the fact that what we are discussing is the *key* to understanding mysticism. If you understand the "phenomenology" of ego, you will understand everything! You can pick up a Bible and it will become crystal clear. The Koran will become crystal clear. The Gita will become crystal clear. You can pick up Einstein's *Special Theory of Relativity* and it will be clear. You can read the Torah and it will be understood. It is the key that will unlock *all* of the mysteries. It is the great knowledge, the great understanding, because in reality, spirit is all that this universe is. What we call "reality" is nothing but a "manifestation" of spirit in a multitude of forms, shapes and fashion. Understand spirit and you have understood all that can be understood with this intellect. The motivation will then be to go into your meditation where you will get a taste of *God-realization*.

Sharon: *You made a statement before the break how about once you understand the sense of going to that new level where you drop the feeling of separateness and the ego expands, you would then be able to understand everything as far as the Bible, relativity, what have you. Is this (witnessing state) the state you were speaking of?*

Actually, that occurs much sooner. Bibles issue out of the state that we just discussed. When you reach the seventh stage of total ego maturity, your understanding will increase by leaps and bounds. However, even in that "pre-transegoic" state, you will get a key insight into unraveling a lot of these mysteries. Now, we are going to go even beyond the mysteries, and next week I will have a chance to put a model before you, because I always have to give you a model, and we will work through it. I just wanted you to get a feeling of your breath being taken from you, because it is a breath-taking trip that we will take! You are going to have to start learning how to think "non-rationally"; not irrationally, but transrationally! Please make a distinction between the two. Most of you already know how to think irrationally, you have that down pat! I now want to see if we can go to *transrational* communication, and then we will be able to get into this. This is a very, very profound subject. It is not unusual for it to take a lifetime of study to simply get a tiny glimpse into this, but the rewards are worth it!

These things shift paradigms, the way you see things, the way you actually *experience* things. This understanding *transforms* people. Remember, *understanding* is what transforms you, nothing else! There is no "mechanical" means of transformation that does not grow from the use of your understanding! That is what this whole spiritual trip is about. This is spirit unfolding itself in the drama called "evolution" and "creation," but remember, it is spirit from the top all the way down! It is immanent. There is nowhere you can turn where there is not spirit, and it is *spirit* becoming *self-conscious!* You see, at a certain stage in the unfoldment of spirit from matter moving upward, spirit becomes increasingly *conscious* of itself. Creation is conscious of *itself!* It is spirit unfolding and seeing itself! You are a phenomenon where spirit is looking back at itself in the form of a Bhai Rani Ra. It is profound!

With each unfoldment, from the lower dimensions of creation upward, spirit is looking back at itself, what Rick called "looking in the mirror." Looking at it at the level of a rock, you see nothing, because you *cannot* see anything. You can only get a sense of, for lack of a better word, what I am calling "Self," but you cannot see that thing in you that is purely spiritual. I am talking about the *spiritual* part of you. This witnessing Self, as Rick has pointed out to us, itself cannot be perceived at all. It is the ground of all experience. It is the ground from which everything emerges, but which itself cannot be experienced.

Do you see how this language does not make sense? So you cannot work off only the definition of language, because it is going to confuse the hell out of you. But we simply have no other way to talk. We are going to coin terminology, we are going to have to temporarily suspend the colloquial connotations of these words and use them in a very specific way. Otherwise, we will become very confused, because we will keep pouring old definitions into words that are being used very differently. Keebah, make it plain for them!

Rick: *I was wondering if there is a possibility of a person who, having had no interaction with humans, spiritual consciousness be at a higher level, or would he even have a spiritual consciousness? He has never been taught and has never had any dealings with human-kind whatsoever. This is only hypothetical, but let's say animals took*

care of him, sort of like a "wolf boy," and he was able to continue to
live—would his consciousness be at a spiritual level?

Would his ego unfold? No. In fact, it would remain pre-egoic.
He would remain at a pre-egoic state—the egocentric
state—unconscious.

June: *So, you need other humans to evolve?*

Your ego is "fed" off your relationships with other people! That
is why you cannot handle being alone! What happens? I can take
either one of you and isolate you for seventy-two hours, and you will
be mad at the end of those seventy-two hours, because your ego will
start dissolving. You will start regressing. You will start "de-
egotizing," dissolving back into a pre-egocentric stage, and when we
open the door after seventy-two hours, you will be making all kinds of
incoherent sounds! The point is that the ego requires support, because
it is a *relative* thing. You are a relative to somebody else! There is a
relativity of ego! Go on and get deep, Rick. The man is talking about
the relativity of ego!

Rick: *The "man" is certainly aware of this. That is why when*
you are incarcerated they will put you in solitary confinement to break
you down. Actually, your morality has already had a breakdown and
that is why you are incarcerated in the first place, and I am not saying
that everyone is guilty who is in jail. Anyway, they will throw you into
solitary and let you beat yourself up and dissolve yourself.

When they drag you out, you are no longer a problem. You will
do everything you are told. You don't have any more ego!

THE VALUE OF MEDITATION

So many of you missed the opportunity to meditate this morning.
These opportunities that we have are so precious and so rare that we
want to take as much advantage of them as possible. It is a tremendous
opportunity to meditate. Without a proper understanding of the value
of meditation, one will not meditate. This understanding is impeded
by the fact that we do not have a solid grasp of the dynamics involved
in spiritual effort. It is this immaturity of ego that makes your

meditation so difficult. We are having problems with our meditation because our egos are too immature, too weak to enter into the practice. We are too centered in the lower dimensions of our being to free up the energy necessary to be applied to the practice of meditation, to sadhana.

There have always been only two possibilities to solve that problem. One has been *bhakti*. If one has sufficient love for the Master, meditation becomes less problematic; you are doing it because the Master has asked you to do it. Out of your love for the Master, you do your meditation and, of course, you derive the benefits therefrom. The reality is that most of us do not have that kind of devotion to the Master. So, we cannot do our meditation out of devotion, out of love, with the recognition that our initiation is a gift that has been given to us by the Master. *None* of us is worthy of initiation. Make no mistake about that. There is nothing we have done to warrant or justify having the good fortune of being initiated. Initiation is a gift that the Master gives to us, and when we receive a gift from someone, we should be appreciative of that gift. When our child gives us ugly ties, we still wear them because the child loves us and they gave us that tie out of their love. Yes, perhaps the tie is ugly or clashes, but because the child gave us the tie out of love, we wear the tie.

We very often really do not appreciate all of the preparations, thought and energy that the Masters have put into bringing the teachings to us. We do not know all of the sacrifices, trials and tribulations that are undergone just to be able to give us the initiation. Therefore, we do not receive the initiation in the spirit in which the initiation was given. We do not value it. We do not wear the tie because it is "ugly." We do not meditate because it is "inconvenient." You have to understand that so much suffering has been undergone in order to share the teachings, to share the gift of initiation, or *Nam*, as the Masters call it. So much work has been involved.

I notice that every week Pam asks the *sangat* for a "love offering," and I have never understood that. I even asked Bilal about this. I said, what is this "love offering"? It was explained that the sangat wanted to give something to express their love and gratitude for what they have received. It is difficult for me to understand. First of all, there is nothing you need to give me in the material realm. If you truly appreciate *satsang*, you will meditate. If you are not meditating, you do not appreciate me. You do not really appreciate the legacy that is being handed to you; hence, there is no real gratitude.

The *only* thing that pleases the Master is when we meditate. That is the only currency in which the Guru deals. On the one hand you say, "Master, we really appreciate you and are grateful for all that you have done for us. We are grateful for the initiation." Then you do no meditation. What kind of gratitude is that? The real thing to give to a Master is our meditation. Give the Master our effort and energy through our sadhana. That is all that the Master wants: for you to become *fully awakened*. That is payment enough. There are never any monetary charges for initiation. Initiation is a gift, a gift to be enjoyed. It is a gift to be *used*.

Someone has to talk to Pam about that and tell her to stop this "offering" for Bhagwan. Bhagwan does not require any offerings in that form. Yes, take up an offering, but collect meditation for me! That has some value to me. Even if you could pay for what the Master has given us, two dollars would not cover it! If you are going to make a donation thinking that you are giving money in return for what you are receiving in satsang, you have a very poor concept of the value of satsang. You would have to give *millions* to come close to compensating in a material way for what has been given us. There is no way to materially compensate for it. We have to really understand *seva* in the truest sense of the word. Yes, keep the sangat alive; you should be supporting the sangat. That is what your money is for. It has nothing to do with me. It is to support a context that is for your own benefit. If you would like to give *me* something, give me your meditation.

You do not know what price has been paid to be able to sit here today. You do not have a clue as to what has been gone through at all. You do not know the sacrifices that have been made in order to sit in these satsangs and share these teachings with you. You have absolutely no concept of what suffering was undergone. A lot of sacrifice has been made. A lot of things had to be given up or denied. A lot of battles had to be fought to be able to share these teachings with you. The only appropriate gratitude for the level of sacrifice that was made is your meditation.

What to say of the satsang? Even these peripheral activities such as these tapes, these videos and these books—Bilal and Sat Ra have spent hours transferring these tapes from one form to the other. You do not know how many hours have been spent in numerous bookstores all over the country, searching out these pearls of wisdom as they appear in printed form. You do not have any idea that sometimes a book was purchased when there was no food to eat. You do not know that the book you throw in the back seat of your car was a meal that was missed. Because of the immaturity of your ego, you have no understanding of that whatsoever. I want you to begin to understand that someone had to pay a price in order to give satsang. The only appropriate response is that you meditate. If you are not meditating, you are simply wasting the sacrifice that has been made. So, meditation is the "name of the game" at the *House of Ra*, and your responsibilities are to display your gratitude in the form of your meditation.

My sister called me and asked, Bhagwan, when are you going to get to the tricks, the technologies? Well, there are no tricks or technologies or magic in dealing with this ego. Simply understand this thing, and that understanding will produce the technology. I said, Emma, you have not been paying close attention. I am not going to pass out a pill at the end of the fifth session that you can dissolve in a glass of water and, presto, your ego will vanish. The ego will diminish in direct proportion to the degree of your understanding.

Ego is the only barrier that separates man-consciousness from God-consciousness and, therefore, the whole purpose of spiritual practice is to somehow, in some shape, form or fashion, deal with this ego. The more understanding you gain as to what this ego is, what the problems are, the better rooted your meditation will become.

Remember, I have to increase your understanding because you do not have the requisite love to meditate. You do not have enough bhakti. If your bhakti was sufficient, you would be meditating. There would be no problem. You do not appreciate the gift. Since you have insufficient gratitude to practice your sadhana out of love, we have to focus on increasing your understanding. The hope is that if your understanding can be increased, that understanding will form the basis out of which your sadhana arises. The objective of these series is to increase your understanding of your predicament. When that understanding becomes more mature, the bhakti will come. Not to worry; sometimes we have to start where we are. These satsangs are useful in a sense in that they can give us a *satori*, a brief glimpse of what it is that these mystics have been continuously saying since time immemorial. It is only a glimpse, but it is enough to inspire us.

Bomani: *Bhagwan, you mentioned understanding. Take a word like "discipline"; from my understanding of what you said, if I don't* *really understand those terms and what they mean, I would not be able to do that.*

It is very difficult. On the Path the emphasis is on two things: understanding and love, *gyan* and bhakti. If you have a deep *understanding* of the sadhana, the methodologies, the paths that are given by these mystics and sages, it is out of that understanding that discipline will fall into place, automatically. There will be no problem. You will not be struggling "to be or not to be." Every time we get out of bed, there is that debate: "Oh, Maybe I will meditate," or "Maybe I won't meditate." Even when we *decide* to meditate, it is with great struggle, great resistance. We cannot wait until the damn thing is over with! Even while we are sitting there, we are not into it, the mind is drifting all over the place. The understanding is not solid, so the sadhana is sporadic; it waivers. It is all ups and downs. That is all right. I am not condemning it. I am simply saying that that kind of sadhana is arising out of an immature state. By "immature" I mean that there is not much understanding there.

The other route is through bhakti, through love. If we have love, we can do things without understanding. Actually, I should not even say that, because love itself is based on understanding, but it is a different species of it. For purposes of discussion, let us assume that there is a distinction between the two. So, if I love you, Bhai Rani, and you ask me to do a thing, whether I understand it or not, just my love for you is enough for me to do it.

You can see, for instance, even in relationships at this level, a little of that dynamic at play, particularly in women, because men are very different animals, "psychologically" speaking. You will find that a woman's actions for her man are always occurring out of her love when it is a healthy kind of love. She cleans the house because she loves him, not because it is "rational." It is love that causes women to put up with all of our nonsense. It is not because we do not have any flaws! The woman is not stupid, she sees his flaws, but she does things because she loves the man. If he tells her, "Go do this, woman," the woman will go and do this. She does this because she loves, and when that love stops, you can't convince her with all the reasoning in the world, because it was never coming from a rational base in the first place!

Similarly, the Guru or the Master will tell us, "Look, I am going to give you a gift that is hued from the rock of my being. I am giving you my 'loins.'" The mystics use this type of terminology, that their disciples are born from their loins, dearer to them than their own kilt and kin. "I have forsaken my world, I have forsaken my life." The *bodhisattva* says, "I could have dissolved, disappeared into this bliss, but I stayed back to give you this thing."

It is almost like the sacrifices you make for David, Bomani. You give him these things, and you simply want him to prosper from them. That is the only thing that you expect from him. If he can receive in the same spirit in which he has been given, he will not waste anything that you give to him. It is like that in the Master-disciple relationship. The Master gives us the *methodology*, a technology. He or she gives us something which no one else can give us. The philosopher will give you all kinds of "theories" and "idealism," but no way for you to have the experience yourself. This is the distinction between them. The Master gives us the methodology, the actual technology for us to have that experience, and out of my love, because my Master is giving me the "gift" of meditation, I meditate.

Perhaps sometimes your mother will tell you to do something. You do what she is telling you to do, but it is not because what she is telling you to do is right. You might be doing something that is even incorrect, but you do it out of the *love* that you have for your mother. When we have that kind of relationship with the Guru, meditation is very, very easy. There can be no problem whatsoever. It becomes *sahaj* (easy). Is it hard to do something for somebody that you love, to fulfill the request of somebody that you love? We knock ourselves out to do it!

Is it hard for you to feed your children, Bhai Rani? The fact is that you get pleasure out of it. You can forego buying a new dress to pay for some courses for your daughter. That is not even a sacrifice. It may look like a sacrifice to someone else, but it brings you great pleasure, because you are doing this out of your love for her. Whenever we are operating out of this dynamic of love, sadhana is very easy!

The problem, of course, as all Masters have said, is that the disciple never loves the Master, just as the child never loves the parent as much as the parent loves the child; nobody does. Bhai Rani, you have never loved your mother as much as your mother loves you. It is not possible! That is the truth. Yes, you will say, "Oh, I love you," but your love for your mother pales into insignificance in comparison to her love for you! It is an inappropriate analogy. It is like comparing a candle with the light of the sun. No child is capable of loving to the same extent as the parent. Dorothy loves those little bad tail boys of hers! She would kill somebody over those boys. Some day those boys will run off and leave you, but you will never run off and leave them, because your love is coming from a higher plane.

The Master's love is like that. The disciple's love can never match the love of the Master, because the Master, like that parent, does so much for us and, like those children, we simply rebel! Just as we do not appreciate the love of the parent until after the parent is gone, it is the same way with the Master. When the Master is no more, then you become conscious, because you feel this immense void in your life, and those of you who have lost a mother or a father understand exactly what I am talking about. That tremendous void descends and, for the first time in your life you realize, "My God, I have lost something immense." What tears you up is you realize that you did not take advantage of it, and this is punishment for the rest of the days of your life! You have wasted a unique opportunity that was called "Mom," that was called "Dad." You lose, and that is it and you cannot survive.

It is like that with us: As long as the Master is in the body, everybody takes it for granted, because you have nothing to contrast it with. So, we do not really have that kind of bhakti. A few people do; please do not misunderstand me. You have a Mira Bai or a Sahjo Bai, or a Charan Das, or a Radha for a Krishna here and there. Every now and then, you will find a disciple who is capable of truly loving the Master. Thus, for that disciple, sadhana is never a problem, because the sadhana is arising out of love: "The Master has asked me to do this, and I love my Master; therefore, it is done! It has nothing to do with my own doubts and skepticism."

The vast majority of us have to be brought to a certain level of understanding. Hence, the necessity of satsang. The whole function of satsang is to increase our levels of understanding so that it can free up the energy necessary for our sadhana. In order to do that, we have to break down all of this ego, we have to mature our ego, because we started off thinking that we *already* know all there is to know! We are our own gurus! We come here every week and say, "Well, you know, I meditate." What meditation are you doing? You don't even know what meditation is! This is just some bullshit you read somewhere; you invented it. You have arrogated to yourself knowledge of a technology that you don't have a clue about! It is like a child talking.

I have a little four-year-old grandson and every day he tells me, "Baba, I'm going to work. I will see you later." He is just talking, because he heard this conversation around the house, and every morning he says this. I play his game and in the evening I ask, "Charsy, what did you do at work today?" Then, he will tell me all the things that he did over at the babysitter's house. This is the concept of a child. You use the same words as a child, but his words are related to an entirely different phenomenon.

We use the word "meditation." Now, let's see what that looks like. Follow that person home and see what meditation they are doing. "Zzzzzz." They read a line from a book and their mind can't even follow the train of thought. They just sit somewhere for X amount of time. You can lie down for five to ten hours a day. Why don't you call that meditation? Some people say they do "sleep meditation." There is no end to this nonsense! They will come in and say, "Oh, I am already a buddha." The Master has to first break down all of this ignorance!

When I was putting the model on the board, so many of you were saying, "Oh, Bhagwan, that's where I am." I heard this. It was all over the room. You were *all* a seven! No one was less than a six! "I'm a number seven. I'm on the verge!" Nonsense! You are bio-centric or you are physio-centric; you may even be pre-egocentric! So, the Master has to first break down all of that stuff. That is the task, but first we need more understanding. If you don't think this is the case, just listen to yourself. Bilal has made all of these tapes. Let a year pass or try to find a tape from two years ago, if you have been around that long. If you listen to yourself from two years ago, you will cut it off and say, "Oh, no! That cannot be me!" You would have seen your growth and that, "My, God, could I have been that stupid?" It starts like this for all of us, and since we do not have the requisite degree of bhakti, the Guru has to *work* with us and break down this *ignorance*, to help us learn how to tell ourselves the truth about ourselves, because most of us do not know how to tell ourselves the truth about ourselves!

Remember, I said that as we are moving through these various stages of ego development and maturation, a lot of us do not always make it to the next stage one hundred percent intact! Some part of us gets caught down on one of the lower rungs of the ladder. A part of us is hanging back at the bio-centric level because it got stuck there. What you will find, for instance, is that we may have developed *intellectually*, but we have not developed *morally*! Have you noticed the distinction between the two? We can do "visual logic"; we can do synthetical thinking; we are very "analytical"; but we can't transcend our adultery, our lying. Why is that? It is because we became *stuck* somewhere. So, the Master has to create a context where he or she makes it easier for us to tell ourselves the truth.

We start off by telling the truth to each other, because we are a community. All of us are "messed" up, so we get comfortable with each other and become a family. Just as when you were growing up, Sat Ra, you could walk around your bedroom in your dirty drawers, and it was no big deal if Rick saw you because he is your brother! It is all right for him to see *your* dirty drawers because you can see *his* dirty drawers! There is an "understanding" and that creates a bond! We share our secrets with each other. What is the secret that we are going to share with each other? That we are not perfect, that we have a lot of stuff wrong with us, that we have been pretending in a lot of areas. That creates that intimacy. We have created a context where we can now *grow*. So, satsang is about that.

Bomani, I have given you the long version, because your question is everybody's question. As this understanding deepens, the sadhana becomes solid. You must remember that those who have been given the "gift" of meditation have taken something like a "vow." It is like vegetarianism. You said, "Bhagwan, I am going to meditate every day." That should have arisen out of the same context as your vegetarianism. You are not vegetarian only on Mondays, Wednesdays and Fridays, are you? Maybe you are, because I do not know. If you are, that means you have a very *immature* concept of what it means to make a vow! *Your* vow means that you are going to do it as long as it is pleasant! You have a very immature ego; therefore, your interpretation of what constitutes a vow is equally immature, because it is coming from the same level of immaturity. If it is coming from a high level of maturity, when you say you are going to meditate, you will meditate! There is no question of "to be"; it is a done deal. You may not make any progress, but you do your meditation! You develop the capacity to keep your word. Most of us do not have this.

So, we are all struggling at various stages, but as our *understanding* deepens, we become straightened out, because now we understand meditation. It is like when you understand vegetarianism, you have no problem. The struggling drops out and your vegetarianism becomes solid. Similarly, when you understand sadhana, the theories behind meditation, when you have come out of your nonsense, out of your own self-deception, when you have gained some clarity and understanding, then the sadhana becomes solid; it becomes sahaj. That is the whole idea behind all of these satsangs. The whole objective is to go on deepening our foundation of understanding, and correcting our misperceptions of these things, because when we really understand, we have no problem.

Enough for today. Ra shekum maat.

CHAPTER FIVE
THE SOUL-CENTRIC STAGE

This is session four of five sessions where we have been discussing the anatomy and evolution of ego. Today we will be going deeper into the anatomy and evolution of ego, and how all of this relates to spiritual progress. We will also talk about some of the practical day-to-day benefits you can expect to receive as a result of working on the acceleration of the maturation of your ego.

Remember, I have said that the problem with most of us is we suffer from an "ego deficiency syndrome." We normally think we have too much ego. No doubt we have too much of the *lower* ego, but the idea in spiritual practice, as well as simply in the normal growth of an individual, is that our ego, our sense of identity, has to go on deeply maturing. If you are functioning out of a very "shallow" ego, you will live a very "shallow" life.

Let us begin our discussion of the nature and evolution of ego with a continuation from last week. We were beginning to look at those states which exist beyond the seventh level, the eco-centric level, where our egos at this point have begun to fully mature. As we begin to mature in terms of our ego and our identity, the experience of separation continues to diminish. I do not want you to forget the fact that as the ego matures, it is an *inclusive* process, and the feeling of separation *diminishes*. Last week I told you that once we evolve to a certain degree of ego maturation, we are now in a position to seriously travel the Spiritual Path.

In ancient times, the Masters would not normally initiate people who were too immature. It was understood that a certain amount of maturity had to be first attained. How would you measure the person's maturity? You would look at their *morality*. People who do not have very solid morals are usually people who are very immature in terms of their ego development. Therefore, the Masters, sages and seers would make the attainment of a certain level of maturity a prerequisite for initiation. If the person has undergone a normal trajectory of development, and their ego is unfolding in a natural course, the moral faculty will very often begin to come into play and take root around the age of twenty-seven. Most often the Masters would, therefore, withhold initiation until a person was in that stage of their life. If you were still at the age of a student, for instance, they normally would not initiate you. Thus, a certain amount of ego maturation is a prerequisite to travel the Path.

You can see, therefore, how a person whose ego has evolved to a point where it has become eco-centric and can now identify with all of nature, can easily follow the vegetarian diet. They would feel, "I am not going to eat other sentient beings simply to satisfy my palate." Their moral would be, "Why should a cow lose its life in order for me to have a hamburger and fries tonight?" To them, it would seem such a vile act! A person who is mature can sacrifice the pleasures of their palate for the life of another sentient being.

The eco-centric person has a certain capacity to experience the oneness with nature, so they are less likely to pollute or destroy the earth. They are much more respectful of nature because, after all, we exist in this "web" of nature. If we destroy all of these trees and the water, we destroy ourselves, literally! We are an ecosystem; we are interdependent. Your existence is dependent upon the existence of the trees. What besides the plants will exchange the carbon dioxide for oxygen in the air we breathe?

Therefore, it is easier for a person who has matured to a level where they can embrace nature, to mold their lives according to the teachings, because the teachings require *ahimsa*, this kind of compassion. If you are locked into one of the lower stages of ego development, where you are still looking upon the world as something that is only there for you to exploit, to reduce to your own pleasure or for purposes of your own entertainment, it is going to be very hard for you to understand this teaching.

The eco-centric level of ego is the "stepping-off point" for the formal practice of spiritual growth. However, there are many intermediary stages between the eco-centric stage (the mature ego) and the so-called "spiritual" stages. I would now like to talk about the next level in the shift of our identities. For lack of a better word, I will call it "soul-centric." Sometimes, we have to invent our own language. I hope you don't mind. However, do not walk around telling people you are "soul-centric," because they will think you are crazy. Keep it among us!

I am reminded that among the Sufis, when the sheikhs or Pirs would initiate a new person into their *sangat*, the Sufi Master or Pir would oftentimes sit down with the new initiate and instruct them as to how they need to now function since they have drunk this "wine." They referred to the knowledge as "wine." It was a code word, because the Sufis had to practice their mysticism within the context of orthodox Islam, which is a very different phenomenon from Sufism.

They had to, therefore, create code words for the knowledge they were dispensing. So, they called this experience of enlightenment "wine." They told the new initiate, "Listen, when you leave the 'Wine Shop'"—they called the place where they met the "Wine Shop" because it is a place where you go to drink wine and you get "high" in there—"you go straight home, because if you linger in the streets, some of these bad boys and thieves will see you as you are staggering away from here and they will rob you. You have to learn the ways to handle this wine." In any event, I don't want you to drink outside of the "Wine Shop." When you leave here, leave our language in here so that the man with the straitjacket does not lock you up!

As I was saying, as we begin to travel from this eco-centric stage in the maturation of our ego, there are many intermediary stages along the way before the ego moves to its next level. Let me point some things out that you might recall. I said before that ego maturation is an *evolution* of your sense of *who* you are, your sense of identity. As you evolve from one stage to the next, you automatically incorporate, integrate and enfold into each higher stage the stage that was below it. The same process is still going on here. As you move from the eco-centric level to the soul-centric level, you are enfolding or integrating all of the other components that have made up your identity to this point into this new identity. The interesting thing is that when your ego becomes soul-centric, your basis of *identification* becomes that with your *soul*.

Most of us do not identify with the soul. You say you have a "soul" or you say, "I am a soul," but we do not find any of that in your description of who you are. I would like for you to take a sheet of paper and on that sheet of paper, write down a description of who you are. If someone were to stop you and say, "Dorothy, tell me, who are you," what would you say? How would you begin to describe yourself? I do not mean to put you on the spot, but please bear with me for a moment. What would be some of the typical ways in which we describe ourselves?

Dorothy: *A female who happens to be black.*

Okay. So, maybe we would first describe ourselves by our gender and race. When we make our race the chief component of our identity, we are really at the socio/ethno-centric level. Remember, at the socio/ethno-centric level our identification is with the group we belong to, our racial makeup. We will say, "Well, I am a black person." What else would you normally say as you go on describing yourself?

Dorothy: *Well, they can see that I am a woman.*

Sometimes, sister, we do not know anymore! We are in very different times! Sometimes we have to ask people to identify their gender for us. They may be confused and be like Dennis Rodman. We don't know what the hell this brother is! We will add our gender, male or female, to our description of ourselves. When we add our gender, we are back to the physio-centric level, those physio-centric qualities that we have enfolded into our overall identity. You can see where we picked up this part of our identity such as, "I am a female." It was at a lower stage of our development and we just rolled that into a higher one. What would be some of the other things that we would include in our description of ourselves?

Dorothy: *Whether or not you were a parent.*

Yes, we would add in our "roles." Again, we are coming back to the socio-centric stage, where we are beginning to form our socio-centric ego and beginning to assume roles: "I am somebody's father (or mother)." You will begin to define yourself in terms of these roles and these roles can be expanded, can't they?

Rick: *Let us say age: senior citizen, middle-aged, etc.*

Yes, sometimes we segregate ourselves based on our age and that is related to the physio-centric person, isn't it? Again, our age is based on our body, right? This is a person who has incorporated a lot of elements that belong to that physio-centric level of ego development. Do you see my point? They think of themselves in terms of the body or some aspect related to the body. What would be some of the other things we would add to our list?

Sharon: *Job title.*

Again, all of that is in this socio-centric area. We still have not gone beyond that. Is anyone beyond the socio- or ethno-centric level of ego development?

Albert: *What about the type of person that you are on the inside?*

Yes, I am a "good" person. I am a "nice" person.

Dorothy: *But that's "ego mythology"! I remember that one, Bhagwan!*

It probably is, but we have to put it in there, because that's what they believe, right? They give us a "myth" about themselves, the kind of person they are, etc. That might even include a lot of elements which belong to the emotio-centric level of development, as well as the psycho-centric level, where you incorporate all of your opinions, beliefs and philosophies, your religion. All of those are mind products. They are rational by-products. They are psycho-centric material. All of that is incorporated, as the brother pointed out, in this description of the kind of person I am. We see that very often, do we not? After we have filled in all of the blanks, we start coming down here: "I am black and a female. I am a mother. I am forty-nine years old. I am a 'great' person!" What are some of the other things you include in your description of yourself?

Bhai Rani: *I hear a lot of people say, "I am a child of God." I wonder where that falls on the scale!*

That could be some more of this "mythological" stuff, because you can't have a higher status than that. When you say, "I am a good person," or "I am a kind person," or "I am an honest person," that is one thing. However, when you say "I am a 'divine' person," you are using some high mythology! But when we look into your life, we will find nothing "divine" about you! That is why we know that, essentially, it is just more mythology. You say, "I am a Christian," or "I am a Hebrew Israelite," or "I am a Buddhist." Yet, when we look for the behavior of a Christian in your life, we find nothing! We look for the behavior of a true Muslim, and we find none of that. Wherever we look for the behavior of a "child of God," we come up short! It probably belongs somewhere in our ego mythology. It is high stuff, it "sounds" good. You will get a lot of action with that one but, invariably, when we penetrate it, it is only some more of that lower development of the ego.

I want you to do this as an exercise. I want you to seriously sit down and describe yourself to yourself and see the things that you are made up of and, after you have exhausted yourself, you will see, "My God, I didn't make it past *this* level!" You will begin to get a self-portrait in terms of where your level of identity is. Remember, your level of identity will dictate so much about you. The level of your identity shapes and determines how you will interact with the world.

If your level of identity is still fairly undeveloped, if you are stuck at a bio-centric level where your identification is only with your bodily sensations, or your senses, you will invariably have a lot of suffering in your life. We pointed out last time that the lower your level of ego development is, the more contracted your sense of identity is, the more out of touch you are with reality. Whenever you are out of touch with reality, you will suffer. Suffering is nothing but your failure to be in *maat* with reality. You are not in harmony with that which is real. Whenever you are not in harmony with that which is real, you will suffer because reality will win every time!

If your identity is still centered in your childishness where your expectation is that the whole world should feel the same way *you* feel, and whenever you encounter anyone in the world who is *not* feeling the way you are feeling, or who is not *thinking* the way you are thinking, or not *believing* the way you are believing, you are bound to experience some conflict and suffering. You can easily measure where you are. If every day you are getting up and you are so depressed and full of so much misery, then that should be a sign to you that you have to do a lot of work on yourself. You are stuck somewhere in some deep unreality, and it is going to cause you much suffering, much pain. You have to grow up! You have to be "born again."

What is this "rebirth"? We go through many rebirths. It is another misnomer, because we think that we go through only one rebirth. In , we talk about being "born again." However, you have to be reborn numerous times because every time you move up the ladder in the evolution of your ego, that is a rebirth. If you move from the bio-centric to the physio-centric, that is a rebirth. If you move from the physio-centric to the emotio-centric, that is another rebirth. It is a constant *process* of growing and being born again. St. Paul said, "I die daily," which means that he must be born daily. It is a constant dying and birthing process that is occurring.

As you began to put together this self-description, the point I want you to note is that at no time did you mention your "soul." Yes, you have told me that your identity is made up of the components of your body and all of the things associated with that. It is made up of this body and its relationship to other people, this body and its function in the world, the society or community. However, what is your soul? I can understand if you say you have a body. That is demonstrated in your list, but you also wrote on your list for me, "I have a soul," and I see no evidence of that! Where is the evidence, the reflection, of your soul in your identity? Have you ever thought about it? Yet, you say over and over that you have a soul. Tell me what part of your identity is a reflection of your soul. What have you incorporated in your identity that is rooted in your identification with your soul? The truth of the matter is that most of us are not in touch with our souls at all! Yes, it is there, but it is not a part of our identity. When we are able to mature to the next level, our locus of identity shifts from all of these lower stages to our souls. We become "soul-centric." Your identity is referenced to your soul? What does that look like?

Bilal, scan the audience. I want you to see your faces if you ever play back this session! I want you to know who you are so that you see what I see. All of these souls here are saying, "Where is my soul? I have lost my soul!" You are right. You *have* lost your soul! You have *no* awareness of your soul. Yes, you are aware of your body. You are aware of the biological processes going on inside the body. You are aware of all of your psycho material. You are aware of your likes and dislikes and all of your emotional material. You are aware of all of your intellectual and mental material, your mind and its opinions, beliefs, values, taboos, etc., but you have lost *all* awareness of your soul. Nevertheless, the objective of spiritual practice is to recapture the awareness of your soul and to shift the center of your identity to that level. Let us investigate this entire phenomenon of becoming "soul-centric."

Let me start by pointing out a few things that you might not have contemplated. We must start with this thing called "awareness." We all have awareness. When you have awareness, you have objects of awareness, right? You are aware of something. These objects of our awareness are usually the things with which we become identified. It is as if I am aware of this chair and in the process of me becoming aware of this chair, I actually begin thinking that I am the chair. Do you see the fallacy? I am aware of the chair, but I am *not* the chair.

Let us revisit all of the materials you just wrote in your self-description, because I want you to see the fact that everything you wrote on your list is an object in the field of your awareness. Is that right, Bauji Ra? Bauji Ra agrees, so I must be on the right track! You experience your physical body as an object in your awareness. Is that right? Don't let me browbeat you! Don't simply agree with me! Don't patronize me! Is that right? You are aware of your body, thus, your body stands in relationship to awareness as an object, does it not? Your body is an object *in* your awareness.

What about your likes and dislikes and all that other emotional stuff, your moods, for instance? How do you experience those? You experience them as objects *in* your field of awareness, correct? You are aware that you are sad or that you are angry: "I'm mad now!" or "I'm sad." That is an act of awareness. You are aware that you are sad, therefore, sadness is an object *in* your awareness, right? Are you with me on this? We have to go very deep now, deep into ourselves.

You cannot run to a book to get what I am talking about today! Do not start thinking, "Well, I guess I will get a book and read up on this stuff and see if I can follow along." No, there *is* no book that you can buy to follow me today. You are going to have to begin looking into your own interiority. That *is* the book. Did Sat Ra set you all straight on that?

THE "SEER"

Just as with your likes and dislikes and everything else of which you are aware, you are aware of *all* relationships as objects in your awareness. It is almost as if you are sitting behind a window and you are looking out of that window at the world, observing the world. There is an observing, witnessing that is going on in you, isn't there? The mystics have called that the "seer." There is something in you that sees that which the eyes see, but itself cannot be seen. Remember, Rick gave us a tremendous insight last time. He said that this seer is of the nature that it cannot be seen. It can see everything, but itself cannot be seen. You cannot experience the seer as an object in the field of awareness. Do you understand? *The seer cannot be experienced as an object in the field of your awareness.* Therefore, if you are looking out here to find your soul, you will not find it, because the soul is not something you can experience as an object in the field of your awareness. Is that right, Rick? Please correct me, Rick, if I should deviate at all. You can experience your soul, but *never* as an object in the field of awareness. There is something that is observing, witnessing all that is taking place in the domain of awareness. *Tat tvam asi*: Thou art that.

To put it in scientific terms, we call this the field of "space-time-causal" continuum. It is a space-time continuum, meaning that everything which comes into this field, this domain of awareness, exists in space. Thus, the soul or seer, by definition, does not exist in *any* space. You have got to stay with me on this one this morning! The body occupies space, right? However, that which *sees* the body is *not* in space. This body was born and it exists in time and, therefore, it will end; but this seer was never born! This is deep! The soul exists *outside* of time. It is not your soul that survives you after your death, because that would put it in time. The soul is *prior* to all time. It was never in time in the first place!

There is something in you that witnesses and observes everything that is going on in space and time, but itself stands outside of the space-time-causality continuum. It is, therefore, *eternal*. By "eternal" we mean outside of time, not a long time, but outside of time completely. It does not exist in time or space at all! Does it move? No, because all movement occurs in the domain of space and time. Therefore, since the soul or seer does not exist in the space-time domain, it does not move. The Greek mystics called it the "unmoved mover." It itself is unmoved, stationary; it is not in time. It simply *watches* those things that are moving.

It is almost like it was when we were kids and we would lie in the grass and look up in the sky at the clouds. Do you remember how those clouds would just drift through the sky? They would come in and drift away and another cloud would come, and maybe a bird would come, and then the bird would disappear. Maybe next a plane would appear. Yet, *we* are not moving; *they* are moving. In the same way, the events of life, the activities of the body, parade across this "window" of awareness. The soul is simply there, *watching*.

When the baby was born that was named "Al," the soul was watching from the inside as well as the outside of the body, and watched it grow up. There was a part that experienced it *subjectively* and there was a part that experienced it *objectively*. It watched you as a little baby, but itself was never a baby! How could it be if it was not in time? It was always simply there: *You* were the baby and it watched you grow up! Please stay with me on this, folks! Didn't "you" watch "yourself" grow up? I am not talking about simply making reference to the data in your memory bank. Moment-to-moment "you" were there and watched "yourself" grow up, but the thing that was *watching* you was never a child. Keebah, are you with me on this? Stay with me! "It" itself does not exist in time or space, but it is watching from that point.

I want you to look at all of the things that you added to the list in your self-description and see how all of those can be located in the domain of awareness, and how they are nothing but pictures that are parading before your eyes. When your sense of identity matures to the level of your soul, it pulls back from its identification with all of those other things on your list: the body and what the body does; the role assigned to the body; the color and sex of the body; where the body lives; its age. The soul begins to understand that none of those things are it! In Hinduism, the expression is *neti, neti*: not this, not that.

THE DOMAIN OF THE SOUL

When you ask the questions, "Who am I?" and "What is the source of my personal awareness?" your answer to those and all of the things on your list is "neti, neti." Is the source of my personal awareness the body? No. From where does the source of your personal awareness arise? The search for that center of awareness is what constitutes the spiritual journey. As you move deeper and deeper into the location of this source from which your personal awareness arises, when you go back as far as you can, you hit the source. When you literally step outside of space and time, you are stepping into the "domain" of the soul. You have found where your soul is, because the soul is not in space and time. So that you can understand this, let me again reiterate that the mind is nothing but this space-time continuum. The mind takes experience and breaks it up into space and time. That is all the mind does. The mind is nothing but the "name" for events that are occurring in space and time.

When you shut down your mind, notice that you have no experience of space and time. When the mind shuts down, for instance, at night when you go to sleep and have no dreams, when you are in that deep, dreamless state that we have called *sushupti*, notice that you do not even know where you are. There is no body, no bed, no world. There is none of this stuff, but you exist, right? There is no sense of space and time in the state of sushupti.

However, you need not go into sushupti, because even in this wakeful level of consciousness when we are having the experience of intense beauty, time-space drops away. Whenever we are having the experience of love, time-space drops out, because these are "no mind" experiences. Isn't that beautiful? These are all experiences outside of your mind, which is why you can never fall in love if you approach love "rationally." Relationships fail today because we are trying to approach our relationships rationally. That "rational approach" is bound to destroy any love. How can you experience love with the mind? You cannot! That is why we call it "falling in love." You fall out of the rational because love is an irrational act.

None of us could understand why Irma would want Bilal as a husband. Her parents couldn't figure it out: "Why do you want to marry *him*?" It didn't make sense. "He is not going to take you anywhere! It doesn't make sense!" It never makes sense! People always ask, "Girl, what do you see in him? He is no good! The man won't even work!" Your daughter will say, "But, Mama, I love him!" That will really get on your nerves, because you can't see it, but you have forgotten that *your* love was also equally irrational. Sometimes you will be so confused: "It must be her hair"; "It must be her eyes." No, it is not that. You are simply trying to find something that will make sense of this. It is not her hair, because her hair is going to fall out! Or, "Well, she has a good shape." In twenty years it will be gone, and you will still be in love. It is not the good shape. You cannot put your finger on it, because it is not in time. It is a timeless, spaceless experience. Love and beauty are timeless, spaceless experiences, and when you have them, you step out of the mind.

I am pointing out all of these things because I want you to begin to understand that the soul exists in the same place as love and beauty exist. It is on that plane. If you are in this world looking for your soul, you are never going to find it. That is the problem for most of us. We have become so enmeshed and entangled in the world that we have lost our souls. Jesus said, "For what will it profit a man if he gains the whole world and loses his own soul?" (Mark 8:36)

The soul can be lost, folks. All of the literature talks about us in terms of "lost souls." There is *nothing* more pathetic than a lost soul. You are not a lost soul because you are not a Christian or a Muslim; you are a lost soul because you are asleep! You are locked down in a lower stage of development. There are millions of Christians who think they have saved their souls and they remain totally lost! There are millions of Muslims who think they have found their souls and they remain lost! Lost souls, found souls, these are not matters pertaining to religion at all.

These are spiritual matters and you will know when your soul is lost, because your experience of *dukkha* will be immense. If you are feeling dukkha in your life, know that you have not found your soul, you have not become soul-centric. The most common characteristic of a person who has reached a soul-centric level in the evolution of identity is that the experience of dukkha drops out. Beneath this level there is dukkha in varying degrees, depending on where you are located in the hierarchy.

However, at this level, dukkha or suffering drops away, because you are no longer identified with any of the components which have been making up your identity to that point. You are simply the observing, witnessing seer; just *vast freedom*. This body, and all of the life and events associated with it are simply passing in the domain of your awareness, and you are simply watching it. You have pulled back from all of these things, you have transcended all of the lower stages. You are at peace, because you are not involved.

Do you know how it feels when you are in love? Have any of you ever been in love? I might be using the wrong analogy here! I am not sure about this crowd! If you have been in love, raise your hands! You know how you feel when you are in love or when you are having the experience of tremendous beauty, perhaps a great piece of music or work of art, a bird taking flight or sunlight sliding down the leaf of a tree, or simply walking through a meadow. At some time in your life you must have had these experiences. Remember how that feels?

That is how it feels when you become soul-centric, but with no interruptions, twenty-four/seven, because you are no longer identified with those things that are suffering. The body is suffering and, therefore, if you are identified with the body, *you* are suffering! Do you understand? *All* suffering is experienced as a result of your identification with the thing that is suffering!

That is natural, because as our egos began to develop in this hierarchy of identities, the first thing that we had access to was the biology of the bio-centric stage, and we became identified with our biological processes—our hunger, etc.—since those were the first objects in the field of our awareness. It almost seems, folks, that awareness is just there, and the first thing that pops up, it becomes identified with and, therefore, has all of the experiences that are associated with that vehicle. As you grow and mature to the next level, immediately the awareness now incorporates that as the foundation of its identity and it has the experiences of suffering that are associated with that vehicle, and so forth.

Vernita: *Bhagwan, is the soul what you were talking about once before when you said that it was who we were before we entered our mother's womb?*

Yes, that was a metaphor, what is called the "original face," the original identity. These are only metaphors pointing to the same thing. They are saying that that which you are, you were before you entered your mother's womb. That which you are, you will be even after this body drops away. That which you are is not subject to decay or change. This body is constantly changing, isn't it? It is in the domain of awareness, and anything that you are aware of, by definition, exists in time and space and, therefore, will perish! We are talking "quantum mysticism" here. Any event, person, place or thing exists in time and space and will perish!

This was the great insight of the Buddha, the insight of "impermanence." Try to understand the impermanence of these things: the wife, the children, the husband, the job, the body—all of this will perish. You do not have to believe it; simply observe it. *It is so.* The little ego that you are trying to cling to will be gone. You are *not* going to heaven. The "you" that you are identified with is made of nothing but your misidentification with the things in the field of awareness. That "you" is going nowhere! It is not going to heaven, it is not going to survive after your death because it is pseudo; it is false. This is the "false" self, but that is the self we all have become identified with. In that process we have lost our identification with our *true* Self, which is the *soul* and, therefore, we suffer.

Let us continue our discussion about the transpersonal levels where our sense of identity is no longer rooted in any of the prior components in our evolution. We are talking about when we reach that level of the unfoldment of spirit that is defined as the level of the "soul." Remember, spirit is immanent in all of the lower stages of evolution. I do not want you to forget that.

Last time we pointed out that even in matter there is spirit, but spirit has not been able to unfold much of itself because of the limitations and restrictions that matter imposes upon that unfoldment. However, spirit is even present in this table, but because the table, the body, the vehicle, the matter, does not lend itself to a great expression of the spirit that is inherent in it, we consider it to be a lower form of life.

In fact, the entire hierarchy of levels of life is based upon how much spirit can be expressed in that form of life. It is how we get our hierarchy. The sages and mystics have told us that there are approximately 8,400,000 different forms in which spirit is inherent, and that these forms differ in the sense that each form will be able to express a different degree of the spirit that is inherent in it. It is this human form we have which allows us to unfold spirit to a very, very high degree, and that entire process of the unfolding of spirit in the human form has been the subject of our talks on the evolution of ego.

Our sense of identity, of who we are, is so critical because wherever our sense of identity is located on this scale will dictate so much of the quality of our life. This business about the evolution, maturation and expansion of ego constitutes the sum total of all spiritual practices. It is the whole objective of Islam, Christianity, Judaism, Hinduism, of any "ism." In its purest form, every religion has had this as its objective: to bring us to a state of what is called "Self-realization."

Now, it is interesting that these mystics will say that you have to work toward "Self-realization," because we have been thinking that we are Self-realized. That is the whole problem, because we feel that my Self *is* this body, its history, its parentage and all of the exploits it has gone through. My Self *is* the collection of my likes, my dislikes, my moods. That *is* my Self. Therefore, we say, "What is this nonsense you are talking, mystic, about 'finding myself'? I already know who *I* am!" This, then, becomes the hardest task.

As Al pointed out to us on a prior occasion, spiritual growth requires a constant dying, doesn't it? In order to be able to attain the next level of your identity, you must forsake your current level of identity. You must die to that level of identification, and this is always painful, because you have become very attached to it and you cling to it. It is really like a death. However, if you have the courage to "die," you will have the experience of being "born again." You cannot be born again unless you are willing to die. These old identities die hard. Therefore, the task is to somehow *cooperate* with this process, to make ourselves amenable to this process, and achieve a certain degree of *detachment*. Detachment becomes the first aid that we can develop in this kind of conscious evolution. We will talk more about that in our last session.

I want to now make sure you have enjoyed the distinction between the level of soul-centricity as opposed to the lower levels. If you can understand the anatomy and evolution of ego, you will have understood *everything* that can be understood about *all* spiritual science. There *is* nothing else! If you can understand this, you will be able to attain that state.

Sharon: *I have a question about the relationship with the soul. In speaking of the soul-centric level, is the spirit and the soul the same? If not, what is the next level?*

You want to go deeper, right? We will address that at the next level of our discussion. I want to first make sure that we have a full grasp of "soul-centricity" before we go into "spirit-centricity," which is the next level. There are also some very dramatic differences. I know that most of us are trying to imagine, "Now, what could be beyond the 'soul' level of identity? When I have been able to reach a center of identity that does not involve the body, the mind or any of its contents, that does not involve any of this, when I am able to inhere in that pure subjectivity without any association with anything—neti, neti—what could possibly be beyond that?" However, as you have already suspected, this is not the final stage, although in many traditions, when practitioners have reached this level of Self-realization, they have stopped and called that "enlightenment." They do not think anything could be beyond that. We will say a few things about that as well, but let us first make sure we have addressed everybody's issues pertaining to soul-centricity.

FREEDOM FROM FEAR

When your awareness finally reaches the level of the soul, it has transcended its identification with all of the lower levels and is now only identified with this vastness, this vastness of freedom. It is a tremendous thing! That is why terms like "the open sky" and "free as a bird in the sky" have been used. All of these metaphors that we see in poetry and literature, across all kinds of cultures, point to a description of that kind of expansive experience upon reaching the level where your identity is rooted in your awareness of your soul. It generates a tremendous sense of freedom. For the first time in your life, you feel free! Real freedom! All of these things are just floating, and you are no longer clinging! It is almost like as a child how you would sometimes try to capture the clouds. That is foolish, because how can you capture a cloud? The cloud has to pass. In the same way, this body will go! It exists in time! It is okay, because the soul is not affected, right? Therefore, when your identity reaches a level where it is centered in the soul, for the first time you experience freedom!

What is this freedom from? Freedom from death! That is your greatest fear. You are afraid to die, and this fear of dying drives all of your behavior. It is the basis of all of your urgency and all of your greed. You are trying to get everything now: "I am going to drink as much booze as I can, and have as much sex as I can, and make as much money as I can. I am going to live it up!" You have truly become a hedonist! "I know death is coming and there is going to be a time when I can't drink, eat, have sex, or make money! Man, I have got to get busy." You are doing all of that because you have lost your *soul*! You have lost *awareness* of the fact that, "I am never going to die. I am not even in the stream of time. I exist outside of the stream of time. I was never *born* and I will never *die*! I am *not* the body. I do *not* need the things that the body thinks it needs. I am *not* going to pander to that."

Yes, let the body go through its thing. Remember, last time I said that you will begin to experience the body as an object in awareness. I am giving you these things, but you have to sit and ponder this one. You have to sit your tail in a chair in a corner somewhere, put your elbow on your knee with a cup of tea, and sit down and think about this. You are going to have to chew it up!

Sharon: *Being afraid of death and learning now that we have to separate ourselves from that. How would one actually free one's self or suspend the fear of death? We know that we are afraid of death, so how do we conquer it?*

That is a very relevant question. The whole function of satsang is to build in us the courage to face this "spiritual death." Remember, it is the "fear" of death, not death itself, the fear of the ending of the ego, the false self, that is so terrifying. The whole purpose of satsang is to encourage each other, to build up each other's confidence.

You must remember that people die for so many things. They conquer their fear of death for the cause of a group, a nation, or a this or that, so people, even in the ordinary sense, can die. The kamikaze pilots could easily move themselves into a state where they could fly their airplanes into a battleship knowing full well that they would perish. Mothers have been known to rush into a burning house to save their child knowing full well that the result could be death. Thus, there are many instances even in ordinary life where people have become inspired, and can conquer the fear of death. If one can have at least that kind of courage on the Spiritual Path, one will then be able to give up this fear of death and to do one's spiritual practices.

Swami Ji Maharaj, one of the great mystics out of India, used to always admonish the disciples to "give up the fear of thy families and friends and do thy devotion." Very often, for us death is simply the realization that we will have to separate from our family and friends, and this idea is too much for us to deal with. Your husband is not on the Path, but you are so attached to him that you cannot follow the Path: To follow the Path you will have to disengage from your husband, and this you cannot do! That is a kind of "death"—the death of relationships.

Remember, death is *not* something that is *abstract*. It is very concrete. Death means that you and your husband are going to separate; the relationship will end. The relationship with your children will end. All of these will end, with no exception. This is very terrifying, because when it ends something in you also dies. Deep down inside you feel that, "Well, if they die, I am going to die." Right! Because you have linked your identification to them. Part of your ego is constructed out of these relationships.

If I separate you out of your relationships, your little false self will simply dissolve, because it is supported by all of these other relationships. If you are primarily centered in the roles that you play and if I remove these actors from that drama, what role would you play? Without your children, how would you be "Mom"? Then, that "Mom" will start dissolving in that abyss and you, too, will dissolve along with it. Therefore, you have to look deeply into this.

In fact, the mystics say that the most sober introspection you can do is to look into your own demise, to introspect the inevitability of your own mortality, to ponder that. The Buddha conducted satsang, like we are having here, in cemeteries, sitting on graves. Why? To make sure we remain constantly aware of the fact that that is where all false selves end. You, too, will end there. Thus, if you can simply understand that the self you are identified with will come to a screeching, abrupt halt, if you can deal with that, you will now move into the requisite frame of mind.

You ask, "How do I conquer my fear?" You conquer your fear through *understanding*! Fear is the result of *ignorance*! Fear exists because your understanding is not deep. You have done no introspection or looked into the nature of impermanence. That absence of knowledge, that "unknownness," is what creates the fear. Have you ever noticed how fearful you always are of that which is unknown? You don't know anything about this person, so you don't let them in your house because, "I don't know anything about this person!" It might be Jesus coming back; but if Jesus rang your doorbell today, you would slam the door and say, "I don't know anything about this guy!" That ignorance will remain unless we consciously investigate it. Therefore, we must deliberately and consciously contemplate and investigate the inevitability of our death, and in that contemplation and investigation, we will gain much understanding and that understanding will eliminate, break down or certainly reduce, the fear. These things have to be dealt with on an individual basis because each of us has different degrees of this fear. However, you can see its presence, because it is your fear of moving to the next level of identity that is called "change," and we *all* fear change.

The fundamental thing is that none of us want to change! Why not? "I don't want to change these habits! Can I continue doing this and still make progress?" What can I say? I try to somehow contribute something to your understanding and, out of that understanding, you can give up these things. If you understand the teachings a little better, that makes it a little easier to give them up, but the fear is there because, fundamentally, you do not want to change. Change means the death of this false self. Change means the dissolving of some part of this contemporary stage of ego development that you are in, and you do not want to do that.

Therefore, you try to bring the teachings down to your level of ego development: You eliminate vegetarianism, you eliminate meditation, you eliminate self-observation, you eliminate satsang. You eliminate all of those things that are in conflict with your "comfort zone," which is based on your level of ego development, and then you wonder why you do not make any progress! Now, what can I say to you? There is no answer to that.

We need to have a very clear understanding of this thing; therefore, we have to study ourselves. Part of your *sadhana* is to study *yourself*. Part of sadhana *requires* this kind of deep introspection because, without it, one cannot give up one's fears. Sister, long before we will conquer the fear of death, the ending of our own ego journey, we will have to first conquer our fear of those around us, our relationships: Those relationships that we are so attached to because they play such a vital role in the maintenance and perpetuation of our false identities, our ego states. That sometimes takes a lot of time. It is a big barrier for all of us; it is not just an isolated occurrence. We all have to go through it and it is very difficult, but it can be done.

The other thing is, if you cannot conquer your fear of ego "death," then you will just have to be killed. In some traditions, the mystics will simply kill you. It is very simple. Either you will slay yourself or the Guru will slay you, but you will get slain one way or the other! If you are afraid to kill yourself, continue coming here. Somehow you will be murdered. We will do "Kervokian" mysticism. We will help you, assist you, to make it pleasant or easier for you.

You will recall that each rung of lower identification has been enfolded into the next higher stage; therefore, when you reach the level of soul-centricity, it does not mean that you lose the experience of the body. Your experience is *expanded* to include those experiences that are transcendental to the body, but it also *includes* the body. Do you understand how the field of experience *expands*? You do not lose anything. "Lost" is another basis of fear; you don't want to "lose" anything: "I don't want to become a buddha if it means I can't have some good food to eat!" Becoming a buddha will eliminate that fear.

Sometimes, Sat Ra, we are like that pig who, when offered the chance to go to heaven inquires, "Is there any mud up there, because I like wallowing in my mud." They said, "There is no mud in heaven." The pig said, "Well, what about some slop? Are there some troughs up there with good garbage? I am not going anywhere where I can't eat some garbage!" They said, "No, there is no garbage up there." He said, "Well, how is the sex up there, because after I have lain in the mud and eaten a bunch of slop, I have got to have me some sex!" They said, "Pig, there is none of that up there either." He said, "Well, I don't want it then! I would rather stay here."

Many of us are like that, because this is our "comfort zone." Hence, it is very difficult for us to move from this comfort zone. We are comfortable at this level of our own ego development. In fact, without *grace*, none of us would move from these temporary levels of ego development. Grace is that force which acts upon stationary objects; it is that thing which comes into your life and shakes you up; it creates great discomfort, and out of that discomfort, you move.

Please make a note: *Over vast periods of time, all of us will automatically evolve.* It may be eons and eons and kalpas and kalpas, time that is immeasurable; billions of more lives may be required. Nonetheless, you too will become a buddha. We really do not have a choice, and by virtue of the fact that we have this human body, we can accelerate our own evolution. We can "step" outside of the laws of mechanical evolution and accelerate it. That is the difference. You can be a buddha right now! You need not wait twenty billion lifetimes for that. The choice is ours, but it is a choice that we each have to make individually.

THE SOUL-CENTRIC STAGE

This soul-centricity that we were talking about becomes the first new level of the shift in identification that can be called "spiritual" in the true sense of the word, because you have now evolved, or expanded, your sense of identity to include your soul. Remember, we have already seen that you have a sense of identity that did not include the soul. That thing which is the most essential part of you was missing from your entire description of yourself, and it was missing because you were not consciously aware of it. It seems that the very basis of your "real" identity, consciousness itself, was missing from your own description. When consciousness becomes the basis of your identity, this is the beginning of true spirituality.

We come now to this phenomenon that occurs as we move deep into this soul-centricity, the "soul-centric" stage. Remember, this is characterized by the fact that you have been able to locate the source of your own personal awareness. You have been able to discover and become identified with the source of your own personal awareness. We are calling this the "state of the soul," where you understand and are experiencing the fact that you are none of the objects that are appearing within the domain of your field of awareness, that that which you are, the seer itself, is unseeable. It sees everything, but cannot experience itself as an object. It is a "felt" sense. You can have a sensation of your being, but you cannot experience the seer as an object. You inhere in that state, you are in that state twenty-four/seven. You live your whole life and its experiences in that state. It is one thing to intellectually understand this, but it is quite a different thing to actually continuously abide in this state of witnessing, in this state where you are the observing self, the seer, where everything is experienced as a parade through the domain of your awareness. When you are sitting outside of this domain of experience, that is what generates detachment, fearlessness, peace.

Nothing is happening to you, but you are so afraid something is going to "happen" to you! "Oh, Bhagwan, I can't do this because this (or that) is going to happen to me!"; "Bhagwan, I can't do that because this is going to happen to me!" You have this whole list of "bad things" that are going to happen to you and, therefore, you have high levels of anxiety. You are constantly contemplating what "bad thing" can happen to you. "I might get sick;" "I might do this," whatever your particular "this" may be. All of these existential anxieties and phobias disappear when we are able to center ourselves at the level of our souls. It becomes the foundation and the locus of our identification, and we are able to live in this state.

Even at night when you are asleep, you will "watch" yourself sleep. This is deep! So, it is not simply an observation of the waking level of consciousness, because you will actually observe yourself going into these states of consciousness. Something sits outside of experience and simply observes it. It observes the waking state, the sleep state with dreams, and the dreamless state. It sees when you go into the dream state; there is no "false" self. There is no experience of the false ego at all. There is no "I" experience. It sees that this self that you are identifying with essentially only manifests itself at the waking level of consciousness. When you dream, you become a different self, and you are less inhibited. The seer sees this whole drama going on. It is a very different thing. Now, let us look and see what happens.

To appreciate this, you must understand that our identity from the bio-centric level all the way up to the soul-centric level has one characteristic in common. Remember, your sense of identity is composed of different components along the way. One part incorporates only the biological processes, one the physical body or the concrete aspect, another your roles, etc. Therefore, they may be different components, but they all bear one thing in common: They are all what we call *dualistic*.

By "dualistic," I mean that all of these identities are based on something called a "subject and object relationship." Something subjective to you observes something objective to you, makes the identification, locks its identity to it. However, notice there is still a witness and that which is being witnessed. Do you see the dichotomy, the "twoness"? There is this sense of "twoness," that which witnesses and observes and that which is being observed. The understanding is "I am not that": *neti, neti*. As you go deep into this state, as this state itself matures, and you inhere in this state, the experience of being an observer dissolves, totally! You have to stay with me on this. There is the experience of the dissolution of the seer, of the witnessing itself. You may be saying, "My God, Bhagwan, what in the world could the resulting state be like?" There is no witnessing, no subject, no object.

When you are in that state, you begin to notice that the witness only comes into being when the object is there. It is a simultaneous thing. That is the first thing you discover: In order for the witness to be in existence, there has to be something to witness. It does not matter that you are not identified with it, however, the witness only exists in conjunction with an object to be witnessed. As you go deep into it, that begins to dissolve and what is left is this kind of "trinity," and this final shift becomes the final stage of identity.

You have the "seer" and the "seen," but what is missing? Yes, unity is missing, but what specifically is missing? The seer is the subject and the seen is the object. What has to exist to make this complete, to connect the two? What connects the seer with that which is seen? Seeing! The sense of identity now shifts from the seer to "seeing."

Remember, our identity was first locked into seeing. In all of the seven stages, our identity was simply locked into a hierarchy of objects that we see in the domain of awareness, and we were then able to evolve from that level to this level. Our whole sense of identity shifted entirely over here to the seer, but there was still this "twoness," wasn't there? The seer and that which was seen, but this is the process that gives rise to both of them. The seer, as well as the seen, emerges out of this seeing. The seer and the seen are two aspects of one thing—seeing—so with the final shift of identity you become identified with the seeing. You are simply the seeing! Meditate on that! You are not the dancer or the dance, you are the *dancing*! You are the process that connects the two.

This is the "oneness" that we talk about. This is the one source of both. It is the source from which the seer emerged and it is also the source from which the seen emerged. It has been called "the ground of being." It has been called so many names: *Amen, maat, Ra, God*—whatever you want to call it. You become identified with the seeing. For instance, when we talk about the seer who sees the mountains, there is still the seer and the mountain. There is still a dichotomy, there is still duality. There is not a oneness.

When one experiences it from this higher point, it is not that there is a seer: You *become* the mountain! It is a very different process. You *are* the mountain! You are no longer simply observing: *The thing is you and you are it!* There is no more dichotomy in this experience. This is called the state of "nonduality," the state of oneness—not twoness in the sense of the seer and the seen. There is no more separation.

That is why I told you in the beginning that ego goes all the way up to the level of the soul. Ego will be with you a long way, but it has to be there. Even at the level of the soul, there is still this fundamental sense of separation. Remember, we defined ego as being the experience of separation from that which is experienced. We defined it as being the "lost" experience of oneness. So, even at the level of the soul, we know that we are no longer those things, because our identification has moved to a very high level, but the fundamental illusion is that we are still separate from that which is being seen and, at the final stage, our identity shifts back to just the pure seeing, where there is no separation.

Sardarji: *That is the trinity?*

Yes, that becomes the "real" trinity: Seeing, seer and seen become *one*. It is a very profound thing. It has been described as the "Father, Son and Holy Ghost." What can really be said about that? Nothing! This is the ultimate stage, where ego has gone from maximum contraction and the maximum experience of separation, all the way back to the experience of oneness. This is what constitutes the whole spiritual journey—and it is a journey because you cannot leapfrog over any of this—and the process to reach that stage is the process that we have called *meditation*. That is why so much emphasis is placed on meditation. However, meditation itself evolves into something that is not even meditation anymore; that technically you cannot call meditation, what Sat Ra calls the "state of tears."

When you try to think about how it feels to be a mountain, it is simply beyond your capacity to grasp that you are the seeing, you are hearing, you are the dancing, you are the process which connects the seer with the seen. You are interior even to the witness. It is profound! You can experience it, yes, but you cannot grasp it with your mind.

Albert: *You were talking about a child being born into the family system or society as a whole and being soul-centric, and you were talking about us being seers, and that we watch ourselves evolve into adults. I am trying to make sense of that, but you also talked about souls becoming wounded right from the start and I guess that is connected with the ego, because we come out and get caught up with all of these things and identify with all of these things. You were saying we must get back to that. I see already why you said that.*

You already see the whole process, and that is why I said the "key." However, it is a key that not only will unlock the mysteries of psychoanalysis and all other forms of therapy, it is a "master" key which, if you understand how to use it, will unlock endless things. It will unlock the Kabbalah, all religious systems, all therapies, all sciences, quantum mechanics. It will unlock anything that is locked, it will open up anything. This is the tremendous gift that these great mystics have given us. They have given us the key to unlock all things. Therefore, it is very important that you understand this thing and use this key of understanding. It will take you through every situation with which you will be confronted in your life. It will heal. It is the panacea that "dissolves" problems; not "solves" problems, dissolves problems! There is a big difference. The "problem" ceases to be a problem. You have been trying to "solve" your problems, and look at the mess you have made.

The Greek mystics called it the "philosopher's stone." If you touch base metal to a philosopher's stone, it is said that the metal turns into gold. Similarly, if anything "touches" this understanding, it becomes converted into a peaceful experience. It reduces *all* conflicts, not simply conflicts between you and the people around you. It is a great thing! Yes, sister? You have another question? Good for you, but I want you to save some of these questions for Sat Ra, for when he drives you home. I don't want him to have any peace!

Sharon: *The masters or the mystics who have arrived at these levels where everything is dissolved, I want to know about that because they have exceeded those levels—and within myself I know that I have not exceeded those levels—conflict is still going on in the world, not just with people that I may meet, but according to the level I may be on. It seems like is it real in a sense?*

I love her thinking out loud, because this is what goes on in her mind! She is simply verbalizing the activities of her mind! This poor woman suffers like this around the clock, and you should have some compassion for her!

You see, as I said before, the key to understanding is that *your* experience of the world is experienced according to the level of your *own* ego development. It is not pre-given. You will see and experience the world from that vantage point, and every time you move to another stage of maturity, an entirely different world comes into being. It is *not* the same world! There are as many worlds as there are stages. *This* very world will be experienced *entirely* different when you move to the next stage. It is wrong to even call it the same world, because it will be so very different. You can imagine that as a child you were living in a certain neighborhood and they were shooting the same dope, etc., but you had no experience of that. You will look fondly back at that same neighborhood and say you had such a good time and so much fun, but they were raping, killing and mugging people all around you! However, you were not developed to a state where you were perceptive of all of that; hence, it was not a part of your experience. So, the world is not something that has its own defining characteristics. Your experience of the world is shaped by the level of your own ego maturation.

Sharon: *So, it is what is happening inside of you, because the world is really inside and not outside?*

That is what the mystics have been saying all along. Jesus went one step further and said, why are you talking about this world? It is such a small thing! He said that the *entire kingdom of God is within you!* The totality of that which exists is inside of you, but it can only be experienced if you are at the right frequency.

Sharon: *That would also be saying that basically it is your belief system.*

Your "belief system" is also generated from your ego level. For instance, let's say you are at a primary stage in your ego development, such as the physio-centric level, where your entire identity is locked into the body. If you are at that stage, do you see how that level would generate a whole set of beliefs or morality system? If you look at the level where you are psycho-centric or emotio-centric, you will again see how each of these stages would generate their own value or belief systems, etc.

Suppose I am locked into my identity as it relates to my likes and dislikes and am very egocentric in that. "Egocentric" is simply the feeling that everybody should feel the way that I feel. It means the inability to see the other, because you have not developed enough, you have not expanded outward. There *are* no other people in the world. What other people feel does not even count! *They* do not have feelings; *I* am the only one who has feelings and only *my* feelings count! If you look closely at this, you will see the kind of morality which will come out of that kind of stage. The feeling is, "To hell with everybody else. I don't care what anybody else is going through." It is a "me" thing; it is "my own thing." You can even see the kinds of needs which will arise out of that stage. Your belief systems, as well as everything else, are dictated by your level of ego development, even your concept of God!

If you are still at a primary stage in your ego development, your concept of God will probably be personalized: Some man—it is usually a "man" because men have created all of this nonsense—up in the sky with long white hair called "God" that is looking out just for you and no one else. He will hear *your* prayers, but he may not hear anybody else's prayers. He is your *own* personal savior. That concept of God was developed when you were four years old, but here you are, forty-five years old, still walking around with this same concept of God.

You can see all of the intricacies and complexities of this thing, and all of that stuff has to be worked through. This is what Al meant when he said you have to work on that. You have to edit and clear up all of that garbage. You have to let it go if you want to move to a higher level of development, an adult level. What are *your* values? Where do your values and beliefs come from and how old were you when you formed them? That would be a good exercise for you: to examine your value and moral systems. Try to locate your age when you developed them. How long have you been thinking that the things *you* feel are wrong, *are* wrong? At what age did you formulate that?

Normally, you formulate your sense of rights and wrongs with a child's mind. Sometimes, it was not even your doing; somebody told you that. It is, therefore, wrong for you to say "my moral system." You do not have a moral system! You have a "borrowed" system, something somebody has told you and it was incorporated in the parenting you received, in your conditioning. The culture taught you that. It is not yours, not original or the result of your own intelligence or conscious investigation at all! All of that has to be looked at.

You say, sister, that it seems as if it is all something coming from you. You are absolutely right! *You* dictate the experience. The suffering is not coming from the world into you; it is just the reverse! I know it is a hard teaching, but it is true: *You create your own suffering!* No one is making you suffer. No one is making you angry. *You* are making yourself angry! No one is making you depressed. *You* are making yourself depressed! You are *pinching yourself*, and then screaming! The mystics say, stop pinching yourself! It is simple, but difficult, because you think somebody else is the cause of your misery: "Well, if so-and-so would only act right!"; or "If my wife would only go along with this!"; or "If my boss would only do this, voilà, I would be in paradise!" Nonsense! However, it is very difficult to deal with reality on that level if you are stuck in one of the primary levels of ego development.

We have traveled quite a distance here, but we have not exhausted any of these things. The intent of the workshops was to introduce to you these topics and things for you to look at. My hope is that you will sit down and go into the nature of these things. You can do whatever reading you need to do to lend support to your insight, but you certainly have a key that will unlock all kinds of mysteries.

Next week we will begin to summarize these things and go into a few of the deeper aspects surrounding meditation and try to tie this together so it will not remain at an "intellectual" level. Otherwise, it will have no value. It will simply remain "theoretical" and theory is meaningless. One ounce of practice is worth more than a ton of theory, because "theory" does not transform anybody. "Practice" is what transforms. Therefore, the whole idea of these workshops was to somehow increase our understanding to a level to enable us to free up the energy to practice. Nevertheless, if you do no meditation, you will have received nothing from me that will amount to anything. All of this will evaporate in a few days or a few weeks. It will be gone, because it is not real, it is not yours; you will have nothing to stand on. You must have meditation, a process that generates this movement in the shifts of identity.

That is what distinguishes "mysticism" from "therapy." Therapy or philosophy has no methodology. Idealism has no methodology. Neither Freud, nor Jung, nor Asaggioli were mystics! Bradshaw is not a mystic. They do not know how to go into the interiority of their own being. They are bright, there is no doubt about it. They are gifted writers and philosophers, but they are nowhere near Buddha. Alice Walker is not a Mira Bai; she does not even come close! Remember, Mira Bai was less articulate. Mira Bai couldn't write a book to save her life, but she was a fully enlightened being! With a Mira Bai, you would not even have to read a book; simply keep company with her and you would become enlightened. That is the *vast* difference with mystics. That is why their company has been such a great value over the centuries for all of us, because by simply being in their *presence*, some kind of *osmosis* takes place.

Ra shekum maat.

CHAPTER SIX
RECEPTIVITY TO THE GRACE OF GOD

This is the final session in a series of five sessions where we have been discussing the management of ego. We have covered an awful lot of ground, and today we will begin to try to summarize this with any questions or topics that still need further exploration. Our aim will be to try to convert it into some kind of practical application. You will recall that our ambition is not to simply spend this time together and theorize. We want to be able to apply these insights to our everyday life, because that is the only way we can derive any real and lasting benefit from the time we spend here in *satsang*. I trust that some of the information that came out of these workshops proves to be useful. If nothing else, it hopefully gives us a very different perspective on this whole business of our egos.

As I reminded you throughout the course of our discussions, the *essence* of spiritual development is directly linked to the evolution of our egos, and spiritual progress is essentially the *transformation* and *transcendence* of our present sense of identity as separate, contracted, recoiled individualism to a more expansive, free and vast experience of totality: *the experience of being God.* As we make spiritual progress, this is the most unique aspect of the entire experience. You actually *experience* a shift in the focus and locus of your identity, and all of this has to do with the ego. Therefore, we have tried to demonstrate how our egos begin in a very contracted, condensed form in a bio-centric state, move on to the body and from the body increasingly incorporate more and more aspects of our being and, ultimately, expand to the level of God.

Last time we talked about "soul-centricity," when the sense of identity has shifted to our souls, and we began to say something about the "spirit-centric" identity. "Spirit-centricity" is where we completely drop or shed the experience of being separate from God. The last frontier of our journey is when we plunge into the ocean, when the "drop" merges back into the "ocean." That analogy, which is very often used by the mystics, still does not truly and accurately reflect what actually happens when we are able to transcend our soul-centricity and move into a state of spirit-centric awareness. A more appropriate analogy would be that *the ocean falls into the drop.* It is very difficult to conceive how the ocean can merge into a drop. You *become* the ocean. It is not so much that you lose your sense of identity; it is simply that your sense of identity expands to include *everything*. There is no more "other" at all. The experience becomes single, full: *one*.

Today, let us review and reexamine any of the various aspects of this whole journey of our egos and try to deal with any problem areas that are still left. Let us open up the floor, and you are most welcome to present anything you would like me to go over with you again.

MEDITATION: "TURNING THE CUP UP"

While you are pondering that, please try to remember that meditation is the most effective means for accelerating the evolution of our identities. We must try not to *ever* forget that. I believe that Sardarji must have mentioned somewhere in the course of this morning's satsang the fact that our meditation *is* the act of receptivity to the Lord's grace. We really cannot talk rationally about opening ourselves to the Lord's grace unless we sit in meditation.

Maharaj Ji used to always say that if there is a rainstorm and we are a cup facing downward, we will not collect one drop of the torrential falling of grace. Meditation is turning the cup up. There *is* no other way. Thus, if you have been praying for the Lord's grace and have been avoiding meditation, please make a note that no grace is forthcoming! If you have been trying somehow to read yourself into a state of receiving grace, please know that no grace will fall upon you. There *is* no other way to receive the grace of your higher being than through the process of meditation!

Very often we are like that struggling fish on the line of the Master. We are struggling not to become caught in this final realization. We are trying to avoid meditation as best we can. We are trying to substitute it with so many things, such as good deeds, charitable donations, and so on; however, none of these are the equivalents of, or substitutions for, this process called meditation. Therefore, we have to remain focused on that. Without meditation, there is no possibility of shaking yourself free from the clutches of your contemporary levels of ego development. So, *everything* comes back to meditation. Ultimately, at the spirit-centric level of development of one's identity, this whole business about grace and effort simply disappears. However, until then, we have to do our part. Let us now discuss any aspect, however mundane, of ego development that you like.

Pam: *Bhagwan, Sardarji's discourse is still ringing in my ears, because it was really beautiful. What he was saying about grace really struck me, but is it true that God's grace flows all the time? So, when we don't meditate and open ourselves up, is that the reason we don't get it?*

You are actually getting it all the time, you are simply not aware of it. Understand the distinction: When we say that we are not getting the grace of God, it does not mean that existentially the grace is not there. The rain is actually falling on the cup. It is not a case where it is not raining, because it is always raining. When we are not receptive to the Lord's grace, it simply means that we are not aware, because grace is happening all the time. Every aspect of your existence down to the tiniest detail is a manifestation of grace. Have you ever thought about it? Can you find any logical reason for you to be alive? It is a profound question! Why should there be such a thing called "human existence"? Why should there even be a thing called a "world"? How did this tremendous mystery come into being? Why shouldn't everything simply be a void? Why should there be any existence at all? We exist because of this grace. We have our being in grace, but we are unaware, and out of that unawareness, we suffer.

Pam: *So it is not a matter of the Creator withholding it?*

It is never a case of the Creator withholding it. God, Allah, whatever you want to use to refer to that source of our being, never withholds. If there was any withholding, you would cease to be, in an instant! The grace is always there. How do we define "grace"? Grace is that which helps you evolve, that which helps you mature, that which takes you back toward this state of God-consciousness. That is grace. Grace may sometimes be bankruptcy, because it then makes you start trying to transcend something. Grace can come in many different forms.

We often think that grace must be a "pleasant" experience, but it is not always pleasant. For some levels of ego development, the experience of grace is very painful. For instance, you may be so attached to someone that you cannot devote any time toward your spiritual practices. You may be so entangled in a relationship that no Gitas, Korans, Bibles, Dhammapadas or Tao Te Chings, no teachings or satsangs—nothing—can snap your clutching to that person, situation, or circumstance. Sometimes it is the Lord's grace that that person dies and you now have no choice. Therefore, anything that brings you closer to the attainment of the state of God-consciousness is grace. Anything that is preventing you from achieving a closer proximity to this state of God-consciousness is the result of your unawareness, your unreceptivity. The whole creation is full of God somehow beckoning to you. God is trying to tell you something, but you are not listening and, therefore, you suffer.

THE "SLAYING" OF THE EGO

Sat Ra: *Before the workshops and a few of the previous satsangs, I was under the impression that you must kill this damn thing, that you must completely destroy it. I didn't know that it was a developmental stage until the full maturation of ego. I thought ego would have to be dropped altogether. So this is a surprise!*

Yes, and hopefully not a contradiction of the previous teachings. You see, the evolution *does* involve the dropping of the ego. Unless we drop the ego level we are on, we cannot go to the next one. Unless we "kill" our current level of ego, we cannot be released to move to the next. In many respects, hopefully, the contradiction is taken care of. There is a "dying" in order to evolve. One has to "die" to be "reborn" into a higher state of ego development. The mystics are hopefully not too confusing when we understand their statements within the backdrops of this whole business about the evolution and maturation of ego.

Swami Ji Maharaj, the founding mystic of the Radha Soami line, used to always refer to our ego as the *homen*, which is a Sanskrit word. He said that this homen or ego has to expand to a state of totality. The more *expanded* the ego becomes, the more total one's experiences, the more *integrated* the experience becomes. Of course, in order to expand, we have to stop this contracting, this clinging to our current level. We have to die to our current level and the sense of who we are. One of the things we have tried to point out is that very often we are clinging to some of the very lowest levels of our ego development. We tried to also show, Sat Ra, how the degree of *dukkha*, or suffering, we are experiencing is directly related to the level of our ego development. All of these things hopefully begin to make sense.

The idea was not to confuse, but to try and give you a bigger picture to look at and to place all of the teachings within that system. When you really understand the role that the maturation of ego plays in the entire process of spiritual development, as I have already said on many occasions, you have, in effect, a key to literally understand the teachings. It is very difficult to understand what these mystics are saying if you do not really fully grasp the significance of the maturation of ego and the shifting of levels of identity. It is a key thing to understand. It makes sense of the teachings. However, you are right.

Hence, it is a shock because, again, our tendency is to think that when the Master says we must "kill the ego," we then enter into a "void." No one wants to enter into a void. There is the feeling that "I" will cease to be, that somehow "I" will go out of existence. Actually, the more you are able to *kill* the ego, the more *alive* you will become; it is just the reverse! You and I have been thinking that we are alive, throbbing, fully conscious, but these lower stages of ego actually obscure the manifestation of your consciousness. You are actually less alive the further down you are in the hierarchy of ego development, so much so that Christ said you are literally "dead." Yes, you have eyes, but you see nothing of this life, of this world. You have ears, but you hear absolutely nothing. You are so egocentric that you are almost "autistic," simply trapped within the confines of your own little mind.

It is a kind of "radical" understanding. However, you need these kinds of radical understandings to become a little more detached, so that you do not take your current identity too seriously, and so that you begin to understand that this sense of who you are, which is made up of various combinations of these different stages of your ego development, this "you" that you are fighting so hard to perpetuate and are so concerned about its future, has no substance at all. It is an *illusion*. That is *enough* to kill you!

LOVE: THE MAXIMUM RECEPTIVITY TO GRACE

Sardarji: *Please say something about how love plays a role in the development of the ego, how it helps you to drop it.*

Yes. "Love" is the full maturation of ego in the sense that we have been discussing. Love is a quality that is only found in people who have matured in terms of the development of their egos. Love makes you *sensitive*, because love essentially is the ability to identify with the "other," the ability to become very sensitive to something other than yourself. In that sensitivity, you become very receptive. People who are not very receptive usually have difficulty in their relationships. Have you ever noticed that? They never notice *anything* about the person they are in a relationship with. You do not know how your wife looks, because you have not even looked at the woman in twenty years! However, she is not the same woman as she was when you married her. Much water has flowed since then, but you are in a relationship that existed twenty years ago! The same is the case with your husband. He is not the same person he was when you first met. There is such an absence of awareness in relationships, because of an absence of love, and love is the ability to be sensitive.

You asked, what is the role that love plays? Love is nothing but *maximum* receptivity to grace! We call that state of maximum receptivity "love," because that is what it is. Your ego has grown from where your concerns are simply about you. Please understand that as long as your concerns are centered on you, as long as "you," "me," or "my" dominates your whole style of life, know that you are at a very, very undeveloped state of ego. You are simply centered on yourself and no love is possible. Love means that we are able to expand. Love is a state of expansion. It is a state of increased sensitivity and perception, a state of increased awareness.

When we are "in love" with someone, Sardarji, it means that we now have the capacity as well as the willingness to relieve their suffering. We are aware of their suffering. Most of us are not aware of the other person's suffering at all. You are aware of *your* suffering, yes, but you cannot feel the suffering of another human being. You are alienated from life. You are "emotionally" autistic, you are wrapped and enfolded back into yourself and, therefore, no experience of love is possible. Love, then, is something very rare among men and women. It is only found in very mature individuals who have transcended all of the lower stages of ego development.

Remember, when that maturation becomes complete, one is able to love not only other *human* beings, because it is not so much related to or based on other human beings, but *all* sentient beings. Love now becomes a part of your character, like the nature of a flower is simply to emit perfume; whether a dog smells that perfume or whether a poet does, it makes the rose no difference. It is a part of the rose's nature to be sweet. Similarly, when we have evolved to a full state of ego development and maturation, *love* becomes our *nature*. It is not the result of a transaction. It is not contractual. It is unconditional. We simply love, we "feel." There is a kind of oneness, a kind of *maatic* relationship with life. Thus, you feel for the animals, you feel for the plants. You feel "life." Now, we do not feel anything at all. Love, Sardarji, is the highest state of receptivity. When we have this capacity to love, it is a manifestation of God's full grace. You can almost tell those individuals who are in a state of receptivity to God's grace. You will know them because they can love.

Jesus said in the scriptures, "Love ye one another because in this way they will know that ye are my disciples." (John 15:12) There is no other way for anyone to recognize that ye are my disciples except that you love each other. You cannot just say, "Oh, I am a Christian. I have been baptized and saved by the Holy Ghost." This is nonsense! That is no evidence of your relationship with Jesus at all. The only evidence of your relationship with a Jesus, or a Buddha, or a Mahavira, or a Kabir is that you love. The same is the case with God. The clearest evidence that you are receptive to the grace of God is found in your demonstration of love. So, it is a *very* deep thing.

To say a few more things about love: If there is not much understanding, how will you love? Love *never* occurs outside of the context of understanding. Please make a note of that! Love requires a "solid" understanding. You do not understand your husband, or your wife, or your neighbor; therefore, you do not love them. You do not understand their suffering or dreams or ambitions. Because you do not understand, you are not capable of loving. Yes, you may *want* to love, but that is another issue. You may be *willing* to love them, but the reality is that you *cannot* love them. You have no capacity to love, because you have no understanding.

What is it, Sardarji, when we truly love someone, other than an effort to relieve them of their suffering? Is there any other way in which we interact with those whom we love? When we love someone, we are concerned about relieving their suffering. But *your* interaction with other human beings is not based on the relief of *their* suffering; it is based on the relief of *your* suffering. It is just the opposite! Have you ever noticed that the more you try to *relieve* your suffering, the more you *suffer*? The more focused you become on just relieving *your* suffering, the more *you* suffer! This is the mathematics of spirituality. This "loving" is a very different matter.

Theresa: *You were discussing the "mathematics of spirituality," and I wanted to make sure I was clear on that. What are the components of the mathematics of spirituality?*

Well, I must have been alluding to the fact that the suffering we experience in life is almost always due to the absence of an adequate degree of love. Suffering *means* the absence of love. Have you ever noticed that? The point I was making, Theresa, is that the more you are trapped in your own egocentricity, the more you are locked into simply providing relief for your own personal suffering and the hell with everybody else, the mathematics of spirituality ensures that you will suffer even more. Your suffering will go on increasing to the degree that your selfishness goes on increasing. At the opposite end, the more energy you begin to devote to the relief and alleviation of the suffering of other people, to that same degree, your own suffering disappears. Your suffering is going on because you are simply focused in on yourself. You are contracted, you are isolated. In that sense, we can say that in the math of spirituality, the more *you* love, the more love is given to you, and the more your own capacity to love *increases*.

Everything else is a very different kind of math. For instance, at the material level, if I am going to share something with you, Dorothy, since matter is finite, that means that I will lose whatever portion of my material possession that I am sharing with you. If I have one hundred pounds of gold and I give you half, I will have only fifty left. That is the mathematics of "material" sharing with other people. If I have one hundred dollars in my pocket—which I do not in case anybody wants to see me as I leave—and I gave you fifty of those dollars, the mathematics of money means that I only have fifty dollars left, so I diminish myself every time I share with you, on a material level, that is.

If I now share my *knowledge* with you, I do not lose any of it. If I know something and I share that knowing with you, I do not lose anything at all, because I have now moved to a higher level of sharing and my loss, therefore, is less. In fact, there is zero loss. If I can go to the next level and can interact with you in such a way that I can share my *love* with you, not only do I not lose any of my love, but once my love is received by you, it comes back to me and, therefore, *increases* my own store of love. Because when I love you, you have no other choice but to love me back. This is the law! If you love, the beloved has to return it in kind. There is no other way.

Very often when we are walking around saying, "You know, I love so-and-so, but they don't love me," please know for sure that you do *not* love that person. Know for a fact that you do not love that person, because the law of spirituality is such that when you *love* that person, that person's love has no choice but to *flow* back toward *you!* This is the law and it has nothing to do with your "opinions." When someone is kind to you in a moment of need, you have no choice but to feel gratitude and appreciative. Something in you will begin to arise where you will want to respond in kind in some way. You have no control over that. In the mathematics of spirituality, then, whenever we love, we always experience abundance. There is always an increase. This is a very strange math, isn't it?

Pam: *That is a very strange math, because it says in the Bible that you are supposed to do good to people who spitefully misuse you and so on. Even with that scripture you are saying that in some way those people are still loving and kind?*

Somewhere one of the poets said—I am not sure who, but it is an old cliche—that the *best* way to deal with an enemy is to make them a friend. Making the enemy a friend is essentially the result of your *loving* the enemy. There is no other way to convert that enemy into a friend except through your loving them. It is, therefore, a very practical thing. Jesus was teaching them something very, very practical. All of the teachings of these mystics are very practical. They relate to *this* world. It has nothing to do with the *other* world. Their teachings are to help us function better in this very world that we live in.

Remember, only a mature ego can do that. Because there is no way in the world that the immature ego can love their enemy. They do not even love their *friend*. They do not even love *themselves*; so, how can they love their enemy? That teaching cannot even be put into practice by them. In fact, just *hearing* that kind of teaching causes them to *recoil*. They cannot believe that Jesus was talking this kind of nonsense, and millions of people are still following him? Just that one statement of his has caused millions of people to *not* follow Jesus to this day, because that seems so crazy to them. This is nonsense! Love my enemies? They feel somehow insulted by that kind of thinking. It is only the mature individual, one who has somehow moved higher in the hierarchy and maturation of their egos, that can begin to implement that. In fact, Pam, when the maturity is complete, one ceases to make any distinction between "enemies" and "friends." That drops out, because it has no meaning. You can no longer distinguish between who is your enemy and who is your friend. Even this categorizing of people as "friends" versus people who are "enemies" itself belongs to a lower level of ego development, which simply disappears as we mature.

"CLEAR" THINKING

Pam: *Last week you were talking about thinking and how thinking does not help you solve your problems and that when you get to a state of ego maturity, you learn how to "dissolve" problems. You also said something to the effect that when you are at a deep level of meditation, what you come to realize is that the whole thinking process is something that is independent. You were saying that things happen to you not so much because of you or even because of your thinking.*

I must have said something to the effect that the realization descends in deep meditation that you are not your mind; that this whole business in the process called "thinking" and all of the thoughts which go with it, are just objects in your consciousness; that there is a distance between you and them; and that these things never truly impact us. When you are able to come to that level of identity called "witnessing," you become more soul-centric. For the first time, you are able to see that this entire mind, as well as the mind process, is something very foreign to your reality.

The problem, Pam, is not thinking; it is "unclear" thinking. Thinking has a legitimate function, purpose and role in this whole business about living. The mystics are not "anti-thinking." The mystics say to learn *how* to think. The reality is that most of us do not know how to think *clearly*. We do not have what the mystics call *viveka*. Viveka means the power to distinguish between that which is real and that which is not real. When we do not have the capacity to distinguish between that which is real and that which is not real, our thinking is always muddled, always of a very confused quality, because we essentially do not have the foundation to do "good" thinking. We are confused, and the result is that we *think* out of this state of confusion. The mind that is purified, that is disciplined, is probably the best tool a human being can have! When this mind of ours has been *trained*, disciplined and cleaned up, we could not have a better *friend*. However, when this mind is in the state in which it is for most of us, you could not have a worse enemy! Part of the process of meditation is that your mind starts becoming clearer. For those who have the tenacity to hang in there, you will begin to notice that your meditation enables you to think clearer and clearer, until you reach a point where you can think very clearly. Ninety percent of enlightenment is based on clear thinking. I want to correct any misunderstandings about thinking *per se*, because the problem is not thinking; the problem lies in not thinking *clearly*, and meditation helps to correct that problem.

Pam: *Bhagwan, I think that is what Bhagwan Rajneesh meant when he talked about "no mind." Are we only capable of that in meditation?*

"No mind" is a condition, a state of being. It is not just something that occurs in meditation. We have to again revisit the meaning of the statement "no mind." You see, it is very difficult to see reality through the activity of the mind. Try to understand this.

I am reminded of an incident that occurred with Mahakasyapa and the Buddha. There is a famous *sutra* in Buddhism that depicts this event. The story is that the Buddha one day appeared for satsang and he was simply holding a flower. He was uncharacteristically silent that day, because the Buddha was famous for seven and eight hour discourses, laying out *very* deep stuff. However, at this particular satsang the Buddha was silent and simply held this flower in his hands. Naturally, the monks and nuns who were assembled were trying to interpret the meaning of this flower, this symbol, and Buddha just listened to their minds tumbling and wondering, "Oh, I wonder what the Buddha means by this. Maybe this flower is a symbol of purity and maybe he is trying to show us that we need to be pure." Someone else thought, "Let's see what the Buddha means by showing us this flower." Throughout the assembly in the minds of all of the monks and nuns who were there was this activity of the mind going on, trying to think of what this flower symbolized, its meaning, except for one monk, Mahakasyapa. When Buddha's eyes fell upon him, Mahakasyapa simply smiled at him. Mahakasyapa simply saw the rose. Now, you must meditate on this. There was nothing going on in Mahakasyapa's consciousness like "mind," therefore, he was able to see "reality," and the reality was to just look at the rose. Mahakasyapa said that when someone is showing you a *rose*, they are simply showing you a *rose*! It's simple. Nothing else!

We are the ones that add on stuff. We obscure the reality with the meaning that we project onto the event, do we not? Thus, "no mind" means not doing that. It means having a direct encounter with reality without any interference of your mind, because your mind simply interferes with your contact with reality. When we are trapped in the mind, we never touch reality; we only touch our minds! This becomes the problem. Someone says something to you and you do not even hear what they said. You hear what you "think" they said, what they must have meant by that smart remark and how you are going to deal with them because of that smart remark, and so forth. You have not "heard" anything, because you have never gone beyond your mind. Or, if someone does something for you, immediately your mind begins to wonder, what is the ulterior motive? They must want something, because why else are they doing this thing? The person is just being nice to you, and you have missed the person being nice to you because of your mind! The Buddha said to go *beyond* the mind.

We should have as a goal the ability to be here in this state of "no-mindness," because the ability to abide in this state of no-mindness is to always be in contact with reality, to always be available to reality. Sardarji was talking about the fact that most of us are not receptive and available to grace. In the same way we are not receptive or available to reality. God *is* reality; grace *is* reality. However, we are never available to reality; hence, the suffering.

Whenever we are experiencing suffering, it is only because we are out of touch with reality! If you are in touch with reality, you will not have any experience of suffering at all! On this point, all mystics and saints agree. When one is in synch, in oneness with reality, when one is adapted to reality, there is *never* any experience of suffering. It is actually the opposite experience, the experience of bliss, because reality is God and anywhere you touch God, you will taste bliss! How can you taste anything else? God *is* the energy called happiness and whenever you touch it, you experience happiness. So, if you are not happy, realize that you are just "autistic," just closed into your mind. You are doing what I call "pinching yourself." You are inflicting your own pain. You are *trapped* in your own *mind*.

Bhai Rani: *Everything does not have to be defined. That is what Tiffany and I were talking about, that people have a tendency to always want this extra step and it has to be defined, it has to be categorized, instead of just seeing what is right there in their face. There still has to be more added to it and I was telling Tiff that's crazy because everything doesn't need a definition. It does not have to be broken down.*

You see, Bhai Rani Ra, this is the same thing that Lao-tzu told us. You are speaking very much in the tradition of the great Zen masters, when they tell us that that is the whole key. Do not *add* anything to it. Do not mix mind into it, simply have the experience! Now, if something is beautiful, nothing needs to be added. Just enjoy it! Life is also like that: simply enjoy it and do not add anything to it! Stop tinkering with it. We tinker with reality through our minds and the more we tinker, the worse it gets! We just tinker (think) ourselves into a state of madness, which leads to suffering! Then we wonder why we have anxiety attacks.

All of these things, Bhai Rani Ra, are indicative and reflective of our lack of maturation. The immature ego will *always* be tinkering, will always be into something. It is like children when they are small, they are just always into something. They stick their hands and spoons into sockets and into fire. It is miraculous that any of us make it past the age of two! Thank God for our parents, because if it were not for them, we would have killed ourselves a long time ago! However, that goes with that level of ego development. When we become adults and have carried over these same levels of ego, we just tinker and tinker and scratch and scratch until we turn moles into mountains.

Pam: *That brings to mind another question I wanted to ask. A lot of black nationalists would be stuck at the socio-centric levels and just inherently seeing the difference between white and black, for instance. That came to mind when you were talking about the way we think about people. Because as I started to study our history, I always thought of white people as being a little bit under us in terms of their mental capacity and maybe even the way they conceptually think, always having to break things down, lacking imagination and creativity. I always thought of them as being different from us, maybe not as evolved as we are. You are saying that someone who thinks that way is at the socio-centric level?*

Yes!

Pam: *That is going to be hard for me, because I just kind of think of us as being superior. I really think that!*

One of my friends who is a minister gave a very beautiful example. He said, for instance, that if you take this human body and reduce it to its seventeen fundamental elements of matter, then put a price tag on it, you are talking about approximately one dollar and forty-seven cents worth of material, the matter that actually makes up your body. He said that the interesting thing is that you have this lump of one dollar and forty-seven cents of dirt which thinks it is better than that lump of one dollar and forty-seven cents of matter. This is madness! It is one dollar and forty-seven cents of matter, and that is it!

Your level of ego development shapes your perceptions, your world view, your morality, your sense of needs, all of those things. Now, at the socio/ethnic-centric level of ego development, your morality is that, "Hey, if they are not a part of my group, f--- them!" That is the moral stance of people who are socio-centric: It is just "me" and "mine" and the hell with everybody else!

Pam: *Isn't there a gray area? You might think you are a little better, but you wouldn't want to kill them!*

Pam, trust me: We are not better than *anybody!* It is almost like one table leg saying, "I am better than the wood I am made out of." This is a nonsensical statement, at a higher level. However, at a lower level, it makes perfectly good sense. It is a relative thing; it depends on where you are.

Pam: *It really is relative, because maybe when I look at what has happened to black folks throughout history, I guess I try to make some sense out of it and I think to myself that there must be some reason why we are in this situation.*

You have to understand something really important, Pam, from the historical perspective, because there is a lot of fantasy associated with the rediscovery of our Afrikan history. You have to realize that there were a lot of people in ancient Afrika who were just absolutely insane! The Ptah Hoteps, the Imhoteps, the Kajamis, have always been there, with no exception. However, what we tend to do is compare the best of the past to the worst of the present, and this is an unfair analogy. Plus, it paints a distorted picture of the past, of those glorious "good old days," and you start trying to get back to the past. You become past-oriented. In any epoch, there is always only a *small* percentage of these highly developed human beings. Whether it was three thousand years ago in Kemet, or whether it is three thousand years later in America, there is always only a small percentage. That does not change. The vast majority of us will remain stuck at one of those lower stages of ego development unless we are receptive to the grace, as Sardarji pointed out. A Ptah Hotep *is* superior to ninety-nine point nine percent of all white (*and* black) people. But you? No!

Pam: *Bhagwan, I really want to thank you because I have dealt with this issue for years! I can see the light breaking in and this has been particularly helpful for me. Thank you for really clearing it up. It has just been misperceptions.*

You are most welcome, sister. It is simply *misunderstanding*. Remember, I have said over and over that our suffering is the result of our misunderstanding. There is nothing else to do, but simply work on our understanding. Hence, that is the tremendous value of satsang. Satsang is our opportunity to come together and help each other to try to deepen our understanding, and out of that understanding the transformation occurs, with no struggle at all. When there is that struggle in the transformation, that means that the understanding is not yet mature; hence, the struggle. "I am struggling to do my meditation." You are struggling because the understanding is not yet mature. When the understanding is mature, there is no struggling. It becomes *sahaj*. It becomes easy, natural, like when spring comes and the grass grows by itself. The grass need not do anything. Nature takes care of everything. Similarly, understanding takes care of all transformation. There *is* no struggle. So, it is our great fortune if we can come into contact with the teachings, as Sardarji has told us. That is simply grace, and it deepens our understanding and makes our life a little smoother. And the more our understanding goes on increasing, the smoother our life becomes.

Theresa: *I also have a problem like what she was talking about, but I try to not be bitter and forgive, like the Bible says. Some people try to be on white people's level because they seem to have it all materially, to try to be like them and be accepted by them and at the same time try to stay black. Some of us feel we do not need to be accepted by them, and some feel we should be able to live in an area of mostly white people because we have the same income. It is hard to deal with all of these issues and at the same time understand that they may have caused our suffering.*

I don't know much about the socio-ethnic philosophies. You will have to speak to someone who is much more versed in that. All I can tell you is that at each of these various degrees and levels of ego development, there will always be a justification for a person's moral stance. Their whole philosophy, their whole world view, will be justified based on that level. When one goes to another *level* of ego development, it is simply not an issue. You are living in a very *different* world. Remember, I said that in each shift in identity, you are actually living in a different world.

For example, your son is sitting there, and he is not even concerned with any of this stuff, whether to go to Afrika or the suburbs. Neither of these issues concerns him at all, because his concerns are related to his level of ego development. Now, he is very concerned about that paper, and how that paper will fold into an airplane. However, outside of that, his concerns are small. His morality is that anybody who interferes with him playing with this paper is essentially behaving immorally! His needs are different. He needs some paper! Again, all of our needs, our moral stance, our world views, and the way we rationalize and justify things, are relative to our level of ego development. They are not absolute at all. They are relative.

KARMA OR "MORALITY"?

Pam: *You also said something about how things would happen to you anyway even if you didn't think and that we place too much importance on the thinking process.*

Things are happening to you because of your *karma*. Your thinking is nothing but your reaction to your karma. Karma happens.

For instance, you are going to die under certain circumstances, certain situations. Whether you think about that or not has nothing to do with the fact that that is how you will die. In the same way, things are just happening and your thinking is *your* interpretation of the events that are laid out for you in your karma, your *pralabdh* karma. And the way you are *interpreting* the events of your karma, the way you are thinking, *determines* how much pain you will undergo from each of these events. If I am to have a broken leg, I can agonize over that as much as I like, but if it is in my karma to have a broken leg, I am going to simply have a broken leg. However, I can add anxiety and panic *thinking* to the whole event and, therefore, double and *compound* my own suffering.

You will find, for instance, that people who suffer from anxiety attacks are people who are constantly trying to prevent something "bad" from happening to them. They do not have very deep understanding. What you call "bad" things are going to happen to you; that's life! Life is made up of these so-called "good" and "bad" things. These events themselves are actually "neutral." They are neither good nor bad. It is our interpretation, the spin we put on these neutral events, that results in our experience of bad versus good.

Pam: *So, the thoughts we think are not the things that will ultimately manifest or is that something down the line? Are the things that are happening to us now the things we have already made through karma?*

It is already incorporated in that section of karma you are undergoing in this present birth. Think about it. You have thought about so much stuff. You think about making a million dollars and all kinds of things. You think about being happy, but are you happy as a result of thinking about it? There is no causal connection.

Bhai Rani: *This is probably dumb, but you know how so many of our young black kids are just being killed. Those killings are simply based on karma, Bhagwan? You know, for every action, there is a reaction; you reap what you sow, etc.; all the little cliches that go along with that. There is no accidental anything, shootings, whatever! That is karma?*

You must understand that karma does not have any kind of moral component. Karma is strictly a description of cause and effect. Now, we interpret whether that is right, wrong, moral or immoral based on our own level. Karma simply means that anything going on is the result of some cause. It does not get into a moral thing. Very often, you see, we confuse and/or mingle morality with an understanding of karma. Karma has nothing to do with morality.

Bhai Rani: *That's what Tiff and I had discussions about. This boy's mother buys him a leather jacket and the boy didn't do anything wrong. That is the way it was presented, that he was innocent. He was killed because he had this leather jacket and someone approached him and wanted to take his jacket, but he refused to give up the jacket because he said his mother worked hard for it, and "Why should I have to give up my jacket?" So, he ends up getting shot as a result of that. Is it his karma, because he did something bad in another life?*

Not "bad." You have to be careful about adding that to it. You have to look at it like a physicist. The refusal to give up the jacket triggered the homicide. That was the cause of it. However, karma in a larger sense deals strictly with the physics of it all, not with the moral aspects of it. We add in that moral quality ourselves. Karma simply says that the events, circumstances, and situations which fill your life are the direct outcome of your own actions. Period! Case closed!

Does that mean that when someone does something to you, they do not inherit some consequence from the action towards you? Of course not. They must also play by the same rules. Does that mean that you cannot create new karmas? No, we are constantly creating new karmas. We talked to some degree in the past about these categories of karma and things of that nature, and I am sure we have tapes somewhere. So many of us confuse karma with "morality." The important thing is to simply remember that karma has *nothing* to do with morality.

*   *   *

I want to thank all of you for hanging in there and bearing with me for these past five sessions. I hope you have enjoyed being in this beautiful environment, and we will see what the Lord has in store for us next. I apologize for any boredom I may have caused you to undergo. Life is boring enough, and I certainly do not wish to add to your boredom! In any event, I hope that you got something useful out of these workshops.

Ra shekum maat.

GLOSSARY

Abhyas — lit., "practice"; esoterically, spiritual practices or discipline: meditation; morality; ahimsa, e.g., vegetarianism

Abhyasi — one who performs spiritual practices

Adhikara — qualifications which must be met before one is considered fit to receive sacred knowledge

Adhikari — entitled; worthy; deserving; "marked souls" who are ready for the Path

Adi — primal; first; original

Adi Granth (Adi Granth Sahib) — lit., "primal scripture": sacred scriptures of the Sikhs compiled by Guru Arjan Dev, the fifth Guru in the line of Guru Nanak which contains the teachings of the Sikh Gurus as well as other saints. After the death of the tenth Guru, Guru Gobind Singh, no successor was found, and the book was given the title "Guru Granth Sahib"

Adi shakti — primordial consciousness or energy

Agyani — ignorant person; one who has not received spiritual enlightenment

Agam Lok — unfathomable; inaccessible region; the name of the seventh spiritual region

Aham Brahmasmi — "I am Brahman": a Vedantic saying exclaiming the oneness of the individual soul with Brahman (God); one of four *mahavakyas* ("great saying"), one in each Veda

Ahankar (ahankara) — egotism; the root cause of dualism or illusion of maya; pride; vanity; see *Five Passions*

Ahimsa — the practice of nonviolence toward any living being, either by thought, word or action

Ajna chakra — the spiritual center located between the eyebrows, described as a "two-petalled lotus," which once reached is the beginning of the final stage of sadhana leading to the ultimate attainment, union with the Divine; the sixth of seven energy centers located in the subtle body along the spine; also referred to as the "Guru chakra," since the inner Guru can be envisioned here

Akal — "timeless"; beyond birth and death

Akal Purush (Akal Purkh) — Timeless (*akal*) Being (*purush*): the Lord who is beyond the limits of time; this name is particularly used in the Granth Sahib and means the same as *Sat Purush*

Akasha — ether: sky; heavens; matter that surrounds the earth beyond the air

Akashic records — from the Sanskrit, *akasha* (ether): It is believed that in akasha, or ether, a record of all actions is inscribed, and can be accessed at higher stages of consciousness; a record of the soul's journeys through all of its lifetimes

Allah — the Arabic (Islamic) name for God

Amen — ancient Afrikan term for the state of pure consciousness; nonduality; God-nature

Anahata (anahat) chakra — the "heart" chakra: gives the knowledge of the mind

Anami (Anami Purush) — the "Nameless One;" the Absolute; the Lord of the eighth region

Ananda (anand) — bliss. Also, Buddha's cousin and closest personal companion among his disciples, who was instrumental in preserving the teachings after the Buddha left this world because he was able to remember everything he had heard the Buddha say

Ana-ul-Huq (Ana'l-Haq, An-ul-Haq) — "I am God" or "I am Truth": Arabic phrase proclaimed upon realization of oneness with God

Anda — the lower portion of Brahmand above the physical region (Pind); astral region

Andi man — the second level of mind which houses all psychic abilities, and corresponds to the Anda region; astral mind

Anuk Ausar — ancient Afrikan phrase which means "I am this (God)," exclaimed upon realizing oneness with God

Anurag Sagar — lit., "ocean of love"; the title of a book by Kabir

Apar — boundless; without form

Aparigraha (apregreha) — freedom from greed and covetousness

Arhat (arahat, arahant) — one who has traversed the Eightfold Path and attained the highest level of the Hinayana path, beyond rebirth, and enters nirvana at the end of his or her life

Aristotle (384-322 B.C.) — one of the most famous philosophers of ancient Greece and student of Plato; tutored Alexander the Great

Arjuna — the hero of the Mahabharata and chief disciple of Lord Krishna. It was to him that Krishna explained the doctrine known as the Bhagavad-Gita

Arupa (arup, aroop) — without form

Asana (asan) — posture for sitting in meditation or yoga. Proper posture should be with the back, neck and head erect, in an easy and natural position, which makes it possible to forget the body and concentrate the mind on the mantra or object of contemplation

Ashram — a center of spiritual study or meditation; retreat; monastery

Asteya (astaiya) — not to steal; abstaining from theft

Astral body — the "subtle body," which houses the mind and all psychic abilities; one of three bodies possessed by animate beings, which corresponds to the astral region

Astral region — the level of consciousness between the physical and causal planes; also known as *Sahansdal Kanwal*; Anda region

Atma (atman) — Supreme Self; spirit; soul

Ausar — the indwelling Self

Avatar (avatara) — an incarnation of divinity. According to Hindu belief, God as Vishnu descends into the creation in various ages. Avatars take birth as the result of free will, not as a consequence of past deeds and tendencies; among those widely accepted as avatars are Buddha, Christ, Krishna, Rama and Ramakrishna

Avidya (avijja) — ignorance; the fundamental root of evil, and the ultimate cause of the desire which creates the dukkha of existence

Awagawan — "coming and going"; cycle of birth and death; reincarnation; see *Chaurasi*

Ba — ancient Afrikan word for the Universal Spirit; total consciousness; bliss

Bachan — word; discourse; instruction; command

Bani — lit., "sound"; teachings, particularly of the Saints, whether oral or written; esoterically, the inner sound or shabd

Banknal — lit., "crooked tunnel"; the path, smaller than the eye of a needle, through which the soul passes when ascending from the first to the second spiritual region

Bhagavad-Gita — lit., "Song of God": a dialogue between Lord Krishna and His friend and foremost disciple, Arjuna, in which Krishna reveals the nature of the Self and the paths to achieve God-realization; part of the Indian epic poem, the *Mahabharata*; the Hindu bible

Bhagwan — Lord; also a term of respect and esteem applied to great spiritual personalities

Bhajan — esoterically, the practice of listening to the sound current or shabd, and with the Guru as a guide, one can traverse higher spiritual realms; hymns or devotional songs; see *Surat Shabd Yoga*

Bhakti — devotion to the Divine; worship; spiritual practice

Bhakti marg — path of devotion

Bhakti Yoga — the path of devotion to God; the discipline of love. One of the four main yogas to achieve union with God, bhakti yoga is the most natural path to God-realization; see *Jnana Yoga, Karma Yoga* and *Raja Yoga*

Bhana — the will or pleasure of the Lord; to be content with one's lot in life, accepting it as Divine will

Bhanwar Gupha — revolving (Bhanwar) cave (Gupha), the fourth spiritual region; the stage of Self-realization

Bhikkhu (bhikshu) — a member of the Buddhist sangha, usually a mendicant monk, who has devoted himself to following the path by renunciation of the world; nun, *bhikkhuni*

Bodhi — enlightenment

Bodhichitta — lit., the "mind of enlightenment." On the relative level, the wish to obtain buddhahood for the sake of all beings; on the absolute level, the direct insight into the ultimate nature of reality

Bodhisattva (bodhisatta) — one whose sole wish is to benefit all sentient beings and who has put off his or her own attainment of complete enlightenment, or buddhahood, for the sake of the enlightenment of all others; the ideal of the Mahayana Path, as contrasted with the arahat of the Hinayana. Bodhisattvas are often called "Buddhas of Compassion"

Bodhi (bo) tree — the sacred fig tree at Buddh-Gaya under which Gautama Buddha attained *nirvana*

Brahm — Lord of the second spiritual region (Trikuti); the ruler of the three worlds (physical, astral and causal); the power that creates and dissolves the phenomenal world; the Universal Mind; Kal

Brahma — one of the Hindu Trinity, the God of creation, the creator of this universe; in Buddhism, defined as ruler of the gods of the world of form

Brahmacharya — the practice of celibacy

Brahman — in Hinduism, the Ultimate Reality; the Absolute Existence of Godhead, the transcendental Reality of Vedanta philosophy. Brahman (or *Brahmin*) also refers to a member of the priestly class, the highest in the ancient Indian caste system; see *Caste*

Brahmand (Brahmanda) — lit., the "egg of Brahm"; the grand division of the universe extending from *Anda* to *Bhanwar Gupha*, over which Brahm has jurisdiction; home of Universal mind

Brahmandi mind — the highest of three levels of mind in the physical universe; Universal Mind; causal mind

Buddha — lit., "the Enlightened One": derived from the root *budh* (to know), one who has attained *nirvana*, an "awakened one." Specif., Prince Gautama Siddhartha (ca. 563-483 B.C.), who renounced great wealth to become a wandering ascetic in India, and upon whose teachings Buddhism is based. He declared that Dharma was for all regardless of caste or sex, traveled and taught for forty-five years and established orders of monks and nuns; see *Tathagata*

Buddha nature — the pure nature of mind; the potential of buddhahood present in all beings; the nature of everything

Buddhi (*buddh*) — the discriminative faculty in the individual; intellect; spiritual wisdom; Universal Mind; the link between Universal Reality and mind (manas)

Buddhism — religion founded ca. 525 B.C., based on the following doctrines as taught by Gautama Buddha: the Four Noble Truths; Nirvana; and the Eightfold Path. Buddhism declined gradually in India, but attracted an increasing number of followers elsewhere, and there are various sects and practices; a central goal is the attainment of Nirvana; see *Hinayana, Mahayana*

Caliph — "supreme ruler": the title taken by Muhammad's successors as secular and religious heads of Islam

Caste — four divisions of Hindu society: *Brahman* or *Brahmin* (priests and scholars—the highest); *kshatriya* (warriors and rulers), *vaisya* or *vaishya* (merchants, farmers and artisans) and *sudra* or *shudra* (laborers and servants). A pattern of social organization that was intended to define responsibility and patterns of social interdependence, it became a means of oppression by one section of society over another, and even persuaded people that they had less or no right to worship God

Causal body — the third body possessed by animate beings where all karmas are stored, which corresponds to the causal region

Causal region — the level of consciousness above the astral plane; the second spiritual region; region of Universal Mind; Trikuti

Chakra — lit., "wheel": a center of conscious energy in the subtle body, along the central spinal canal (*sushumna*), which can only be experienced through spiritual practice. There are six main chakras: *muladhara*, near the rectum; *svadhishthana*, between the navel and sexual organ; *manipura*, near the navel; *anahata*, near the heart center; *vishuddha*, in the throat; and *ajna*, in the space between the eyebrows. There is a seventh, the *sahasrara*, located in the crown of the head, and when it is activated by the *kundalini*, one realizes oneness with God (*samadhi*)

Charan Das (1703-1839) — eighteenth century Indian mystic from Rajasthan known for his poetry. He practiced Surat Shabd Yoga; Master of Sahjo Bai

Charan Singh Ji Maharaj (1916-1990) — a double graduate in law and arts, He was appointed by Sardar Bahadur Maharaj Jagat Singh, in absentia, and presided over the Radha Soami Colony in Beas (Punjab), India from 1951-1990. During that time, He authored numerous books on Sant Mat and initiated hundreds of thousands of disciples; Bhagwan Ra Afrika's Guru

Chaurasi — lit., "eighty four"; hence, "the wheel of eighty-four": the 8,400,000 species in creation through which souls may have to incarnate before gaining a human form; the wheel of transmigration; reincarnation; see *Awagawan*

Chela — disciple; seeker

Chetan — conscious; awakened; spirit; intelligence; same as *chaitanya*: conscious life force as opposed to *jar* (inert or inanimate) existence

Chit (*chiti*) — divine conscious energy; pure consciousness; the active or creative aspect of God; the power which manifests the Universe

Chitta — in Yoga terminology, the mind-stuff, whose three components are *manas, buddhi*, and *ahankar*

Christianity — the world's largest religion based on the Old Testament and the teachings of Jesus Christ; Christ is the adhesive that holds the differing and sometimes antagonistic groups together

Chuang-tzu (ca. 369-286 B.C.) — Chinese sage, philosopher and leading Taoist authority, noted for his satirical essays, and said to have lived as a hermit

Dadu (1544-1603) — Muslim saint of Rajasthan, a cotton carder by trade, known for his bold speeches in beautiful poetry and the teaching of Surat Shabd Yoga; also known as Dadu Dayal, the "Compassionate One," for his extremely compassionate nature

Dan — charity; service with wealth—use of one's resources for the welfare of the poor

Darshan — lit., "seeing"; implies looking intently at the Master with one-pointed attention (outer darshan); inner darshan takes place when the disciple goes inside through meditation and encounters the Radiant Form of the Master

Daswan Dwar — lit., "the tenth door"; the third region above the physical, which is actually the first level of the spiritual realm; the tenth aperture or door leading from Trikuti; Daswan Dwar is Sunn and Maha Sunn combined

Dayal — merciful; compassionate; an epithet of the Supreme Being

Dhammapada — the famous Pali scripture on spiritual life ascribed to the Buddha

Dharma (dhamma) — various meanings, and is most commonly translated as the "teachings," from all religions, Christian, Hindu, etc. Buddhist teachings are called the Buddhadharma. In its widest sense it means all that can be known, everything that exists; Ultimate Reality; law; truth; duty; righteousness

Dhunatmak (dhunatmik, dhunyatmak nam) — the inexpressible primal sound, which cannot be written or spoken nor heard with the physical ears; the inner music which can only be experienced by the soul; another name for Shabd; see *Nam*

Dhyan — to "see"; attention; namely, to contemplate on the form of the Master at the eye center during meditation in order to achieve concentration, which is the second aspect of spiritual practice in Surat Shabd Yoga, the others being simran and bhajan

Dhyana — "meditation"; the Sanskrit word of which *Ch'an* and *Zen* are Chinese and Japanese transliterations

Dravidians — lit., "the blacks": a race of people of the Indus Valley in India over 3,500 years ago, who were oppressed by an Aryan invasion around 1,000 B.C.

Drishti — a special gaze or merciful glance bestowed by the Satguru; also, inner attention and grace of the Master

Dukkha (dukha, dukh) — suffering; sorrow; the assertion that all life is suffering is one of the "Four Noble Truths" of the Buddha

Ego — the self that believes it is separate from God which, in turn, is the cause of all samsara and suffering; "I"-consciousness

Einstein, Albert (1879-1955) — German-born Jewish theoretical physicist, who formulated the theory of relativity and wrote on religion in his later years; he applied the term Cosmic Religion to his acknowledgment of God

Eye center — also referred to as the tenth door or the "third eye": the space between the eyebrows where a spiritual aspirant focuses the attention during meditation in order to pass to a higher level of consciousness. It is known in different cultures and religions by different terms; see *Tisra til*

Fakir (faqir) — a Muslim sage or holy man; (usually wandering) ascetic or mendicant

Five passions — also called the "five perversions of mind" or "five negative state of mind": lust (*kam*); anger (*krodh*); greed (*lobh*); attachment (*moh*); and vanity or egotism (*ahankar*), which keep man attached to the outer world. The antidotes are: lust–chastity, continence (*shil*); anger–forgiveness, tolerance (*kshama*); greed–contentment (*santosha*); attachment–discrimination (*vivek*) or detachment (*vairagya*); vanity–humility (*dinta*)

Five poisons — in Buddhism, the five negative emotions: (1) bewilderment (ignorance, confusion); (2) attachment (or desire); (3) aversion (including hatred, anger); (4) jealousy; and (5) pride

Four Noble Truths of the Buddha — (1) all existence is suffering; (2) the cause of suffering is selfish craving, desire for separate existence; (3) the cessation of suffering is attained by the elimination of this thirst for separate existence; and (4) the way to the ceasing of suffering is attained by following the Noble Eightfold Path; see *Noble Eightfold Path*

Fromm, Erich (1900-1980) — American psychoanalyst, born in Germany, who explored the individual's sense of isolation and estrangement in modern society and authored *Psychoanalysis and Religion*, 1950

Gaddi — throne; seat where the Master sits while giving discourse or satsang

Guda chakra — the first and lowest of the six chakras in the human body; the rectal plexus, also called *mul (muladhara) chakra*

Guna — lit., "quality" or "attribute"; one of three types of energy: *sattva*—harmony, calmness or purity; *rajas*—activity, restlessness, passion; and *tamas*—inertia, ignorance, darkness, which are present in varying degrees (according to the individual) in human nature; the three attributes or qualities out of which creation proceeds. The predominance of a particular guna creates corresponding tendencies in behavior: *satoguna* produces generosity, kindness, contentment, wisdom, understanding; *rajoguna* produces assertiveness, ambition, competition, envy, pride; and *tamoguna* produces sluggishness, ignorance, selfishness, resentment, vengeance

Gurbani — lit., "teachings of the Guru"; what has been written in a particular book such as the *Ra Ananda Sutra*, *Sar Bachan*, etc., and especially the Sikh scriptures (*Granth Sahib* the *Dasham Granth*); esoterically, Nam, Shabd or Word

Gurdwara — a Sikh temple

Guru — lit., "one who gives light"; Master; spiritual teacher

Guru bhakti (gurbhakti) — devotion to the Guru

Gurumukh (gurmukh) — lit., "one whose face is turned towards the Guru"; one who has completely surrendered himself to the Guru, as opposed to *manmukh*, a slave of the mind

Guru Nanak (1469-1539) — the first in a line of ten Sikh Gurus, whose teachings are recorded in the Adi Granth, He condemned the orthodox creed that was based on rituals and ceremonies and emphasized the spiritual aspect of religion

Guru Sahib — an honorific used to refer to any Guru; used especially in the Sikh community to refer to the ten Gurus in the line of Guru Nanak; whichever Guru or saint is being spoken about or written about is referred to as Guru Sahib, meaning that particular Guru

Gyan — spiritual knowledge or wisdom; true knowledge

Gyani — lit., "one who possesses knowledge"; in modern times the term is mostly confined to intellectuals or those proficient in theological knowledge

Gyan yoga — the form of yoga which attempts to achieve God-realization through the acquisition of knowledge

Haj — pilgrimage to Mecca, sacred to the Muslims; see also *Mecca*

Haq — lit., "truth"; reality; God

Hatha yoga — this yoga derives its name from the Sanskrit *ha* (sun) and *tha* (moon), and involves the attainment of samadhi through the balancing of pranas which flow through the *pingala* (sun) and *ida* (moon) nadis. By diligently performing, under expert supervision physical exercises, including *asanas*, *kriyas* and *pranayama*, the pranas can be made to merge and flow into the *sushumna*; when this energy rises to the *sahasrara* chakra, Self-realization occurs

Hazrat — holy man; a title of veneration among the Muslims

Hekau — Afrikan term for "words of power," i.e. mantras

Heru — Afrikan word for the faculty that determines will in man

Hinayana — historically, the earliest school of Buddhism; also known as Theravada (the "Teachings of the Elders"), its only surviving sect. The teachings of a method of personal liberation which permits one to leave the cycle of suffering (samsara) and attain nirvana, its ideal is arhathood; also known as the "Small Vehicle"

Hinduism — the oldest of the world's contemporary religions, Hinduism began in India ca. 1500 B.C. and has the third largest number of adherents after Christianity and Islam. The major texts are the *Vedas* and the *Bhagavad-Gita*. The only reality is Brahman. Life is viewed as a continuing cycle of birth and rebirth and the goal is Nirvana and reunion with Brahma

Homen (homain) — egotism; I-ness; separateness

Hukam (hukm) — order; command; esoterically Shabd, Nam or Word

Huzur — term of respect used in addressing kings, holy men or high personages

Huzur Maharaj Ji — a term usually used when referring to one's own Master

Ida — the nadi or subtle channel which extends from the muladhara to the ajna chakra running alongside the sushumna and ending above the base of the left nostril; it is referred to as the "moon" nadi because of its cooling nature

Imam — Muslim spiritual leader

Ishta (isht) — the chosen ideal; goal; object of worship

Islam — founded by Prophet Muhammad in 622 A.D., Islam has become the world's second largest religion. It is based on Allah's revelations to Muhammad, which were incorporated into the Koran; followers have five fundamental duties, including prayer five times daily and one pilgrimage to Mecca in one's lifetime

Jagrat — waking level of consciousness, although moments of "genuine" wakefulness are fleeting

Jainism — an Indian religion founded in fourth century B.C. by Mahavira which teaches the potential divinity of every soul. Liberation is achieved through right faith, right knowledge and right conduct, with a special emphasis on ahimsa (nonviolence)

Japa (jap) — recitation; prayer; repetition, usually silently, of a mantra; see *Simran*

Jiva (jiv) — the individual soul or human self. Philosophically speaking, jiva is the atman identified with its coverings: body, mind, senses, etc. Ignorant of its divinity, it experiences birth and death, pleasure and pain

Jivatman (jivatma) — the atman manifesting itself as the individual self; spirit embodied in the physical form

Jnana yoga — the path of knowledge; the yoga of attaining supreme wisdom through intellectual inquiry; one of the four main yogas practiced to achieve union with the Divine; see *Gyan*

Judaism — the term "Judaism" is relatively new; in ancient times it was called *Torah*. Central to the written Torah are the five books of Moses (the Pentateuch), the first five books of the Christian Old Testament. Thirty-four books were added later to form the Hebrew Bible. Judaism encompasses a broad range of beliefs and practices and each synagogue is run by its congregation and is free to choose its own rabbi. Jews consider themselves the chosen people of God

Jung, Carl Gustav (1875-1961) — Swiss psychologist and psychiatrist; founded analytical psychology; propounded a collective unconscious and stressed the individual's need for internal harmony (individuation)

Jyoti (jot) — light; flame; esoterically, the light of the first spiritual region, Sahansdal Kanwal

Ka — ancient Afrikan word for the "inner body," the astral body

Kabbalah — system of Jewish theosophy and mysticism

Kabir (1440-1518) — illiterate Indian poet-saint, born a Muslim, worked as a weaver in Benares. Though the details of his birth and death are vague, it is well known that He denounced the rituals and customs of religion and practiced and taught Surat Shabd Yoga. Early in his life He became a discipline of the Hindu saint Ramananda; some of His writings were recorded in the *Adi Granth*

Kal — lit., "time" or "death"; negative power, the ruler of the three worlds (physical, astral and causal), which are all under the law of karma; also called Brahm; Dharam Rai, Lord of Judgment; and Yama, the Lord of Death

Kalpa — Buddhist term for an age or epoch; an extremely long period of time

Kama (kam) — lust; desire of the senses, especially sexual desire

Karma (kamma; karam)—action; the law of cause and effect; justice. There are three types: (1) *pralabdh* (or *prarabdh*) —fate or destiny karma experienced in the present life caused by past actions; (2) *kriyaman*—the debts and credits created by actions in this life to be reaped in future lives; and (3) *sinchit* (or *sanchit*)—the remainder or store of unpaid karma from past lives. The soul cannot escape from the cycle of death and rebirth and reunite with its source until its karmic account is fully settled

Karma yoga — one of the four main paths to union with the Divine: the path of selfless action; doing karmas without desire for reward

Kaya — "body." In the Mahayana, there are three aspects of a body of a buddha: (1) *dharmakaya*, the body of dharma or truth, the absolute buddha nature; (2) *sambhogakaya*, the body of enjoyment, the aspect of buddha nature which communicates the dharma; and (3) *nirmanakaya*, the body of creation, in which the buddha nature manifests itself on earth, taken in order to free beings from samsara

Khu — ancient Afrikan term for the higher Self, a state of consciousness beyond mind

King, Martin Luther, Jr. (1929-1968) — American clergyman and civil rights leader who won the Nobel Peace Prize in 1964 for his nonviolent resistance to racial injustice; assassinated in 1968

Koan — in Zen, a nonsensical question or problem asked of a student to force him, through contemplation, to a greater awareness of reality, e.g., the sound of one hand clapping

Koran (*Quran* or *Qur'an*) — Holy Scriptures of Islam revealed to Prophet Muhammad

Kosha — sheath, covering of the soul. There are five koshas: (1) *annamaya-kosha*, the gross physical sheath (body); (2) *pranamaya-kosha*, the subtle or vital sheath which vitalizes body and mind (breath); (3) *manomaya-kosha*, the mind sheath which receives sense impressions; (4) *vijnanamaya-kosha*, the sheath of intellect, the discriminative faculty; and (5) *anandamaya-kosha*, the sheath of bliss (ego or causal body), which is nearest the blissful Atman (spirit)

Krishna, Lord — lit., "Dark one": Hindu saint held to have been a manifestation of the Supreme Being and who was the teacher of the *Bhagavad-Gita*; an incarnation of Vishnu, the preserver, one of the Gods of the Hindu triad (Brahma, the creator; Vishnu; and Shiva, the destroyer)

Krishnamurti, J. (1895-1986) — spiritual teacher, born into a Brahmin family in South India, who spent his formative years affiliated with the Theosophical Society and who stressed that the teacher was unimportant—only the teachings—and the need to know one's self (to examine the "I")

Kriya — a gross (physical) or subtle (mental, emotional) purificatory movement initiated by the awakened kundalini. Kriyas purify the body and nervous system so as to allow a seeker to endure the energy of higher states of consciousness

Kriya yoga — ancient form of yoga which utilizes a simple method to decarbonize the blood through control of the breath or life force; preliminary disciplines of raja yoga, which consist of three steps:

austerity; study (the reading of holy books and japa); and dedication of the fruits of one's work to God

Kun — Muslim name for God, meaning Allah, the High, the All-in-All; also means shabd or word; "Be," the command (hukam) God is said to have spoken at the time of creation of the universe

Kundalini — lit., "coiled up," or the "serpent": the energy lying dormant in humans at the base of the spine (*muladhara* chakra), which when awakened by spiritual practice and passes through the chakras, gradually purifies the individual and leads to states of higher consciousness. The practice of kundalini yoga should only be done under the guidance of a qualified Master or Guru. Also called the *adi shakti* or supreme energy; *chiti* (universal Consciousness); in Japanese, it is called *ki*, in Chinese, *chi*, in Christianity the *Holy Spirit*

Lama — in Tibetan Buddhism, a spiritual teacher or Guru

Lao-tzu (born ca. 571 B.C.) — Chinese sage and keeper of the imperial archives in the Chou dynasty, who reportedly wrote the *Tao Te Ching* and founded Taoism. He taught devotion to Nam or the Tao; there is disagreement about whether He is a historical or legendary figure

Lila (*leela*) — the divine play in which God is said to enact all the roles; sport; also means the Relative (which consists of time, space and causation)

Lotus feet — a translation of the term *charan* which lit. means "revered feet," having a connotation of love and respect. When used in reference to a spiritual Master, it designates the Master's Radiant Form

Ma — lit., "Mother"; women saints and the Goddess Shakti are frequently referred to as Ma in India

Maat — various meanings, generally means balance or order; also truth or karma (justice)

Maat Seba — a teacher of maat (spiritual balance) to those who can be taught

Maha — lit., "great," i.e. mahatma, "great soul," or mahadeva, "great god"

Mahakashyapa — one of the Buddha's foremost disciples; according to the Zen tradition, the first patriarch of the dharma. After the Buddha left this world, He was entrusted with the responsibility for maintaining the teachings and the sangha

Maha maya — the highest form of maya, illusion; the appellation of the deity presiding over the throat center; see *Shakti*

Maharaj — lit., "Great King"; a title of respect

Mahasamadhi — lit., "the great samadhi," or superconscious state; usually refers to the final absorption in the Divine of an illumined soul when the body is given up

Maha sunn — the "great void"; an inner spiritual region of impenetrable darkness above Daswan Dwar proper and below Bhanwar Gupha that is devoid of matter. It can only be crossed with the help of a Master

Mahavira (Mahavir) — sixth century B.C. saint who founded Jainism, a sect of Hinduism, and was the first to bring about a change in the social and spiritual status of women in India. Mahavira means "Great Hero"

Mahayana — the school of the "Great Vehicle": the teachings of the Buddha that emphasize the path of the *bodhisattva*, which is the method of attaining buddhahood with the motivation of *bodhichitta*, solely to help liberate all sentient beings from samsara

Mahdi — the expected messiah of the Muslim tradition

Man — mind (pronounced "mun")

Manas — mind; the discriminative or rational faculty in man, which is essentially dual in nature, i.e. lower mind and higher mind

Manmukh — lit., "facing the mind"; one who obeys the dictates of the mind; a person dominated by the ego

Mansur, al-Hallaj (870-923) — Persian Sufi mystic, whose full name was Hussain-bin-Mansur. For proclaiming *Ana-al-Haq!* ("I am God!") in a state of ecstasy, he was executed for heresy

Mantra — holy words given to a disciple at the time of initiation which are used to develop concentration in meditation. Repetition of the mantra (japa) performed regularly and reverently results in purification of the mind and, ultimately, God-realization; God in the form of sound; a prayer; see *Simran*

Maslow, Abraham H. (1898-1970) — American psychologist and educator; authored *Religions, Values, and Peak-Experiences*, 1964

Mat — creed; system; way; religion; teachings

Mauj — wave; will; especially the will and pleasure of the Satguru or Supreme Being

Maya — illusion; phenomena, all of which impermanent, and therefore, unreal, and produces samsara and suffering; name given to the Goddess Shakti

Mecca — city in Saudi Arabia, the birthplace of Prophet Muhammad. The shrine of Ka'ba in Mecca is a place of Islamic pilgrimage called *haj*, and every Muslim is expected to go there at least once

Meditation — technically speaking, the state of prolonged concentration, achieved through repeated practice, which usually consists of the use of a mantra and the focusing of one-pointed attention on an object or deity; there are numerous forms of meditation

Men Ab em Aungk Em Maat — "keeping the heart stable to live truth": the meditation technique for transcending the emotions in the Kemetic tradition; called *satipatthana* (right or stable mindfulness) in esoteric Buddhism

Metu Neter — a two-volume work by Ra Un Nefer Amen I, published by Khamit Corp., based on the Great Oracle of Tehuti and the Egyptian System of Spiritual Cultivation

Mira Bai (*Mirabai*) (1498-1547) — famous Indian mystic, a Rajput princess who married the Prince of Chittor, devoted Her life to spiritual practice, and was exiled by Her husband. Though in Her youth She was a devotee of Sri Krishna, She was later initiated into the mystic path by Ravi Das, the cobbler, and Her devotional songs are still widely sung in Rajasthan and other parts of India

Moksha (*moksh*) — salvation; redemption; ultimate release or liberation of the soul from the cycle of birth and death; *mukti* has the same meaning

Moses — Biblical prophet of the Jews in the Old Testament, is thought to have been born in the late 14th Century B.C. in Egypt. According to tradition, he was brought up in the Pharaoh's court and eventually led his people out of Egyptian captivity to Sinai; received the Ten Commandments from God

Muhammad (570-632) — wealthy prophet and founder of Islam, born in Mecca (Arabia), He was called the "Prophet of Allah." He preached the worship of the formless God and was against idolatry; his revelations are set forth in the Koran (or Qur'an)

Mullah — a Muslim spiritual teacher or leader; a priest

Muni — a holy man; sage; seer; lit. one who hears or experiences within

Muntu — God; man: Afrikan term used to refer to man in all of his different levels of being, all the way up to God, to remind him of his true nature

Mureed — in Sufism, the disciple

Murshid — Sufi Satguru or Master

Mysticism — the belief that direct knowledge of God can be attained, and recognition of the essential unity of life, the goal of mysticism is the "experience of reality" (*nirvana* or *samadhi*) while living in a human body

Nad (*nada*) — divine music or sounds which are heard in meditation; shabd

Nadi — pathway of energy (prana) in the human body. In the physical body, nadis take the form of blood vessels, nerves and lymph ducts; in the subtle body they form a complex system of 720 million astral tubes through which the prana flows, the most important of which are ida, pingala and sushumna; also pertains to nad (shabd)

Nam — the Sound Current; the inner sounds or melodies one experiences during meditation; Nad; Logos; Word; see *Shabd*

Nam bhakti — devotion to Nam

Namaste — lit., "Salutation to you"; a popular greeting throughout India, made by placing the palms together, thumbs against the chest, and nodding the head slightly

Nar narayan devi (*nari narayani deh*) — the human form, in which God resides and can be realized; the "temple of God"

Naropa (1016-1100) — Indian pandita and siddha, the disciple of Tilopa and teacher of Marpa the Translator

Neti, neti — "not this, not this," meaning this is not the Self, not Reality; used by some practitioners to focus the attention during meditation

Nijman (*nij man*) — the real, innermost higher mind, corresponding to the causal body

Nij rup — lit., "one's own" real form

Nirat — the soul's faculty of seeing the light within; see *Surat Shabd Yoga*

Nirvana (*nibbana*) — in Buddhism, the supreme goal: the state of enlightenment characterized by extinction or absorption of the ego; union with Ultimate Reality. Once is attained, one is released from the limitations of existence, from rebirth and suffering

Nirvikalpa samadhi (*nirbikalpa*) — lit., "changeless samadhi": the supreme transcendental state of consciousness in which all sense of duality is transcended, and one is absorbed in the Supreme Reality

Niyama — observance of certain virtues; the second of the eight limbs of raja yoga. The virtues are purity (physical and mental); contentment; austerity; study (reading of holy books as well as japa); and devotion to God

Noble Eightfold Path — the Way to the cessation of suffering as taught by the Buddha, which consists of: (1) right understanding; (2) right purpose (aspiration); (3) right speech; (4) right conduct; (5) right vocation; (6) right effort; (7) right alertness; and (8) right concentration. Note: not to be confused with the Eightfold Path of Patanjali

Om (Aum) — the sound symbol of God (Brahm in Hindu); audible life stream or sound of the second spiritual region; repetition of Om is used as part of the meditation practice in some spiritual traditions

Omkar (Onkar) — Brahm; esoterically, the Lord of the second spiritual region

Pandit (pundit) — learned; wise; member of the Hindu priestly class

Paramita — perfection; the six (or ten) stages of spiritual perfection followed by the bodhisattva in his progress to Buddhahood: charity, morality, patient resignation, zeal, meditation and contemplation, or wisdom. Sometimes the following four are added: skillful means of teaching, power over obstacles, spiritual aspiration, and knowledge, these last four being regarded as expansions of prajna, wisdom

Param Sant — supreme saint; one who has reached the highest spiritual stage

Parampara — spiritual tradition

Paranirvana — "Beyond Nirvana," the state into which one who has attained nirvana passes at death, in which form completely dissolves into the dharmakaya

Par Brahm — lit., "Beyond Brahm"; appellation of the Lord of the third spiritual region

Parshad (prasad) — Grace; blessing; substance or food blessed by a Saint or Master and infused by him with a small amount of his spiritual essence (*shakti*); also, food that has been offered to one's deity before being consumed

Patanjali — the foremost ancient exponent of yoga, thought to have existed ca. 200 B.C., who wrote the *Yoga Sutras*, which is known as the Eightfold Path; see *Yoga Sutras*

Pind (Pinda) — physical universe; the lowest division of creation; physical body

Pindi man — the ordinary (lower) aspect of mind that governs the physical body and senses

Pingala — the nadi or subtle channel which extends from the muladhara to the ajna chakra running alongside the sushumna and ending above the base of the right nostril; it is referred to as the "sun" nadi because of its heating nature

Pir — Murshid, Master in the Sufi tradition

Plato (ca. 428-348 B.C.) — Greek philosopher; the most distinguished and loyal disciple of Socrates; the entire philosophy of Socrates is known through Plato's books

Prajna — transcendental wisdom acquired through contemplation and deep meditation: the awareness that the mind is the basis or fundamental reality of all things

Prakriti — nature; matter as opposed to spirit; jyoti; maya; female energy; the shakti or female energy of any deity

Prana (pran) — life force which sustains the body and universe; breath; primal energy. Yoga divides the prana in the human body into five types according to the functions it performs: *prana* controls the breath; *apana* controls the elimination of waste matter; *samana* distributes nourishment; *vyana* moves the body parts; *udana* is the upward force in the *sushumna* and which, when activated, moves one toward Self-realization

Pranayama (pranayam) — the control of the vital energy (prana) through the practice of breathing exercises; the fourth of the eight limbs of raja yoga. Unless rules of strict continence and diet are observed and supervision by a competent teacher is obtained, the practice of pranayama may produce mental and physical disorders

Ptah Hotep — ancient Afrikan sage and vizier (high government official)

Pundit — learned; scholar; member of the Hindu priestly class

Purush — male creative energy, as distinguished from Prakriti; man; mind; also denotes Niranjan as well as the Supreme Being

Purusha (purush) — the soul, conceived as individual or as universal (the soul of the universe); one of the two ultimate realities postulated by the Sankhya system of orthodox Hindu philosophy, Purusha denotes the Self, the Absolute, Pure Consciousness. In Vedanta philosophy, Purusha denotes the Atman

Ra — ancient Afrikan term for the vital life force symbolically represented by the sun

Radha Soami (or *Swami*) — Swami means "Lord" and Radha means "Soul," hence, "Lord of the Soul"; the Supreme Being

Radiant Form — the inner form of the Master, contacted by the disciple through concentration on the Word

Raja Yoga — lit., "royal yoga"; one of the four main yogas, systemized in the *Yoga Sutras* of Patanjali: path of formal meditation consisting of concentrating the mind on the Ultimate Reality until the ego is transcended and the complete experience of "oneness" is achieved. The eight limbs of raja yoga are: (1) *yama*; (2) *niyama*; (3) *asana*; (4) *pranayama*; (5) *pratyahara*; (6) *dharana*; (7) *dhyana*; (8) *samadhi*

Ram (Rama) — God; shabd; the power that pervades everywhere. Also the name of the son of King Dasaratha of Ayodhya, believed to be an incarnation of Vishnu

Ramana Maharshi — born in 1879 as Venkataraman Iyer in South India, to overcome His fear of death, He investigated the fear by imitating a corpse, distancing Himself from body and mind, and became God-realized. He recommended concentration on the "I" or meditation on "Who am I?" as a way to God-realization

Ra shekum maat — a gesture of respect for the "power" of God and the Divinity residing in everyone; same as the Hindi *namaste*

Ravi Das (Ravidas) — cobbler saint of the sixteenth century India, who was a brother disciple of Kabir and the Master of Mira Bai, and who taught the Path of devotion to the Word; some of His compositions were included in the *Adi Granth*

Reincarnation — the succession of birth, death and rebirth which results from man's ignorance of his divinity. This ignorance is the result of his mistaken identification with the body, mind, intellect and ego

Ren — Kemetic (Afrikan) word for name

Rigpa — the true nature of mind; "buddha nature"; enlightenment; the realization that everything is a manifestation and projection of one's own mind

Rinpoche — a term of respect meaning "Precious One," given to highly revered teachers in Tibetan Buddhism

Rishi — lit., "seer"; any of the ancient Hindu seers to whom knowledge of the Vedas was revealed; sage or saint

Roshi — Zen Master

Rupa (rup, roop) — form, one of the five skandhas

Sach Khand — "true region," the fifth spiritual region presided over by Sat Purush (the true Lord); the realm of pure spirit where the soul merges into its source; also called *Sat Lok* or *Sat Desh*

Sadhana — spiritual practice or discipline, e.g., meditation, morality, ahimsa

Sadhu (sadh) — holy man; a monk or ascetic, usually a wanderer; mystic; esoterically, one who has reached the third spiritual stage and crossed the region of mind and matter

Sahaj (sehj) — easy; natural; the natural state of the soul

Sahaj (sahaja) samadhi — lit., "natural meditation": the state in which one remains fully alert and experiences divine consciousness throughout all daily activities

Sahaj yoga — same as Surat Shabd Yoga

Sahansdal Kanwal (Sahasradal Kamal) — the "thousand-petalled lotus"; the first spiritual region above the physical; the astral region

Sahasrara — the topmost spiritual center located in the crown of the head and described as a "thousand-petalled lotus", by which after being reached by the kundalini, the soul attains the state of samadhi; in the spiritual practitioner, the exit for the spirit (consciousness) at the time of death

Sahib — Lord or Honorable Sir; a term of respect

Sahjo Bai (Sehjo Bai) — eighteenth century female poet-saint of Rajasthan who lived as a householder and was a disciple of Charan Das; Her poems are full of love and devotion for the Master

Sakya — the tribe into which Buddha was born

Sakyamuni — the sage of the Sakyas, i.e. Buddha

Salat — Sufi term for prayer

Samadhi — deep state of concentration in which all consciousness of the outer world is transcended and one experiences the Supreme Reality and becomes Self-realized, which occurs once the sahasrara chakra is activated. There are various levels of samadhi; see *Nirvikalpa samadhi, Sahaj samadhi, Savikalpa samadhi*

Samsara — the ceaseless cycle of birth, death and rebirth to which one is subject as long as one remains ignorant of his true identity (God-nature), which is characterized by suffering

Sangat — Hindu term for community or congregation of disciples and seekers

Sangha — Buddhist term for community of disciples; the monastic order founded by the Buddha, the male members being called bhikkhus and the females bhikkhunis

Samyama — lit., "control"; a technical term describing the process by which dharana, dhyana and samadhi—the last three steps of raja yoga—are brought to bear upon an object. The mastery of samyama leads to illumination

Sannyas — the monastic life, dedicated to the complete renunciation of the Self and the attainment of knowledge of the Supreme Reality; or initiation during which the aspirant takes vows of renunciation; a monk who has taken the final vows of renunciation according to Vedic rites is called a *sannyasin*; a nun, *sannyasini*

Sanskaras (samskaras) — impressions or tendencies, positive and negative, from previous births which form the outlook and behavior of an individual

Sant — Hindu word for saint; one who has reached the fifth region; God-realized soul

Sant Mat — teachings of the saints; the science of God-realization. It is the science of merging one's soul in the Supreme Creator, under the guidance of a perfect living Master; has also been called *Surat Shabd Yoga*

Sant Satguru — a saint who is also a spiritual teacher. Everyone who has reached the fifth spiritual region is a saint, but not all accept followers or are designated to teach. Hence, every true Master or Satguru is a saint, but not all saints are Satgurus

Sar Bachan — lit., "essential" or "true" (sar) words (bachan); the name of a book by Soami Ji Maharaj

Sariputta (Sariputra) — one of Buddha's chief disciples

Satavik foods — foods that produce satavik qualities of peace and tranquility, i.e. lacto-vegetarian foods, based mainly on milk and plants, to the total exclusion of all animal products and eggs, fertile and infertile

Sat — true or truth; real; everlasting

Sat-chit-ananda — state of absolute bliss; absolute consciousness (sat, truth; chit, consciousness; ananda, bliss)

Sat Guru (Satguru) — "true Master": a spiritual adept who has access to the fifth spiritual region. The true Satguru is internal and is realized with the assistance of the outer, physical Guru or Master, who acts as a "window" to the Divine

Sat Lok — true (*sat*) region (*lok*); another name for Sach Khand

Satori — a state of intuitive illumination, momentary enlightenment, sought in Zen Buddhism

Sat Purush — "True Lord," who presides over Sat Lok and all universes below it; God; also called *Akal Purush*

Satsang — "true association." Most commonly translated as a congregation assembled to hear spiritual discourses (external) of a Master; the highest form is association of the soul with the Radiant Form of the Master or the shabd (internal)

Savikalpa samadhi — the first stage of transcendental consciousness, in which the distinction between subject and object persists

Seba — ancient Afrikan word for Master or teacher

Self — atman (*atma*): the Supreme Self; Universal Consciousness; Ultimate Reality; Buddha nature; lower case: the ego

Sephiroth — Jewish Kabbalistic term meaning God's emanation. There are ten sephiroth that emerged from *Ain Soph* (Ein Sof), each of which points to a different aspect of God's creative nature and together they comprise the content of Divine light in the chain of Being. The whole concept is an attempt to explain how a transcendent God can interact with the world

Seva (*sewa*) — voluntary service to the Master or disciples, to humanity; there are four types of seva: monetary, physical, mental and spiritual

Sevadar (*sewadar*) — one who does seva; one who serves

Shabd — in Sant Mat, term for the Sound Current, the divine, inner sound which reverberates throughout the creation. There are five forms of the Shabd within every human being. It also manifests through mystic practice as inner light; the audible life steam; the Word in the Bible; Nad (Nada) in the Vedas; the Tao; see *Nam*; *Sound Current*

Shabds — hymns, paragraphs or stanzas of sacred text put to music and often sung

Shah rag — lit., "royal vein," the central current or canal in the finer body which is located and traversed by means of spiritual practice according to instructions of a Master; also called *sushmana* or *sushumna*

Shakti — spiritual energy; in Indian philosophy it is always female, e.g., God as Mother of the Universe; the Goddess; the highest form of maya or illusion (maya, maha maya, shakti)

Shaktipat diksha — a yogic initiation in which the Siddha Guru transmits his spiritual energy into the aspirant, thereby awakening the aspirant's dormant kundalini. There are four different way in which the shaktipat can be received: *sparsha* diksha, through the Guru's physical touch; *mantra* diksha, through his words; *drik* diksha, through his look; and *manasa* diksha, through his thoughts

Shambhavi diksha — the rarest of spiritual initiations in which, as the result of receiving shaktipat from a Siddha Guru, an aspirant immediately experiences the Supreme Reality

Shanti — peace

Shastras — Hindu scriptures; books of philosophy and moral code

Sheikh — "chief"; a Muslim holy man or spiritual Master; head of an Arab tribe, principality, etc.; a courtesy title among the Muslims

Shunya (*shunyata*; *sunya*; *sunn*) — emptiness: the ultimate nature of all phenomena, which is their lack of inherent existence; void; vacuum; esoterically, the third Spiritual Region which is devoid of matter in any form; see *Maha Sunn*

Siddha — lit., "perfected one," one who has attained the state of awareness where he experiences himself as all-pervasive and who has achieved mastery over his senses; an enlightened Master

Siddhis (*iddhis*) — spiritual perfection; supernatural or occult power (clairvoyance, telepathy, recalling one's past lives, etc.) obtained by means of yoga practice or spiritual discipline. It is forbidden to use these psychic powers for one's personal benefit

Sikh — lit., "disciple"; the followers of Guru Nanak and his nine successors are known as Sikhs; the term also applies to one who has reached the first spiritual region within, and means the same as *chela*

Sila — in Buddhism the system of moral development

Simran (*sumiran*) — "repetition": the (usually silent) repetition of the holy names (mantra) one receives from the Guru upon initiation to focus attention at the eye center in order to withdraw attention from the body and outer world; see *Japa*

Skandhas (*khandhas*) — the five aggregates (form, feeling, perception, intellect and consciousness) that compose mental and physical existence which support ego-grasping and are the basis for suffering, which are inherent in every form of life, either in an active or a potential state

Soami Ji (*Swami Ji*) (1818-1878) — born Shiv Dayal Singh in Agra, he was a disciple of Tulsi Sahib of Hathras, and was the founder of the Radha Soami line. As a child he was raised on the scriptures of the *Adi Granth*. He started teaching the way of *Surat*

Shabd Yoga after spending 17 years in a room meditating. He
authored two books, *Sar Bachan* (poetry and prose)

Socrates — Greek philosopher, condemned to death in 399 B.C. at
about the age of seventy for impiety and corrupting youths. Most
of Plato's (one of his disciples) works are based on Socrates'
teachings

Sohang — lit., "I am that": conscious realization of oneness with God;
appellation of the Lord of the fourth spiritual region

Sound Current — the inner sound or music one hears, after initiation
by a Master, when in deep concentration or meditation; Word in
the bible; Logos; Nad of the Vedas; Nam in Hindu; see *Shabd*

Sufi — an adherent of Sufism

Sufism — a mystic sect developed in Persia that believes in a living
murshid (Guru); Islamic mysticism

Sukha (sukh) — pleasure; happiness; comfort

Surah — a chapter in the Koran

Surat — the ability of the soul to hear on the spiritual planes inside the
body; this faculty is developed through the practice of *Surat Shabd
Yoga*

Surat Shabd Yoga — the practice of joining the soul (*surat*) with the
Word (*shabd*) and merging (*yoga*) with it. Through the practice of
listening to the Sound Current or Divine Music, the soul reaches
the highest regions, beyond all duality, and becomes one with the
Absolute; also called *Sahaj Yoga*

Sushmana — also called *sukhmana* and *shah rag* ("royal vein"): The
central current in the finer body, starting from the eye center and
leading upward into the higher spiritual regions. It is located and
traversed by means of the spiritual practice taught by a Master.
The current to the left is called *ida* and that to the right, *pingala*.
According to Radha Swami literature, it is not to be confused with
sushumna (below), which is the central canal along the spine in the
lower body

Sushumna — the hollow canal (nadi) which runs through the center of
the spinal cord in the subtle body and which connects the six lower
chakras or centers of consciousness with the sahasrara chakra at
the crown of the head. When the kundalini awakens due to
spiritual practice, it rises through a smaller nadi known as *chitrini*,
located within the sushumna. Sushumna is also called the *Brahma
nadi* (channel of the Absolute), the *samvitti* nadi (channel of
Consciousness), and the Pathway of the Great Kundalini

Sushupti — deep, dreamless sleep; sound sleep without dreams or any interference of thought; also, when all attention has gone up to Agya center (the first spiritual region), which condition is known as Turiya, and one is as dead to the world but wide awake within

Sutra (sutta) — lit., "thread; " a precept summarizing Vedic teaching; a discourse of the Buddha

Swabhava — the true Self; inner nature

Swami — lit., "Lord"; the Supreme Lord or Supreme Creator; esoterically, in the *Radha Soami* tradition, the Lord of the eighth spiritual region; a title given to religious teachers

Swapna — sleep with subjective dreams

Tan — the physical body

Tanha — craving; desire; selfish or blind demandingness, which is the cause of unhappiness or suffering, one of the Four Noble Truths of the Buddha

Tantra — ancient religious philosophy in which Shakti is usually the main deity worshiped, and the universe is regarded as the divine play of Shakti and Shiva. Tantra deals primarily with spiritual practices and ritual forms of worship, the goal of which is liberation from ignorance and rebirth through direct knowledge that the soul and the Godhead (Shiva-Shakti) are one. The admission of women led to charges that Tantra was a "yoga of sex." The Buddhist tantric text is based on the original purity of the nature of mind, whose fruit is the realization of that nature

Tao — various meanings, one commonly used is the "Law," it also refers to the inner sound and light (shabd). The Tao is lit. the movement of all life; also translated as meaning the Way; truth; Dharma

Taoism — once one of the major religions of China; based on the *Tao Te Ching*, a book credited to Lao-tzu (ca. 600 B.C.), Taoism advocates a simplistic way of life and noninterference with the natural flow of events; effortless action and freedom from desires are viewed as virtues

Tao Te Ching — translated as "the Way" or "the Path," sacred scriptures written by the Chinese mystic Lao-tzu, who founded Taoism and taught devotion to Nam or the Tao

Tapas, tapasya — the practice of austerities; penance; self-control; spiritual discipline

Tathagata — a name for the Buddha, which means "the Perfect One"; "One who has fully arrived"; "One who has attained (spiritual perfection)"; see *Buddha*

Tat tvam asi — "That thou art": a Vedantic expression of realization that first, there is no distinction between this individual and that individual, and second, each individual is the supreme Lord; see *Aham Brahmasmi*

Tattwas (tattva) — the five elements present, in varying degrees, in all of creation: earth, water, fire, air and ether. Only in humans are all five active, and the greater the number of active tattwas, the greater the responsibility involved in killing that form and the greater the burden of karma assumed

Theravada — "The Way (doctrine or teachings) of the Elders"; see *Hinayana*

Three jewels — in Buddhism, the taking of refuge in the dharma (teachings); in the Guru (spiritual teacher); and the sangha (the community of spiritual seekers)

Tisra til — the third eye; the tenth door; the seat or headquarters of the soul located between the eyebrows, upon which one concentrates in meditation; see *Eye Center*

Trikuti — the second spiritual region above Anda; the home of the mind; the causal region

Triloki — lit., "the three worlds (physical, astral, causal), which are all within the domain of Kal; also called *Brahm Lok*

Tukaram Maharaj — a great poet-saint of seventeenth century Maharashtra who composed thousands of poems denouncing outward forms of worship and describing all aspects of spiritual life, and who emphasized japa as a spiritual practice

Turiya (turiya pad) — lit., "the fourth," the superconscious state which transcends the three ordinary states of consciousness: wakefulness, dreaming and dreamless sleep; the "here and now"; Sahansdal Kanwal; the consciousness of the astral plane

Upanishads — lit., "to sit near or close," because the teachings were directly imparted to the disciple by the teacher; the philosophical and mystical part of the Vedas which describe the spiritual experiences of the ancient Indian sages, of which one hundred and eight have been preserved; also called Vedanta, "end of the Vedas"

Vairagya (vairag) — detachment from the world and its pleasures; renunciation; asceticism

Varnatmak (varnatmik) — expressible; names of God which can be spoken or written. There are four types: *baikhri* (oral—spoken with tongue and lips); *madhama* (silent: repeated silently in the throat); *pashyanti* (meditated mentally in the heart); *para* (current or wave which the yogis raise from the navel); see *Dhunatmak*

Vasana — mental tendency; a "groove" in the recording equipment of the mind

Veda — lit., "knowledge"; the most ancient sacred scripture of the Hindus, regarded by the orthodox as the supreme authority in all religious matters. There are four Vedas: the *Rig*, the *Yajur*, the *Sama* and the *Atharva*

Vedanta — lit., "end of the Vedas." A religious philosophy which has evolved from the teachings of the latter, or knowledge, portion of the Vedas (the Upanishads). In this sense, it is the common basis of all religious sects of India. Vedanta teaches that the purpose of man's life is to realize the ultimate Reality, here and now, through spiritual practice

Vidya — knowledge

Vipashyana (vipassana) — insight; "clear seeing": in the Mahayana, a form of analytical meditation on the nature of things that leads to insight into the true nature of phenomena: shunyata

Viveka (vivek) — discrimination between real and unreal, between the eternal and the ephemeral

Word — known in different religions under different names, it designates the dynamic power of God which created and sustains the universe and through which the soul returns to its source; see *Shabd, Nam*

Yama — "Lord of Death" who takes the uninitiated soul at the time of death; see *Kal*. Another meaning is "self-control," the first of the eight limbs of Raja Yoga. Yama includes ahimsa, truthfulness, non-stealing, continence and abstention from greed. It is to be practiced in thought, word and deed

Yoga (yog) — lit., "union" or "yoke"; the state of union with God; the practices (sadhanas) which enable the soul to achieve oneness with God. A male yoga practitioner is called a *yogi*; a female, a *yogini*

Yoga Sutras — the famous aphorisms on Yoga philosophy and practice, compiled by Patanjali, between the fourth century B.C. and the fourth century A.D., known as the Eightfold Path. They consist of: (1) *yama* and (2) *niyama* (require observance of ten negative and positive moralities of body, speech and mind, study and devotion to God); (3) *asana* (right posture); (4) *pranayama* (control of prana); (5) *pratyahara* (withdrawal of senses from external objects); (6) *dharana* (concentration); (7) *dhyana* (meditation); and (8) *samadhi* (absorption; superconscious)

Yuga (*yug*) — age or cycle of time. The Hindu scriptures have divided time into four yugas: *Sat* (Satya) or *Krita* Yuga (the True or Golden Age); *Treta* Yuga (the Silver Age); *Dwapar* (Dwapara) Yuga (the Cooper or Bronze Age); and *Kal* (or Kali) Yuga (the Dark or Iron Age). It is said that we are now in Kal Yuga

Zen — one of the schools of Chinese and Japanese Buddhism, emphasizing abandonment of striving as the way to enlightenment

Zend Avesta — the sacred writings of the ancient Zoroastrian religion and of its present-day form among the Parsees, a sect descended from a group of Persian refugees who fled from the Moslem persecutions in the seventh and eighth centuries

Zikr — Sufi term that refers to the highest form of remembrance or repetition, the simran or inner invocation of the holy names under the direction of a Master; also used for many other kinds of repetition practices that pertain to the lower chakras and lower regions

Zoroastrianism — religion founded by Zoroaster, a prophet and teacher of ancient Persia, which is practiced by relatively few people, most of whom live in India and Iran. The Supreme Lord of creation is called Ahura Mazda and the Avesta contains its hymns, prayers and doctrines

INDEX